Kansas Quilts & Quilters

Map of Kansas by Harriet Angelia Deuel, Wallulah, Wyandotte County, 1887.
Pieced and embroidered wools. Collection of the Kansas Museum of History.

Publication made possible in part by the Kansas Quilt Project:
Documenting Quilts and Quiltmakers

Kansas Quilts & Quilters

Barbara Brackman

Jennie A. Chinn

Gayle R. Davis

Terry Thompson

Sara Reimer Farley

Nancy Hornback

University Press of Kansas

© 1993 by the University Press of Kansas

All rights reserved

Published by the University Press of Kansas (Lawrence, Kansas 66049), which was organized by the Kansas
Board of Regents and is operated and funded by Emporia State University,
Fort Hays State University, Kansas State University, Pittsburg State University,
the University of Kansas, and Wichita State University

Library of Congress Cataloging-in-Publication Data

Kansas quilts and quilters / Barbara Brackman ... [et al.].
p.   cm.
Includes index.
ISBN 0-7006-0584-3 (alk. paper : hardcover)
ISBN 0-7006-0585-1 (alk. paper : paper)
1. Quilting—Kansas—History.
2. Quilts—Kansas. I. Brackman, Barbara.
TT835.K36   1993
746.9'7'09781—dc20   92-43108

Printed in Hong Kong

10 9 8 7 6 5 4 3 2 1

The paper used in this publication meets the
minimum requirements of the American National Standard for
Permanence of Paper for Printed Library Materials Z39.48-1984.

Design by Christine Mercer

Contents

Kansas Quilts & Quilters

House, pieced by Mary Schenck Ellison (1857–1952), Kansas, 1900–1930.
Quilted recently. Collection of Judy Zinn.

The Papers of Mary Ellison

MARY SCHENCK SPARKS ELLISON'S LONG LIFE SPANNED MUCH OF THE PERIOD WE DISCUSS IN THIS BOOK. BORN IN INDIANA IN 1857, SHE CAME TO KANSAS IN 1870. SHE WAS AN AVID QUILTMAKER. WE CANNOT CALL HER TYPICAL BECAUSE HER PRODUCTION WAS PRODIGIOUS. WHEN SHE WAS NINETY-TWO SHE ESTIMATED that she had made over three hundred quilts. She was also atypical in that she left many written references to quiltmaking over her ninety-five years. From February to June 1876, she kept a diary. As an eighteen-year-old housekeeper for her father and six of her brothers and sisters in Leavenworth County, she recorded her daily housework and sewing, mentioning quilts on thirty days. She described the cutting, piecing, quilting, tying, or binding of at least eleven different quilts or comforters in those months. She also included references to her later quilting activities in a round-robin letter that began circulating to family members in 1903 (it still circulates), and the family has four newspaper clippings about her that refer to her quilts.

In a 1907 letter she jokingly referred to quiltmaking as her "perfession." Despite the joke she did consider herself a professional quilter. In the 1880s, she supplemented her income as she raised two children alone by weaving rag carpets, baking bread, knitting mittens, and taking in quilting, which netted her "a neat little sum of pin money," she recalled in a 1908 letter to *Metropolitan and Rural Home* magazine. During her second marriage, to O. A. Ellison, a man known in the family to begrudge money for household expenses, she mentioned buying a washing machine and a set of dishes with her personal money earned from quilting. After she divorced Ellison about 1909, she supported herself and two children by farming, supplementing her income by selling silk stockings door-to-door and quilting on winter days when she could not make her rounds. In a 1914 letter she wrote that she made only about twenty-five cents a day from her quilting, but "that is better than hundreds of men are doing this winter."

Mary Ellison described her quilts as "plain" (or "common") and "fancy" (or "nice"), an aesthetic differentiation not often found in written records of the past but often heard from today's quiltmakers. She did not leave us much information on her criteria for distinguishing between plain and fancy; however, the quilt in the photo of her daughters is remembered as the "very fine one" made for Esly, an appliqued floral wreath, set with bleached muslin and quilted with complex designs. We can assume that "common quilts" were the "dark" quilts she described in a 1904 letter—pieced scrap quilts of cotton or wool that were tied or quilted in straight lines or fans. The diary is also valuable in that it describes quilts by pattern names: Winding Blade, Nine Patch, and Crowfoot, evidence that these names were established in the vernacular in the 1870s although they were not recorded by publications until later.

Mary Ellen Schenck (pronounced "skenk") was born in Whitestown, Indiana. Her mother was a Quaker who left the church to marry a Baptist, the religion in which Mary was raised. She died when Mary was twelve, leaving ten children. Mary's father married a woman with three children, and in 1870 the fifteen members of the Schenck family traveled to Kansas, a trip Mary often recalled for her grandchildren. They settled on a farm near Springdale in eastern Leavenworth County. Mary and her brothers and sisters had an unhappy relationship with their stepmother, who died within a few years of arriving in Kansas, leaving Mary to care for the children still at home. The diary was written in the months before her father married for a third time. In it she mentions her husband-to-be, Will Sparks, several times. The cast of characters included her brother Firman, who had moved out of the house, presumably to live as an apprentice; brothers Isaac, Zenas, John, and Levi; and sisters Zeruiah and Edith, who lived at home. Sister Esly was married and lived elsewhere, and sister Naomi (nicknamed Omy) spent much of her time at Esly's.

Mary seems to have done most of the housework, but the family divided some of the

Mary Ellison's daughters with the "very fine" quilt mentioned in a 1936 letter. Courtesy of Marjorie Beems.

chores. In the weeks Mary cooked she had little other work to do, although she was responsible for most of the family's clothing and bedding. Her father was a preacher and justice of the peace who heard lawsuits in his home. Many of the guests Mary mentions were his fellow church members and preachers.

Soon after she ceased her diary Mary married Will Sparks. They had three children, and because both had unpleasant memories of stepparents, they agreed that if either died the other would not remarry until the children were grown. When Will died Mary kept her word and raised the children alone on her needlework income. With her second husband she had a second family and lived in Effingham and Muscotah in Atchison County; after the divorce she lived in Topeka and nearby Oskaloosa and Grantville.

Mary Ellison spent her later years with daughter Ursula in Grantville. Ursula's daughter, Marjorie Beems, who has generously shared Mary Ellison's papers and photographs, remembers growing up with her grandmother and her quilts. Mary taught her to piece quilts at six or seven years of age. In her later years Grandmother Ellison used a frame designed for her by her

brother Isaac, who had envisioned it in a dream and sent her a model from Wyoming. Brother John, who lived near Oskaloosa, built it for her. So tiny her feet did not reach the floor, she quilted with a box under her feet. She quilted alone; she was a member of the Predestinarian Baptist Church, which had no organized quilting groups. Although her sister Esly quilted too, they rarely quilted together.

People sent Mary Ellison boxes of scraps to make into quilts, and Marjorie Beems remembers her as never happier than when she received gifts of fabric. She never sewed on Sunday, warning that every stitch taken on the Sabbath would have to be removed in the next world with one's nose.

Few of Mary Ellison's quilts remain in her family. She told Marjorie that they were meant to be used, and the family did as she wished.

Mary Ellen Schenck's Diary, 1876. Copied by her granddaughter Marjorie Beems
February.
1st Tu.
Weather very cold. Knit on John's socks. B.
Wed. 2nd.
Knit some and quilted on'a comfort.
Thurs. 3d
Pieced a comfort a piece for Isaac and Firman and knit a little. Washed ironed and cooked for traveling.
Fri. 4th
Helped get the folks started to Nemaha Co. and then pieced a comfort apiece for Isaac and Firman. Red a letter from _____. Weather a little warmer.
Sat. 5th
Finished piecing another comfort and Ba[by] quilt and knit some.

Weather very windy.

Sun. 6th
Staid at home all day. E. and M. Swaim and A. and J. Sparks here. The day very warm.

Mo. 7th
Did a large washing. Picked the geese and commenced stockings for Edith.

Tu. 8th
Ironed, cut and made a garment for Esly put a quilt in the frame then knit till bed time.

Wed. 9th
Commenced washing but company came and I quit and quilted till nite and then sewed for Firman.

Th. 10th
Finished washing and quilting cleaned off the north yard and then sewed for Firman till bed time. He is fixing to go away.

Fri. 11th
Sewed awhile and finished the yard then papered the kitchen and knit some.

Sat. 12th
Sewed some and did the baking and went to meeting [to]night to hear Mr. Brundridge and See _____.

Sun. 13th
Went to meeting at _____ and _____ and E here for dinner. Firman went to Mr. Jones' today to commence work for one year.

Mo. 14th
Sewed all day for Firman and went to Frank Sparks's at night and staid till bed time.

Tu. 15th
Sewed for Firman till evening knit awhile. I mended some of the children's clothes and did a little mending for—Number one.

We. 16th
Washed and sewed on my basque [a dress bodice] till night and then patched Edith's dress and knit till bed time.

Th. 17th
Helped to iron and finish my basque.

Fri. 18th
Took my knitting and went to Mr. Ernhart's and stopped to see the sick at Mr. Wells.

Sat. 19
Went to Wilhelm to meeting and to Housh's for dinner. Went to meeting again at night and to Mr. Miller's to stay all night.

Su 20
Went to meeting & to Mr. Woodard's for dinner. Went to meeting at _____ at night and then came home.

Mo 21st
Fixed my dress "set a hen" and tied a comfort for Isaac and quilted till night then knit till free.

Tu 22
Finished quilting and knit awhile.

Wed 23rd
Washed and churched in the morning and went to see _____.

Th. 24
Ironed and patched for myself & commenced making John a shirt.

Fri 25th
Finished the sewing and went to Mr. Peters's for supper and then went to Mr. Thornbrough's to meeting and staid all night.

Sat 26
Went to Little Hope to meeting and to Mr. T's for dinner and went to meeting again in the evening then went to Mrs. Vanpelt's and staid all night.

Sun 27th
Went to meeting and to Mr. Peters's for dinner and then came home. Isaac came home.

Mon 28th
Finished Firman's shirt and cut two for Zenas and one for John. Lawsuit here to day.

Su 29
Made a shirt apiece for J. and Zenas. Knit a little.

March

Wed 1st
Bound a quilt and fixed Isaac pants and knit.

Th. 2nd
Bound a comfort swept up the upstairs and knit. Georgia South here.

Fri 3rd
Washed and knit. Wrote to Esly.

Sat 4th
Helped to iron and finished knitting.

Sun 5th
Staid at home. E. Jones, W. Sparks, W. Elliot, W. Jones, A. Sparks and Firman here at night.

Mon 6th
Cut and sewed carpet rags and patched Zenas' pants at night. Rain nearly [early?] and snowed lightly in the evening.

Tu 7th
Cut carpet rags till noon and after then went to Springdale got back sewed till night.

Wed 8
Washed and commenced making a fine shirt for father.

Th 9th
Helped iron finished the shirt and cut quilt squares.

Fri 10th
Pieced on Firmans Winding Blade quilt.

Sat 11th
Baked finished a piecing F's quilt and began a Crowfoot for myself. Went a ne——ing at night and then went with Nan Van to Mr. Wells' and *sat* up all night.

Su 12th
Came home & went to meeting at eleven o'clock. W.S. AS, O.S., and W.E. and C.R., and Firman here for dinner. Went to meeting again at night.

Mo 13th
This is my week to "cook and wash dishes" consequently I will not do as much other work. Pieced on my quilt.

Tu 14th
Pieced on my quilt. Lawsuit here to day. got dinner for four. Went to Mr. Wells's at night to sit up

Mary Schenck, age eighteen, 1875. Courtesy of Marjorie Beems.

and they had company so came back.

We 15
Finished piecing my quilt and commenced one for Isaac.

Th 16th
Finished piecing Isaac's quilt and went to Wells's and sat up all night.

Fri 17th
Came home this morning and pieced on my nine patch quilt till evening and then mended Isaac's waist received a letter from A. C. beby.

Sat 18
Cleaned up the house and scrubbed the floors. Wrote a letter to FMH.

Su 19
Staid at home and the snow fell nearly all day. Wrote letters to L.H.F. & RJL.

Mo 20
Pieced on my quilt. J.P. & E.V. here.

Tu 21
Pieced quilts awhile and fixed father's fine shirt and Zenas's gloves. Firman came home this evening and I fixed his suspenders, vest & gloves.

We 22
Pieced quilts. L.S. here.

Th. 23rd
Washed and fixed John a pair of

sox, & fathers glove & sewed a little.

Fri 24th
A snowy, wet day. Cleaned up the upstairs ironed a little hemmed a stand cover and wrote to A.E.B.

Sa 25th
Didn't do any thing much till night when I scrubbed the floor as it has been a wet sloppy week. L.S. went away this morning.

Su 26
Staid at home J. and C. ___ W.J. and Firman here for dinner. A very pleasant day over head but muddy underneath. Read some in ___ nearly every night for a while.

Mo 27th
Patched Levi's pants and Zena's pants and coat. Commenced some tatting. Today is the beginning of my cooking week again & the mo. A disagreeable day I ever saw.

Tu 28
Patched Isaac's white shirt and made myself a ruffle and chemmazette.

We 29th
Commenced washing but Frank Sparks's all came on a visit so dispened with the washing for to day. The boys killed a goose and a brant [a wild goose] today.

Th 30th
Finished washing and cleaned up the kitchen and ironed. The weather is pleasant again.

Fri 31st
Patched in the morning and in the evening went to see Mrs. Hicherson came home and churned The wind is high.

April

Sa 1st
Fixed up my little cupboard & straightened up my drawer and done some mending. It has rained nearly all day.

Su 2nd
A cloudy, dark day. I staid at

home all day. Wil Sparks here. I commenced writing some but didnt get done.

Mo 3rd
A pretty a day as one could ask for. I washed, ironed & patched & finished my writing.

Tu 4th
Cleaned off the bedsteads and scrubbed upstairs and down. Cut and sewed some on John's fine shirt. Windy day

We 5th
Done some patching and went to F. Sparks's & Mr. Wells's to take some seeds and flowr. Sarah Story's here today.

Th 6th
Sewed on J.'s shirt and after noon went to see Georgiana South & they gave us some Snow ball sprigs which we sat out after we came home.

Fri 7th
Sat out beets and raddishes for seed turnips for greens and also set some hollyhocks and rose bushes. After dinner set out onions and planted lettuce peas and raddishes.

Sat 8th
Scrubbed and baked and went to meeting at night. Firman came home with us

Sun 9th
Went to meeting again. W. here for dinner. Another dark day.

Mo 10th
Washed and cleaned up the kitchen. Warm day.

Tu 11th
Ironed and cut and sewed on Zeruiahs dress. Weather windy.

We 12th
Churned & sewed for Zeruiah. Rains very hard for a while then drizzle & drizzle.

Th 13th
Finished the dress & watched _____ drawers did Levi's coat

Fr 14th
Fixed Zena's & Levi's pants & father's coat & scrubbed the

kitchen and porch & baked light bread. CD Mr. _____ came yesterday but went away to day. it has been clear nearly all day.

Sa 15
Blacked the Stove baked pies and light bread and scrubbed and cleaned up generally. Received a letter from I. H Furnas.

Su 16
Went out to Wilhelm to meeting. Firman came home with us. Saw S.J. baptized. Went to meeting at ____ at night. Messrs Huffman Mendenhall and Peters & Mrs. Hufman & Vanpelt came home with us and staid all night. The roads all pretty muddy.

Mo 17th
After our visitors left I done up the work & then went out and planted beans and beets and cucumbers which kept me til noon and after noon I pieced on Omy's quilt. She has bin at Esly's ever since February.

Tu 18
Washed and churned and pieced on the quilt & wrote a letter to Esly's folks. Pretty windy day.

We 19
A very windy day indeed. Mended somesocks in the after noon and read in the dictionary. Looked thru my box in the for noon. Rain and hail in the evening.

Th 20th
Ironed cleaned out closet and commenced patching but Georgia South came up and I set out flowers and laughed the rest of the day. Wrote a letter to N F. Wright. A very pleasant day.

Fri 21st
Hoed the onions, planted beans beets and cucumbers got done at 4 p.m. Rec'd a letter from Esly. Some indications of rain.

Sat. 22
Patched made Levi a doll, fooled around awhile. Isaac killed some dux today. Firman came home

this evening & now it is raining hard.

Sun 23rd
Cloudy day. Firman Zeruiah & I went to Mrs. Story's this afternoon and they came home with us.

Mon 24th
Still Cloudy. Washed & did part of the ironing. C. Hale here tonite.

Tu 25th
Patched & went to Springdale & got me a dress.

We 26th
Took my dress & went to see Georgia and staid all day.

Th 27th
Sewed on my dress.

Fri 28
Sewed & fixed father's coat. rec'd a letter from T. AB

Sa 29
Sewed & baked & iron & read a paper.

Mo May 1st
Cut carpet rags. rainy day.

Tu 2nd
Washed made a chicken coop & wrote a letter to Esly. tolerable fair day.

We 3d
Ironed. Scrubbed the porch & cut carpet rags. C. Hale's here.

Th 4th
Patched. It has rained nearly all day.

Fri 5th
Cleaned up the upstairs and finished my dress. Mr. Styp—— here last night. patched my dress.

Sat 6th
Made a little apron & pin cushion. A rainy rainy day. Mr. Peters Huffman & Mendinghall came here last night.

Su 7
Wrote some verses from a book, a dark cloudy morning but clear & cool in the evening, our visitors went home this am.

Mo 8
A pretty day. I washed, ironed,

scrubbed the kitchen & porch & hoed in the garden.

Tu 9
Scrubbed & scalded downstairs & hoed _____ and fixed my dress, G.F. South here _____.

We 10
Finished hoeing and planted some tomatoes peppers beans & watermelons. Went to see Sallie Story in the evening.

Th 11
Went to see Mollie Swain & staid all day.

Fri 12th
Patched & planted flower seeds.

Sa 13
Have done a little of almost every thing. Went to meeting at night. Firman came home with us.

Su 14
Went to meeting. J.H. McGee, OA South W.T. Sparks & O Hale & family here for dinner.

Mo 15
Cut and helped to piece an old quilt for the lounge.

Tu 16
Washed 10 bed covers & churned & finished piecing the quilt, & set out some tomatoe plants. It has been a pretty day.

We 17
Scalded & scrubbed upstairs, cleaned out the closet fixed a lining for the quilt & cut some squares for another. The weather showery.

Th 18
It rained some this morning then cleared off and I washed but it clouded up and rained again so I did not get the clothes hung out. Cut and pieced on an old quilt the rest of the time. Our peas are in bloom & onions have sets.

Fri 19
Finished washing pieced some on the old quilt, and hoed the garden. Rec'ed a letter from Omy & Esly. Weather about the same.

Sa 20th
Ironed, patched & baked. Geor-

gia South here.

Su 21st

Went to Wilhelm in the morning & then came home got dinner & went to the Donneley School-house at 5 oclock & to Mr. Jones' & staid all night. Firman C. C. Megee was here for dinner. Clear, this evening.

Mo 22

I came home this morning about 10 o'clock A cloudy day _____ a paper nearly all day. Mr. Stypes here. I fixed fathers pants.

Tu 23rd

Dropped corn in the forenoon. Mrs. Hickerson came in the afternoon & staid till evening during which time I fixed Edie's dress after she went away, dropped corn till night. a cool day.

We 24

Commenced washing but Isaac came in and wanted help so I left the washing for Z. & plant corn for him all the rest of the day.

Th 25th

Dropped corn all the forenoon & fixed to put milk in the cellar, slopped the hogs & c. & c., J. Peters here last night.

Fr 26

Patched Levi's pants & went to Springdale. A letter from N F Wright with _____ pictures

Sa 27

Took out the stove & scrubbed. cut and made _____ a _____ & a quilt _____ & ironed some

Su 28th

A pretty day. John Wilsy & Matty, and Wil, Bert & John Sparks here.

Mo 29th

Sewed for Levi. A slight rain today.

Tu 30th

Washed & cut out & commenced a garment for Edie. So E. Swaim here.

We 31st

Sewed & Edies dress—finished

the other. A lawsuit here this morning at _____ o clock before which I hoed in the garden. Mr. ——ird came here this pm to board till he can finish a bridge.

June

Th 1st

Picked the geese. finished Edies dress & ripped some tucks out of skirts fixed pants for Isaac & father.

Fri 2

Washed the sacks & patched pants for I.J. & L. Slite rain.

Sat 3rd

Took the lounge upstairs straightened around, & patched sacks & ironed a little. Rec'ed a letter from Hennie hardin.

Su 4th

Warm day. W. A & J. Sparks, Firman & W. F. Jones & family here on a visit.

Mo 5th

Did a larg washing & ironing.

Tu 6th

Washed 12 pairs of pants & c. in the forenoon went to Hickersons in the afternoon.

We 7th

Cleaned up the kitchen, patched, & cleared up some drawers.

Thu 8th

Went to town, got back at 3 o'clock, & finished the shirt I commenced for John some time ago.

Fri 9

Did a little washing & ironing & patched pants. Scrubbed the kitchen.

Sa 10th

Scrubbed baked, patched Firmans pants. We had a good rain tonight which was badly needed.

Su 11th

Went to meeting in the morning & to Mr. Jones after Firman that evening. Father was married today & I wanted him to come down. Ella came too.

Mo 12

Scrubbed the porch & fixed for

father to come home but it rained so he didn't get here till evening.

Tu 13

Fixed Isaac's shirt & socks. a rainy day. Firman & Ella went home today.

We 14th

Churned & commenced washing in the evening but didn't finish.

Th 15

Finished washing & . . .

Excerpts from Schenck Family Round-Robin Letters
12/11/1904

I quilted twelve quilts this year but cant quilt any more til my hand and arm gets better of rheumatism, five or six were fancy ones and some were just dark every day ones for myself & I put as little work on them as would do at all. I have been wanting to get a washing machine when I get pay for the last fancy one but seems like they will never come after it.

10/21/1906

Blue ribbon—$1 at Effingham fair

Class—Best bed quilt, any material but silk

1st prize based on finest quilting 2nd prize based on smallest piecing

There were so many quilts there that I thought prettier than mine.

7/22/1907

(at Oskaloosa) Tine (?) Clark was going to have a quilting next day. She had invited over 50. And at the quilting was the most aristocratic place I nearly ever struck, but they all had a good time. I guess I acted pretty well unless it was at dinner. It was a course dinner, and I didn't know how many courses there was to be so I didn't hardly know when I was done! but I capped off on ice cream and hot strawberry sauce, though all the rest had been just as nice.

1907

Well, I reckon you'll all be glad to hear that I am still working at my "perfeshion" while I rest. That is, quilting. I have the seventh one in the frames now for this year, but only one of them was mine, and they were all fancy quilts but two. You would all be interested in this one I am at now if I was to describe it, but I guess I won't just now. I had got to needing some dishes and I thought I would quilt enough to get me a set.

1/8/1908

Now all dear sisters and nieces
I'll tell you for well I do know
You wonder what went with the
    pieces
You made into quilts long ago
I delivered them both in
    September
And very much pleased both
    appeared
But I do wish they both had
    remembered
And told you so in their own
    words.

1/8/1911

[after her divorce] If I had room I could at least do quilting, but I didn't even get my quilting frames from up there and don't know yet whether I will be allowed to go back there to get anything else that I left there or not.

8/1/1911

(Oskaloosa) Ursula often reads to us while I quilt. It will be a month the 6th since we got here, and I have quilted one quilt, helped quilt another and got the third one about one third done.

4/13/1913

I had a pretty good time most of the winter even if I didn't have means to buy quilt stuff all the time. A lady brought me a nice quilt and I made some hair switches, and sewed about 65# of carpet rags.

2/4/1914

I have quilted 3 nice white quilts that is joined with white and quilted in fanciful patterns—one with a wreath in each square, the others I called the wild rose pattern. I just finished one yesterday that was pieced of buff gingham and white. It looks real pretty. It was joined with strips and I quilted the border like this

and the rest of it kind of this way.

Just before I got that one done yesterday, a lady came out from town with another, all blue and white. She said she had several and hoped no one would get in ahead of her. It means about 25¢ a day to me—but that is better than hundreds of men are doing this winter.

8/8/1914

Well, I'm still quilting but I don't think I will ever again try to quilt anything I am very particular about in such hot weather. I quilted 12 through the winter and six of them were white ones, one was my own. I had these two to quilt lately and I will be glad when they are done. I tell Ursula I have to quilt in the morning while it is cool and about the time she gets the work done it is getting too hot to quilt.

1915

I have as much quilting engaged as I can do for all winter I expect for I just work at that when the weather is so bad I can't go at all.

1916

Had "2 red & white Irish Chain quilts & a Star quilt" in house.

1931

As far as I can tell now I am doing my last quilting.

Mary Schenck Ellison, age eighty-nine, 1946. Courtesy of Marjorie Beems.

6/18/1935

I have not given up quilting but have not had material to do with for a good while, so I still piece some and wish some one else would send me quilting to do.

7/17/1936

I have been quilting all summer. I have done 2 common ones for Dell, 3 nice ones for Dora, one for Florence and 1 very fine one for Esly and 1 for Lovejoy.

9/19/1937

As for me I still *putter* mostly with my quilt pieces, but sometimes it is hard to keep from losing interest.

8/5/1941

I am and can still keep busy *most* of the time with my pen or my needle. I cannot quilt anymore but I still piece, only when I get too nervous because it is so useless.

Constitution and Union Forever by Elizabeth Moffitt Lyle with help from John (Jack)
Moffitt (1837–1864), Kewanee, Illinois, 1860. Appliqued, embroidered,
and quilted cottons. Smoky Hill Museum.

This quilt seems to reflect Union patriotism during the Civil War, but because it
has only thirty-three stars (Kansas was the thirty-fourth state, admitted to the
Union a few months before the start of the war in 1861) it may have been made
before war was officially declared.

As with many mid-nineteenth-century quilts now in Kansas there are stories that it
was made here, but the truth is that it was made in the more-settled eastern states.
Elizabeth Lyle was assisted by her brother, Jack Moffitt, who cut out the stars. Jack and
Thomas Moffitt went to Kansas in 1864. They were among the first group of European
settlers in Lincoln County, building in an area considered unsafe because of threats
from the Native Americans who hunted the area. While on a buffalo hunt the brothers
and two friends were killed. Seventy years later, the Moffitt family sent the quilt
Jack had helped make to a museum in the state where he died.

Chapter One

Introduction

Barbara Brackman and Mary Madden

WOMEN, IT IS OFTEN SAID, HAVE RARELY TOLD THEIR OWN STORIES. OUR EXPERIENCE WITH THE KANSAS QUILT PROJECT, HOWEVER, HAS SHOWN US THAT WOMEN RECORDED THEIR STORIES THROUGH THEIR NEEDLEWORK, THEIR WRITING, AND THE TALES THEY TOLD THEIR CHILDREN. IT IS ONLY NOW, AT THE END OF the twentieth century, that we are ready to listen. In this book, the Kansas Quilt Project tells the story of Kansas quilts as well as the story of Kansas women through their quilts.

The "Kansas Quilt Project: Documenting Quilts and Quiltmakers" was organized as a nonprofit corporation in 1986, the year of the state's 125th anniversary. Eleanor Malone and Nancy Hornback of Wichita's Prairie Quilt Guild, quilters with an interest in antique quilts and women's history, had conducted a survey of quilts for an exhibit in Kansas City. They decided to celebrate the Kansas anniversary with a quilt project modeled on those that had been carried out in Kentucky, North Carolina, and other states (at that point eleven states had organized research surveys; now all fifty states have at least one). The two women called a meeting of representatives from Kansas quilt guilds and the Kansas State Historical Society. Of those twenty-five women, the eight who became the board of the Kansas Quilt Project, Inc., were Eleanor Malone (president), Nancy Hornback (secretary), Helen Storbeck (treasurer), Barbara Brackman, Barbara Bruce, Mary Margaret Rowen, and Jennie Chinn and Mary Madden from the Kansas State Historical Society. Dr. Gayle Davis of Wichita State University

and Dorothy Cozart of Phillips University served as advisers.

Financial assistance for the project has been in the form of grants, most notably from the National Endowment for the Arts and the Kansas Arts Commission. Twenty-three Kansas guilds contributed, as did hundreds of individuals (see Acknowledgments). The Kansas State Historical Society agreed to provide professional and financial assistance as the cosponsor for the project.

The project set multiple goals: to heighten public awareness of quilts as examples of Kansas folk art, to document the lives of Kansas quiltmakers and their work, to collect data and establish a repository at the Kansas State Historical Society, to promote the art of quiltmaking through public programs, and to promote the conservation and preservation of quilts. The means for fulfilling these objectives were as numerous as the goals themselves.

As the principal method for documenting quilts and quiltmakers, Quilt Discovery Days began in the summer of 1986. Kansans who owned quilts were encouraged to bring them to central locations and share their stories about the people who made them. The criteria for accepting quilts were very broad. The Kansas Quilt Project (KQP) was interested not only in old

quilts but also those fresh from the quilting frame. By specifically including contemporary quilts and quiltmakers, the KQP fulfilled its goal of documenting and preserving current quiltmaking activities. No geographical restrictions were placed on a quilt's place of origin. The KQP sought to study quilts brought to Kansas as well as those made here.

The board enlisted ten regional coordinators to organize the Quilt Discovery Days in their assigned regions of the state (see Acknowledgments for a listing of coordinators and other volunteers). The coordinators in turn recruited legions of volunteers to aid in the exciting but often laborious process of registering quilts. Interviewers questioned those who brought quilts about the history of each quilt and the quiltmaker's biography and motivation. Trained documenters examined each quilt; recorded information on technique, fabric, and size; and determined a range of dates during which it was most likely to have been constructed. Staff assigned a pattern name from standardized references to allow for later computerized retrieval, and photographers documented each quilt in black and white prints and color slides.

The public response was tremendous. An average of 183 quilts was brought to each of the

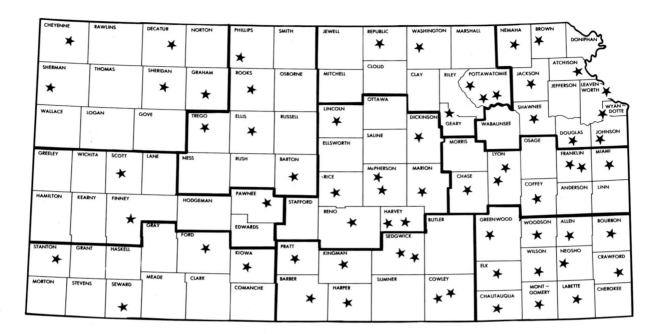

Each star represents a city where the Quilt Discovery Days were held.

seventy-two Quilt Discovery Days. In sixteen months, the project recorded 13,107[1] quilts and tops from every corner of the state. The benefits were equally overwhelming. The project succeeded in acquiring a comprehensive collection of information, much of which has been entered into a computerized data base at the Kansas State Historical Society. Many of the people who brought in their quilts left with a new appreciation of them.

Such a broad survey has inherent limitations. Interviewers with minimal training and documenters processing so many quilts in a short time may miss important facts. Some quiltmakers will not bring their quilts to a Quilt Discovery Day; others will neglect to bring a range of their own or their family's quilts. Realizing these limitations in collecting data solely through Quilt Discovery Days, the project

planned for a second research phase in the summer of 1988. In-depth interviews with quiltmakers were held in their homes or in club meeting rooms to obtain a more diverse and deeper discussion of quiltmaking than was possible at the public quilt days. To confirm and enhance family histories, the project staff also did extensive research into historical sources such as census records, diaries, letters, and photographs. It was at this time that we uncovered the papers left by Mary Schenck Ellison (1857–1952), which are presented in detail in the Prelude.

During 1988, the project also entered its dissemination phase, sponsoring many quilt shows, seminars, and lectures around the state to present preliminary findings. A major exhibit, Textile Diaries: Kansas Quilt Memories, opened at the Kansas Museum of History in 1990 and traveled nationwide under the auspices of Exhibits USA. The spring 1990 issue of the journal *Kansas History* featured findings from the project and a catalog of the show. The Kansas Museum of History collaborated on a curriculum package for grade-school children that focuses on quilts and state history.

With this book, we present further information obtained from the Quilt Discovery Days, the computerized data base, the follow-up interviews, and additional historical research. The contributors to this book provide both a broad view of Kansas quilts in their historical and cultural contexts and a closer examination of specific aspects of quilts and quiltmaking.

We found in our survey of Kansas quilts that the history, geography, and social life of the state have profoundly affected the story of the quilts in Kansas: those made here, those brought here, and—just as important—those we did not find. Interestingly, the early story of Kansas quilts is one of omission. We found remarkably few quilts made in Kansas before 1875, and few fine applique quilts made here at any point in the nineteenth century. We had hoped to find quilts made by women involved in the political and moral movements so important in Kansas—the nineteenth-century abolition, temperance, populist, or suffrage crusades—but we did not. Further, we found no distinctive Kansas quilt, one that could be categorized by its color, workmanship, style, or fabric as typical of the state. It appears that once Kansas women were settled enough to begin any significant quiltmaking activity, their work was typical of that being done elsewhere. Turn-of-the-century Kansas women fol-lowed national trends because they had access to the same fabrics, magazines, and pattern transfers as women throughout the country.

During the twentieth century, however, it may be argued that Kansas women have done more than follow others: They have led the way and developed trends that have created various national styles. Several of the women mentioned in the book, among them Carrie Hall, Rose Kretsinger, Scioto Imhoff Danner, and Terry Thompson, are a few of those whose patterns have achieved national circulation, giving the state its well-deserved reputation as "quilt country."

We chose in this book to feature representative quilts and quiltmakers; thus the book is neither a catalog of all the quilts recorded by the KQP nor a selection of the most unusual. The wide range of quilts we recorded made it clear that quiltmakers produce both plain and fancy quilts, quilts for function and for show. We hope in our selection of quilts and quilt-makers that we have presented this broad range rather than setting up a hall of fame in which the state's "best" quilts and quiltmakers are represented. This book is not the final word on Kansas quilts. We hope that the archives at the Kansas State Historical Society will be used by researchers who will further explore the place of quiltmaking in the state.

A Note on Pattern Names

The authors as Kansans and quiltmakers have long noted the many quilt pattern names that refer to Kansas (for instance, Kansas Trouble, Rocky Road to Kansas, Kansas Dugout, and Kansas Dust Storm), an abun-dance that may be due to the state's location as home to several twentieth-century pattern outlets, such as Mrs. Danner's Quilts and *Capper's Weekly*. The state has also benefited from close proximity to Kansas City, where the *Star* and the Aunt Martha and McKim studios were located. Missouri has many pattern names for the same reason. By comparison, Maryland and Delaware, important to nine-teenth-century quiltmaking but home to no commercial pattern companies, can claim few pattern names in the pattern indexes.

The geography of pattern studios and publications is not the only reason for the numerous Kansas pattern references. Both California and Texas boast many patterns yet have never been home to significant pattern studios. State image appears to be a factor. Like Kansas, Texas and California were more than mere places in the last century. They were crusades, as Robert Smith Bader has noted in his study of the Kansas image.[2] The nineteenth-century press painted vivid pictures of California and its gold, Texas and its Alamo, and Kansas and its pre–Civil War troubles— images with broad appeal to Americans fascinated with the west. Kansas may have many patterns named for it for the same reason that the American vocabulary has included phrases like Kansas Fever (the urge to move here), Kansas Idea (prohibition), and Kansas Dirt (the dust storms wherever their source).

We chose "Rocky Road to Kansas" for the project logo and a chapter title, although we real-ize that most of the names associated with quilt patterns are fairly recent and that pattern names reflect the influence of the popular press only since the very end of

Ladies' Aid Society in Elk, Chase County, ca. 1900.

the nineteenth century. We have no evidence that women making quilts in the years 1854 to 1861, when the Kansas Troubles were the talk of the United States, called their quilts by that name. We doubt that women living in Kansas dugouts actually called their quilts Kansas Dugout, and we don't believe that any pioneers taking the road to Kansas when it was truly rocky made the string quilt in that design, since the pattern appeared after railroads facilitated trips to Kansas. In fact, the names Kansas Troubles and Rocky Road to Kansas record events that were only memories by the time the patterns were first published in 1889. Other names that might seem to have 150 years of tradi-

tion behind them, such as Kansas Sunflower and Kansas Dugout, actually date only to the 1930s. And it was during that decade, as pattern companies and pattern names multiplied, that the naming of patterns for current events began. Quiltmakers living through the Dust Bowl and the 1936 presidential campaign recorded those events with the Kansas Dust Storm and Landon Sunflower designs they found in the *Kansas City Star*. Today's quiltmakers, with access to thousands of patterns, continue to choose designs like Jean Mitchell's Love for Kansas for the symbolic meaning of the names.[3]

We have used conventional pattern names where appropriate

Sewing class in Osborne, Kansas, 1899.

in the photograph captions for the quilts in the book. Most of the patterns we found were published at some point in the popular press over the past century, and we have used the name that seems most familiar to today's readers. Occasionally the family gave us a pattern name, and we have noted that. If we found no specific name, a circumstance quite common with applique designs, we have used a generic name such as *floral applique*.

Note also that the dates in most of the photo captions are estimations based on family history as well as on the fabric and style of the quilts. When we use the word *circa* as in "ca. 1890," we mean ten years either side of that date. We usually prefer a

range of dates, however, such as 1890 to 1925, that better reflects the style changes that we used for comparative dating.

Notes

1. The project recorded forms on 13,107 quilts but entered data on only 12,862 into the computerized data base. The discrepancy is due to two factors: (1) some quilt owners did not sign release forms, and (2) we had incomplete forms on a number of quilts, primarily because some owners tired of the wait and left before the documentation process on their quilts had been completed.

2. Robert Smith Bader, *Hayseeds, Moralists, and Methodists: The Twentieth-Century Image of Kansas* (Lawrence: University Press of Kansas, 1988).

3. Jean Mitchell, *Quilt Kansas* (Lawrence: Jean Mitchell, 1978), contains traditional patterns named for Kansas and several original designs.

KQP Df024. *Rocky Road to Kansas, pieced, embroidered and tied by friends of Mary Elizabeth McCreight (1882–?), Osage County, 1890–1910. Wool, silk, and cotton. Collection of Doris Hetrick.*
This four-pointed star is known as Rocky Road to Kansas. It is a string quilt, so called because seamstresses could make use of long, thin strings of scraps.

Chapter Two

Rocky Road to Kansas

Barbara Brackman

T HE STORY OF KANSAS QUILTS IS A STORY OF ROADS—THE IMMIGRANT ROADS INTO AND THROUGH KANSAS AND THE EQUALLY ROCKY ROADS OUT OF THE STATE IN HARD TIMES. WHILE KANSAS WAS STILL A TERRITORY, PATCHWORK QUILTS CAME TO IT WITH THE FIRST EMIGRANTS FROM THE UNITED STATES, WHO CARRIED quilts in bedrolls, on pack mules, and in wagons. During the westward migration, quilts were among America's utilitarian bedding, but they had many functions other than providing warmth. To people living on the frontier, quilts offered shelter when draped as tents or hung as room dividers; they became shrouds after death; and they served as luggage, as one did for Mary, a former slave whose last name was not recorded by her employer, Elizabeth Bacon Custer. Mrs. Custer recalled that as her husband, Gen. George Armstrong Custer, was posted around the West, including Kansas for five years, Mary invariably prepared for travel by bundling her possessions into a quilt made of souvenirs of her Kentucky friends' dresses.[1]

For women like Mary, living hundreds of miles from family, friends, and home, quilts held meaning far beyond their utility. Some were figurative autograph books called "album" quilts; many were collections of sentimental scraps from clothing; most were reminders of the hands that had made them. Their combination of function and meaning is a primary reason why so many quilts made in so many other states journeyed to Kansas, where they eventually were recorded by the Kansas Quilt Project.

During the time that Kansas was a territory, between 1854 and statehood in 1861, quiltmaking was a popular pastime in the United States. During the first half of the century, as America's cotton industry matured to compete with European imports, calico prints became so affordable that quilts, once a form of needlework only for the wealthy, became commonplace. By 1832 they were so established a part of household textile production that a woman living in Delaware could confide in her diary, "Lydia Sims . . . assisted me in putting in my first quilt. Cry shame! to think that I have been married and a housekeeper for more than fourteen years and never before was thus occupied."[2]

Quiltmaking was associated with a variety of social functions throughout an American woman's life. Patchwork was a foundation for needlework education. Girls learned to piece nine-patch blocks before they learned to read, acquiring the basics of clothing construction through seaming scraps of fabric. Young women created patchwork quilts to set aside for future housekeeping. Women of all ages found in sewing circles and quilting parties a recreation with a purpose. Men also had a place in the social aspect of quilting; they were often invited to the party for supper and dancing after the quilting frame was put away.

Of the approximately 13,000 quilts brought to Quilt Discovery Days, 315 were judged to have been made before the Civil War. No quilts, however, were recorded as having been made in Kansas or brought here before the territory was open to non–Native American settlers, nor have any written records been found from those days. The absence of Kansas-made quilts before 1854 is not surprising, since quilts were not typically used by the Indian tribes native to the state or resident here after 1825. However, given quiltmaking's popularity in the United States, one might assume that women accompanying missionaries, Indian agents, and traders made quilts here, and it is possible that girls in missionary schools were taught patchwork as a part of the sewing curriculum typical of girls' education at the time. Clara Gowing, a missionary with the Delaware Indians, remembered only that "the girls were taught to sew."[3]

The Road to California

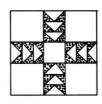

Women traveling through Kansas on the pioneer trails left many records in their diaries, letters, and memoirs of the quilts they carried with them. Although we found no quilts in Kansas left by

Strip quilt by unknown maker, 1825–1850. Helen F. Spencer Museum of Art, University of Kansas, The William Bridges Thayer Memorial.

Very few such everyday quilts made before the Civil War are in Kansas today. Quilts pieced in simple designs of recycled clothing and furnishing fabrics were undoubtedly brought here but used and used up.

Not one family brought an early-nineteenth-century pieced quilt like this to the Quilt Discovery Days. This one came to Kansas after it was purchased by Sallie Casey Thayer, who donated her quilt collection to the art museum at the University of Kansas in 1917.

these travelers, a considerable number must have passed through on the Santa Fe and Oregon trails. Records of quilts on the Santa Fe Trail, the trade road that crossed the state from northeast to southwest, are sparse because few women took the road; it was traveled primarily by merchants, teamsters, and traders delivering goods between Independence and Santa Fe. However, the Oregon Trail that cut across the northeast corner of Kansas was a road for families moving west in search of fortune and fertile land along the Pacific Coast. Between 1841 and 1866, over a quarter of a million people crossed the plains.[4] Many began their trips at the edge of Kansas in "jumping-off places" along the Missouri River from Westport north to St. Joseph, Missouri. "I could not begin to tell you how many there are in St. Joseph that are going to Oregon and California but thousands of them," wrote Mary M. Colby to her family in 1850. "It is a sight to see the tents and wagons on the banks of the river and through the country. They are as thick as camp meeting tents twenty or thirty miles and some say for fifty miles."[5]

Most of the early travelers had little idea of what lay ahead of them on the trail that went west to the Little Blue River and wound north to Fort Kearny to join the Platte River Road. Concepts of Indian Territory were shaped by childhood geography lessons like those recalled by future Kansan Sara Robinson, who remembered the continental map that identified the Great Plains as "the Great American Desert, inhabited only by savages and wild beasts."[6] Oregon-bound Abigail Scott Duniway must have had a similar preconception when she

recorded in her diary, at a camping spot east of the Big Blue River on a May day in 1852, "The *plains* certainly wear a charm that I never expected to see."[7] The treeless hills of Kansas, at their best under a carpet of May wild flowers, looked to travelers like a manicured park. Many wrote home about the beauty of the country. Mrs. Tamsen E. Donner, in the first week of a journey that would end horribly in an early California snowstorm, was enthusiastic about the land's potential: "The prairie between the Blue and the Platte rivers is abundant beyond description. Never have I seen so varied a country—so suitable for cultivation."[8]

 Emigrants who were tempted to cut short their five-month journey and to settle just over the Missouri line were prohibited from doing so by the federal policy of maintaining the central plains as a home for Native Americans, both native tribes like the Kanzas and Wichitas and transplanted tribes like the Shawnees and Delawares. Most white people spent only a few nights in the territory, and it is evident from their travel diaries and letters that many spent their nights under quilts. Men writing of their travels occasionally mention their bedding, using the general term *blankets*, but women in their diaries and memoirs are more specific. They describe blankets, Indian blankets, Mackinaw blankets, Mexican blankets, quilts, coverlids (a common term for coverlets, which may be woven spreads), comforters, and comfortables (synonyms for what are probably heavy quilted or tied quilts of

patchwork or whole cloth).

Susan Magoffin accompanied her trader husband to Santa Fe in 1846. At Lone Elm, in what is now Johnson County, on the first night of her seven-hundred-mile trip, she contentedly took inventory of her bedding in her diary. "Now the prairie life begins. . . . Our bed is as good as many houses have. Sheets, blankets, counterpanes, pillows &c."[9] Rebecca Ketcham did not sound quite as satisfied when she awoke after her first night in Kansas. "How would you who have so many comforts at home, like to have an India-rubber cloth spread on the ground, then a quilt or blanket, and with your carpet bag and clothes for a pillow lay yourself down to sleep, while your only protection from the cold night air was a cloth tent? Over our bed clothes we have an India-rubber cloth which protects us from the dampness which comes through the tent."[10] Ellen Tootle on her first day on the road described her typical wagon home: "We are not as comfortable today as we expect to be. Things were just put in every way. The inside of the wagon is filled nearly to the top with boxes, trunks, comfortables, blankets, guns, a mattress, all the etc. of camp life."[11]

We can imagine that among the possessions that women tucked into their wagons were scrapbags of fabric for making quilts along the way. However, little evidence supports the image of sewing circles held around campfires or patchwork pieced in wagons. The California Heritage Quilt Project recorded a quilt that commemorated an 1859 overland trip. Inscriptions (probably added later) include: "Left Illinois for California, April 15, 1859"; "Pieces cut out in the

Family and wagon, Johnson County, 1908.

Miriam Davis Colt, 1902. As a young woman she went to Kansas to join a vegetarian commune.

winter of 1859 by Grandma"; "Seven Months on the road. Arrived in Columbia. October 28, 1859." This quilt, which was assembled decades later from blocks presumably sewn on the trail, is a rare example of quilt-making en route.[12]

Diaries, letters, and memoirs of women on the trails provide no evidence of quiltmaking. In seventy-four diaries and letters describing western trips between 1841 and 1865, not one woman mentioned sewing a quilt on the road.[13] Sandra Myres, after extensive reading of trail diaries, concluded that "sewing was a favorite pastime," but only a few diary entries support her thesis.[14] The omission of mention of sewing has two possible causes—either travelers did little sewing, or it was so commonplace it was not worth mentioning.

The most likely time for handwork would have been at night or during daytime rest stops, which were sometimes hours long, especially when temperatures exceeded 100 degrees. Susan Magoffin wrote in her diary, "I have opened a regular mantuamaker's [dressmaker's] shop on The Plains. I am sewing on a dress everyday at noon and will finish it soon."[15] Magoffin had an advantage over women on the emigrant trail. As the lone woman in a trade caravan, she was required to do little cooking, laundry, or other family maintenance. More typical of women on the Oregon and California trails was Tamsen Donner, who cataloged her time when the wagons were not rolling: "I botanize and read some, but cook a 'heap' more."[16] Some parties laid over at camps every Sunday because of religious objections to traveling on the Sabbath; although that day might have provided hours to stitch, keeping the Sabbath often extended to handwork, too. Outside Marysville, Louisa Cooke regretted after a Sunday of traveling that the only sign of the Sabbath was "the ladies have laid by their knitting and sewing &c."[17] Rebecca Ketcham customarily did not do handwork on the Sabbath, with one exception, which she noted on a Sunday night: "This morning I so entirely forgot the day I took my knitting and sat down to work."[18]

A popular myth imagines women sewing while riding in the wagons, but most healthy emigrants walked to conserve the strength of their draft animals. John Mack Faragher, after reading eighty-seven women's diaries, letters, and memoirs, writes that riding was not common, but "when they did choose to ride, women busied themselves with mending or knitting."[19] Knitting, which can be accomplished under low light, on a bumpy ride, or under other adverse conditions, was the type of handcraft most likely done. Riding inside the wagons was rough enough to make sewing difficult, especially the precision seaming that patchwork often requires. Helen Carpenter, moving from Franklin County, Kansas Territory, to the West Coast in the 1850s, complained in her diary after her first week on the road, "It has been too cold for sewing and the road has been so rough and uneven that I accomplished but little with the needle."[20] Lucy Rutledge Cooke, on the other hand, did manage to sew at least once while she rode, an incident she reported in a letter to her sister. "Yes, we were sewing as we rode along. I have made sis a little sunbonnet today." But she later complained that she was at a loss as to how to amuse herself, for, although she had sewing to do, it was "what I cannot do well while riding. I might knit but have only red yarn which I bought for Sis but it is too near summer to commence woolen socks. If only I had some muslin. . . . "[21]

Her longing for materials illustrates an additional reason why few quilts were made on the trail. Immigrants were forced to bring the minimum necessary for survival. Yardage for clothes and scrapbags for patchwork were not a necessity. There is mention of buying fabric at outposts like Lawrence (Kansas), Fort Laramie (Wyoming), and Salt Lake City (Utah) in the late 1850s, but fabric for quilts appears to have been as much a luxury on the trail as was time to sew.

Kansas Troubles

 In 1854 Kansas became a destination rather than a mile marker on the road to the West Coast. Glowing descriptions of Kansas sent by overland travelers to family members and newspapers back east encouraged the U.S. government to forcibly remove most of the Native American tribes to a smaller Indian Territory (in present-day Oklahoma) and to open Kansas and Nebraska to settlement. The new Kansas Territory quickly became a pawn in the intensifying confrontation between the North and the South when the Kansas-Nebraska Bill mandated that settlers would vote to open the territory to slavery or declare it a free state. Partisans from both sides joined emigrants looking for fortunes and fertile land, and Kansas became a crusade with battle cries in print, sermon, and song, such as Lucy Larcom's "Call to Kansas":

> Sister true, join us too,
> Where the Kansas flows;
> Let the Northern lily bloom
> With the Southern rose.
> Brave brother, true sister,
> List, we call to thee:
> We'll sing, upon the
>   Kansas plains
> The song of liberty.[22]

Far more "northern lilies" than "southern roses" eventually answered the call. New Yorker Miriam Davis Colt and six members of her extended family were free-state sympathizers persuaded to join a vegetarian commune near what is now Humboldt. From her diary of the 1855 trip, later published as *Went to Kansas: A Thrilling Account of an Ill-Fated Expedition to That Fairy Land*, we learn that immigrants to Kansas brought much the same goods as those heading farther west. Like Oregon- and California-bound travelers, Colt referred often to her bedding, since it was among her few possessions aside from the wild flowers that grew in abundance on the prairies. Colt had disposed of nearly everything else in the weeks before her departure, converting most of her household linens and clothing to carpet rags, which she gave away as she attempted to "reduce down, bringing everything into as small a compass as necessary."[23] She repaired old clothing and sewed new with the help of friends, hoping to build a supply to last her husband, two young children, and herself two or three years. She packed the clothes into trunks with quilts and other bedding and set out for Kansas, riding from New York to Saint Louis in "the cars" (the train);

Clarina I. Howard Nichols, ca. 1855. Clarina Nichols, a fighter for women's rights and abolition, moved from Massachusetts to continue the struggle in the Kansas territory.

steaming on the Missouri River to Kansas City on a passenger boat; and riding the last hundred miles or so in a wagon pulled by a team of oxen purchased in Kansas City.

Colt was heartbroken to discover that the glorious Octagon City planned for the banks of the Neosho River was only a collection of tents and a single log cabin. After a hot, dry, mosquito-plagued summer, she persuaded her husband to abandon the ever-dwindling settlement, which suffered from malaria, cholera, a lack of building materials, and conflicts with Native Americans and southern sympathizers who called themselves Border Ruffians.[24] Her nightmarish journey out of Kansas was arranged by a drunken, swearing Border Ruffian who pinned quilts to the top of his wagon to keep out the rain.[25] By the time she returned to New York, only she and her daughter survived.

The vegetarian settlement and its Octagon City were failures, but better-organized and better-funded settlements survived to thrive. Abolitionists in Boston focused on Lawrence, to which the New England Emigrant Aid Society sent hundreds of free-state zealots, many of them women devoted to abolition, a cause that had received much financial and emotional support from New England's numerous female anti-slavery societies. Hannah Anderson Ropes was one New Englander who made a commitment to support the free-state cause with her presence in the territory even though she could not vote. She lasted six months in "Bleeding Kansas," suffering the austerities of frontier life as well as typhoid fever, fleas, and the terrors of the first guerrilla battles of the Civil War.

The quilts Ropes brought in her trunks provided emotional comfort in their link to the maker, her "dear mother," and physical comfort as well.[26] Imported bedding was a necessity, as manufactured bedding was apparently unavailable for purchase in Kansas. The *Kansas Herald of Freedom*, a free-state newspaper widely read in New England, urged emigrants to pack "good clothing, suited for service not show, such as is adapted for this section of the country, also bedding (not beds on account of their bulk)."[27]

Jane Carruth, arriving in Osawatomie, and Clarina Howard Nichols in Lawrence both wrote that they were forced to borrow bedding since they had not brought any, a mistake caused, Nichols admitted, by "my ignorance of the customs of the country . . . as 'woman's sphere' here is out of doors, I may be allowed to suggest that those who emi-

grate here ought to know before coming precisely what they will find here as materials for a comfortable home here and their cost. Many have been sadly disappointed, not with the country, but in the means necessary to avail themselves of its advantages."[28] New Yorker Mary Tenney, courted by Edwin Gray in 1857, wrote in her diary of their plans for a "home in the Far West." Quiltmaking was part of her preparation for marriage and their trip to Kansas: "I have 5 ready and 3 partly."[29]

The emphasis on bringing sufficient bedding to the territory is a primary reason why so many quilts made in the eastern states during the mid nineteenth century were later recorded by the KQP. It also explains the lack of quilts made here in the first years of settlement: Because most Kansas pioneers owned little but their clothing, cooking utensils, tools, and bedding, their first years here were likely spent producing other necessities.[30]

Although no quilts could be proved to have been made here in territorial years, secondhand accounts of quiltmaking appear in women's writings. Hannah Ropes noted several examples in her letters. An English woman worked on a comforter as Ropes visited her near Lawrence; in another home Ropes noted a workbasket of patches hanging from the ceiling beam next to a side of venison and the potato basket; and she described the furniture in the hotel parlor of Lawrence's Cincinnati House as lounges of unpeeled wood, upholstered with cushions of prairie grass and "nicely covered with patch."[31]

The rustic furniture was a measure of the roughness of life in Lawrence and the rest of the territory. The free-state newspa-

Fragment of a whole-cloth comforter made to raise funds by women of the Boston (Massachusetts) Emigrant Aid Society, 1855. Tied wool. Kansas Museum of History.

The family story that accompanied this piece when it was donated in 1930 indicates that Dr. Sylvester B. Prentiss purchased it at a charity raffle in Lawrence, shortly after he immigrated in the spring of 1855. Funds raised fed newly arrived Kansans. Active in free-state politics, Dr. Prentiss had many hostile encounters with southern sympathizers during the years the territory was known as Bleeding Kansas. His office was burned in the 1863 attack by Quantrill's guerrillas, but he was not injured and was able to treat the wounded.

He impressed upon his children the historical value of the comforter; at some point it was cut into several pieces, probably so that each child might have a souvenir. Two pieces are now in the Kansas Museum of History.

pers and the correspondents like Ropes, Nichols, and Colt who wrote for an eastern audience kept up a cheery, if gritty, optimism throughout the late 1850s. However, there was no denying that many of the passionate immigrants from the cities of New England were unprepared to confront a life in the farms and towns on the frontier. Their sometimes desperate conditions were noted by one of their antagonists, who affected concern. "Where is their support to come from?" asked the editor of the proslavery *Frontier News* in Franklin, Kansas Territory. "Aid Society, maybe. That is a slim trust. Last winter . . . many of them would have perished of starvation had not the western men fed them. It will be worse next winter."[32] His prediction was all too accurate. In December 1855, the temperature fell to minus 30 degrees.

During the difficult winter months, the New England Emigrant Aid Society provided relief shipments of supplies, food, seed, and Sharp's Rifles, known as Beecher's Bibles. Packed in one 1855 shipment was a quilt—a comforter. Back in Boston, the ladies of the aid society cut up what were purported to be military cloaks worn by Revolutionary War soldiers to sew a tied coverlet that they donated to the Lawrence settlers, who raffled it to raise funds in support of the destitute.[33]

The role of the fund-raising coverlet in Lawrence's fight for survival as a free-state stronghold is an indication of the importance of quilts in yet another aspect of American women's lives—the moral cause. In the early nineteenth century, American women who had traditionally met in groups to sew clothing and linens for the poor added a new component to their sewing circles—selling the needlework made at meetings to provide funds for reform. Pen wipers, pincushions, embroidered slippers, and quilts were sold at Ladies Fairs, the ancestors of church bazaars and today's holiday craft boutiques. Pennies raised from such sales accumulated to fund missions, church building programs, and abolition, temperance, and antiprostitution campaigns. Women's groups also quilted for hire, charging a fee to customers who had supplied the patchwork top. By midcentury, women all over the United States used such genteel fund-raising methods, congruent with the concept of a woman's domestic sphere, to influence the moral direction of the country.

In New England, the success of the female antislavery societies motivated some to break through the boundaries of what was considered proper and venture into public life, actively organizing for social change through speaking, writing, and campaigning for the vote.[34] Although New Englanders were a minority of Kansas settlers, the state reaped the harvest of lessons learned by women active in the antislavery movement. From the early days of settlement, Kansas women continued the tradition of combining needlework with social activities. In May 1856, Sara Robinson recorded two women's events that served, as she noted, to join "newcomers from almost all the states in the union . . . in strong bonds of friendship" and also served higher purposes. She enjoyed an entertainment at a Lawrence hotel given by the ladies of the Literary Charitable Association and, while visiting in Topeka, attended a sewing circle/temperance meeting.[35] In 1859, Henrietta Woodford and her brother, the Reverend O. L. Woodford, reported the establishment of a Ladies Sewing Society in Grasshopper Falls (later Valley Falls), "the object being to furnish the Congregational Church."[36] Such ladies' aid societies were to flourish with the state, providing a strong social network for quiltmaking activities that continues to the present day. Although no quilts and few records of quiltmaking activity survive, quilts were likely a part of the work of some territorial and early state ladies' aid organizations. By 1863, the women of the Wyandotte (later Kansas City, Kansas) Ladies' Aid Society had been organized long enough to finish a quilt that won second prize at the first Kansas state fair.[37]

While some Kansas women raised funds, others raised eyebrows with their less-traditional activism. The first Kansas Equal Rights Association was formed in 1859 in the hopes of influencing the framers of the state constitution to include a provision for women's suffrage. Clarina Howard Nichols was at the Wyandotte Constitutional Convention, "a self-appointed delegate, uninvited and uninstructed," remembered Mary Tenney Gray. "Often she sat knitting, but more often busy with pencil or pen and with bright eyes always on the alert for the 'business before the house.'"[38] Despite considerable support for the petition, Nichols's request that women be granted the right to vote in the free state was denied, with the justification that women should be relieved from "merely political" rights and duties so "that they may have more time to attend to those greater and more complicated responsibilities which . . . devolve around women."[39] The one concession granted by the first legislature—that white women could vote in district school elections—made Kansas in 1861 the first to give women universal suffrage in the domain of education.

Kansas Dugout

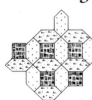
During the Civil War, the road through Kansas grew less rocky with the advent of the stage lines and the beginning of the railroads. Catherine Wever Collins, on her way to join her husband in Fort Laramie, recorded that the trip from Cincinnati took only eleven days. She rode the train to the Kansas line, disembarked, crossed the Missouri River on a ferry, and boarded an-

other train that took her the few miles to Atchison, where she caught a stage coach for the last, long leg of her trip. The same year Hallie Riley Hodder and her sister took a similar trip to Denver, boarding a stage coach in Atchison. By "changing horses every ten miles at little stations on the way and riding nights as well as days we made 100 miles in 24-hours and reached Denver on the evening of the seventh day."[40]

The Homestead Act of 1862 gave would-be settlers free title to public land, superseding the old preemption laws that required payment. Much Kansas land was given to railroad corporations as an incentive to build lines through the West; to finance construction they sold the land that lined their routes. Thus, the railroads indirectly encouraged post–Civil War settlement with easier travel and the promise of access to eastern markets and goods, and they directly influenced immigration by advertising their land. The Kansas Pacific, with four million acres to sell, was typical in flooding eastern states and eastern Europe with free promotional pamphlets in several languages. Inflated accounts of the wonders of Kansas encouraged land-hungry people to invest in "a well-watered country."[41] Such foreign-language pamphlets were effective in bringing European settlers, who came individually or in colonies, such as the Mennonites who came to central Kansas. In the 1870s, the Kansas population tripled.

The three thousand miles of track laid across Kansas by the late 1870s meant that emigrants could ship more of their goods to their new homes. The KQP recorded several stories of emigrants who rented railroad cars to send their possessions, including their quilts. Quilts and bedding remained high on the list of items to bring. Abbie Bright, who planned to homestead in 1871, recorded instructions from her brother in her diary: "I am only to take heavy, strong clothing and whatever I will want for a bed."[42] Six years later, Howard Ruede made the mistake of arriving with nothing for a bed. He and his brother slept close together with their army coats as blankets. "Hope I can make another $2 tomorrow," he wrote his family. "Then I'll buy a blanket. Our overcoats are hardly enough." He advised his brother and sister who followed them to bring bedding: a shawl, pillows, quilts, and blankets.[43]

The KQP recorded several quilts brought to the state in these years. One that has survived is Jennie Gildersleeve Montgomery's friendship quilt, signed by twenty Pennsylvania friends. She packed it when she brought her four children to McPherson to live with a sister after her husband's death in the 1870s.[44] The KQP also recorded an increased number of quilts from the 1870s that may be reliably attributed to Kansas quiltmakers. A comparison of date-inscribed quilts with known origins indicates that a shift from imported quilts to Kansas-made quilts took place during that decade. Nine dated quilts made in other states before 1875 were recorded but not one made in Kansas. For the years 1875 through 1899, the project recorded fourteen dated Kansas-made quilts and nine from elsewhere.

The Kansas-made quilts inscribed with dates in the 1870s and those attributed to the decade are similar to those made elsewhere, as all post–Civil War quilts differed from earlier quilts in several significant ways. Women used fewer fine details, such as stuffed quilting and corded bindings. They abandoned chintz prints and relied on small-scale calicoes. They typically increased the number of prints per quilt and decreased the size of the pieces, a reflection of the continuing deflation in the price of cotton prints. They lost interest in making whole-cloth, appliqued albums and medallion quilts. By the time Kansans began making quilts in large numbers, the increasing number of national magazines had begun to standardize quiltmaking styles across the country.[45]

Written records also indicate an increase in quiltmaking activities in Kansas in the 1870s. Luna Warner, who settled south of Downs in 1871 when she was sixteen years old, wrote in her diary four months later, "I have 22 squares of an album bed quilt done." This is the earliest personal reference to quiltmaking in a Kansas diary or letter found by this author.[46] Luna Warner was certainly not alone; many memoirs and fiction works set in Kansas in the 1870s and 1880s describe quiltmaking, as do newspaper articles, especially accounts of fairs.

The agricultural fair was an established American tradition by the time Kansas became a territory. Prizes for quilts were a standard feature. The first state fair in Leavenworth in 1863 offered two dollars for the "best and most tastefully executed quilt or coverlet," one dollar for second best, and a subscription to the new *Kansas Farmer* magazine for third. Clara Gowing, visiting Leavenworth for a teachers' convention, recalled the needlework

Crazy quilts were popular at the 1894 Finney County Fair.

display there as a "one-day exhibit of fancy domestic articles, a very good but not very large exhibit. The fruit and vegetable exhibit was very large."[47]

Local agricultural fairs were organized for numerous reasons, among them a desire to create a sense of community, a purpose advocated by the *Abilene Chronicle* in 1870: "We have been asked 'Can we hold a Fair this fall?' We will not be able to make as large a display as older counties can, but we can hold at least a small exhibition. . . . A good Fair even if it be but small . . . will bring our people together and . . . cement the bonds of friendship which should always exist between citizens of the same county." The citizens responded, and a week later the *Chronicle* advertised the premium list for the first annual Dickinson County Fair with four prizes for quilts in two categories—"the best and neatest made fancy quilt" and the "best and neatest made white quilt."[48] In addition to their social role, fairs also popularized new crops, equipment, and farming and housekeeping methods with competitions and educational exhibits, which farmers and their wives were encouraged to copy. Prizewinning quilts undoubtedly inspired imitations and set standards for craftsmanship and design.

The early descriptions of quilt premiums at Kansas fairs give little information about the kind of quilts displayed. The 1871 Douglas County Fair gave premiums in only one category—"for the best and most tastefully executed patchwork quilt ($3 for first $2 for second and $1 for third)." However, a local hardware dealer offered a special premium, a washing machine valued at twenty dollars, for the best and most tastefully arranged patchwork quilt. The subtle difference in terms—"tastefully executed" versus "tastefully arranged"— may reflect the conflict between craftsmanship and design that is still a matter of discussion in Kansas quilt competitions.[49] Over the years, competitive fairs increased the number of quilt

categories and published descriptions in more detail, giving current historians more insight into popular styles. The 1893 Wilson County Fair included eleven categories for patchwork and quilts, with separate classes for autograph quilts, log cabin quilts, worsted comforters, and Japanese (crazy) quilts or fancy silk quilts.[50]

State fairs in eastern states influenced the Kansas State Fair and county fairs, as evidenced by premium descriptions. For example, during the 1870s the Kansas State Fair included quilts as a subcategory of "Needle, Shell and Waxwork," a categorization found earlier at the Ohio State Fair between 1850 and 1865. As descriptions in Ohio changed, so did descriptions in Kansas, usually with a time lag of a year or longer. For example, the Ohio county fairs were two years ahead of Kansas fairs in offering prizes for the newly popular log cabin quilts in the early 1870s.[51]

We cannot determine whether fair categories created popular taste or merely reflected what

A sewing class at Kansas State Agricultural College in Manhattan about 1900.

A Kansas family poses in front of their dugout home near Waubunsee in Riley county, ca. 1890. The woman on the right has a quilt folded over the back of her chair. Riley County Historical Society.

Cowboys camping out at the W. D. Boyce Cattle Company in Kansas or Colorado about 1900. The cowboy on the right sleeps under a tied patchwork comforter. Cowboys called their quilts "soogans" (also spelled "suggins," "sugans," and "sougans"). Denver Public Library.

women were making. Prizes for log cabin quilts, crazy quilts, or Irish chains could have been a response to the popularity of the designs rather than an incentive for quiltmakers to begin making them, but it seems likely that by offering prizes for specific types of quilts, fairs may have helped to nationalize and standardize aesthetics, encouraging Kansans to keep up with Ohio quiltmakers.

Premium lists often included prizes for quilts by children, an age group usually defined as "under 15." There were also some categories for children younger than twelve, ten, and eight.[52] The KQP recorded numerous quilts with family histories crediting them to children and found many Kansans who re-

called making quilts in their youth. In her memoirs written in 1939, Florence Kniseley Menninger, who left Pennsylvania for Kansas as a teenager, remembered that by the time she was ten she had made a dozen quilts, finishing the blocks for her first one by age five. Carrie Hackett Hall in 1935 recalled her pleasure in winning first prize at a Smith County fair with a star quilt she pieced at the age of seven in the early 1870s.[53]

Reminiscences of Americans born in the first half of the nineteenth century include recollections of making quilts as early as the age of five, but the KQP records of quilts made by Kansas children indicate that nine or ten was a more typical age to learn

Barbara Brackman

later in the century.[54] Interview data suggest that the tradition of children's learning to sew by making quilts persisted through the 1940s and was revived in the 1980s.[55]

The advent of the sewing machine undoubtedly affected the female curriculum. Once the machine reached factories and homes, young girls no longer had to prepare early for a lifetime of hand sewing of a family's clothing and linens. The machine meant that by the end of the century the curriculum for girls had widened; sewing was still important but no longer the focus of their formal education. Early Kansas immigrants were urged to bring machines with them by an advertisement on the back cover

of Redpath and Hinton's 1859 *Hand-book to Kansas Territory and the Rocky Mountains Gold Region*: "Is there a husband, father or brother in the United States who will permit the drudgery of hand-sewing in his family when a Grover and Baker machine will do it better, more expeditiously and cheaper than can possibly be done by hand?"[56] Evidence in women's writing and in their quilts indicates that the machine did not have an effect here until the 1870s and 1880s. Elise Dubach Isely received a machine from her husband in 1873 as a wedding anniversary gift. Looking back, she considered its arrival evidence that for her family in Doniphan County on the Missouri border, "pioneer days

The Watters family in front of their sod house on the Metcalf Ranch in Decatur County, ca. 1880. Can that be a quilt hanging over the back of the rocker?

were over."[57]

Elizabeth Bacon Custer, writing in the 1880s, echoed Isely's opinion that Kansas was no longer a frontier. "I lately rode through the state, which seemed when I first saw it a hopeless, barren waste and found the land under fine cultivation, the houses, barns and fences excellently built, and cattle in the meadows."[58] The frontier, however, persisted in the western counties. Kansas is essentially two states, divided by a line running roughly from Concordia south through Salina, Wichita, and Wellington that marks an all-important difference in annual precipitation. On the eastern side, still part of the continent's fertile central lowlands, farmers successfully adapted farming methods from their home states. But settlers in the western two-thirds of the state, the edge of the unfamiliar Great Plains, struggled through trial and error to make the land productive, and for decades, agricultural disasters loomed over the broad horizon. Years when rain fell encouraged wild optimism and an influx of settlers who quickly learned the folly of the myth that breaking the prairie would change meteorological conditions. Rain did not follow the plow, as many people believed; drought followed good years, and bust inevitably followed boom. Speaking for a generation of western Kansans, Anna Webber wrote in her diary, "July 21, 1881: It is clouding up for a rain, and I do hope We will get it. We need rain so bad, everything is nearly burned up. O, dear, this is a hard place to live, this Kansas is."[59]

Prayers for precipitation were too often rewarded with blizzards like the monstrous snowstorm of New Year's Day 1886,

Unknown Plains Indian woman and child about 1900. A patchwork quilt has been incorporated into her dwelling. The photo was found in Kansas, but the location may be Oklahoma. Collection of Terry Thompson.

A woman identified only as Florence M. stitches a crazy quilt in Wichita at the turn of the century. Courtesy of Jan Sakoguchi.

in which over half the cattle in Ford County froze to death, or with floods like an 1885 disaster, recalled by Mrs. S. T. Roach of Medicine Lodge. As the water rose, her family "climbed to the loft as we could, snatching a few quilts to take up with us we climbed." Her relatives were not as lucky. Their house washed away, they drowned in the rush of water, and "household furniture was scattered everywhere. Their feather beds were hanging in the trees and their lovely quilts, washed full of sand, were picked up along the shore hanging on the bushes."[60]

The vagaries of weather were only one factor in the boom-and-bust cycle; wild land speculation added to the craziness. For years the major commodity traded was real estate. Speculators did a land office business in town lots that *might* be situated in the county seat. The potential profits inspired desperate "county-seat wars" in which citizens of one metropolis-to-be murdered those in another over the all-important designation as the center of county business. Craig Miner, in his history of Kansas settlement, notes that an 1887 survey of the number of real estate transactions across the country placed New York City first, Kansas City second, Wichita third, and Topeka tenth. Wichita, growing 500 percent in a year, was the fastest-growing city in the nation; and Finney County's population increased from about 1,400 to 14,000 between 1885 and 1886. Growth was often, however, a matter of one step forward and two steps back. By 1887, over half the population of Finney County had left for greener pastures.[61]

During the last quarter of the nineteenth century, as in the days

Crazy pillow pieced and embroidered by Ida Stover Eisenhower (1862–1946), Abilene, 1900–1920. Dwight D. Eisenhower Library.

Ida Stover, an orphan living with relatives in Virginia, ran away from home to get an education. In 1883 she joined a Mennonite caravan traveling to Kansas and enrolled in Lane University in Douglas County. There she met David Eisenhower, married, and had the seven sons whom she recorded on this pillow. In a biography, Earning the Right to Do Fancy Work (Lawrence: University of Kansas Press, 1957), Kunigunde Duncan remembered a visit to the Eisenhower home when son Dwight was commander of the Allied forces during World War II.

"Every chair had its extra cushion. What hadn't she mastered possible to be done with needle, sewing-machine, crochet hook, knitting needles, embroidery hoop, tatting shuttle. . . . "

Although son Paul died in 1895, Ida included his name on the pillow. "These reporters," she complained to Duncan nearly fifty years later. "They don't count my little Paul who died before his first birthday. Why, he was my son too."

Ida Stover Eisenhower with her husband and six surviving sons in 1926. Left to right: Arthur, Edgar, Roy, Earl, husband David, Dwight, and Milton.

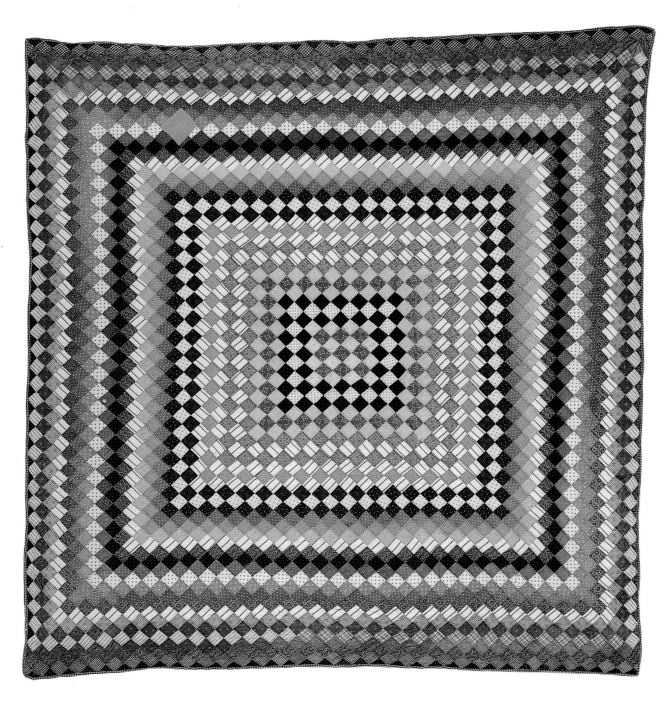

KQP Ga084, Trip around the World, pieced by Anna Moriah Gold Hopkins (1865–1948), New Lancaster, Miami County, 1890–1910 with later repair. Cottons. Collection of Wilma Homrighausen.

Anna Hopkins made this quilt for her son, Omar C. Hopkins, and embroidered his initials on the back. She was born in Illinois of Pennsylvania German ancestry. Both the pattern and the idea of a quilt set aside to go for a son's housekeeping speak of Pennsylvania German traditions.

Anna Hopkins.

when the Oregon Trail crossed Kansas, many eastern quilts passed through the state. Kansas-made quilts—taken with them by optimists moving farther west—were later recorded by projects in California and Washington. Kansas quilts also traveled east to Pennsylvania and Wisconsin, where the discouraged recovered from their attacks of Kansas Fever while "visiting the wife's folks" (the contemporary euphemism for giving up on Kansas).

There are many stories of hardship and sorrow at the end of the century. Our comfortable, twentieth-century perspective encourages us to view women's lives, in particular, as "almost inconceivably hard, dreary, monotonous and uninteresting," words used by Kansan John Ise in the 1930s. However, today's historians studying women's own words tell us, as Glenda Riley has, that "clearly there is great variation in the experiences, perspectives, and outlooks of Kansas frontierswomen."[62] Some women did live the tale of bitter loneliness on their Kansas homesteads. Hattie Humphrey's words in 1873 in

Edwards County are haunting: "Everything is so monotonous, almost unbearable even to me, who am not supposed to have any nerves."[63] Others, like Flora Moorman Heston, who spent a year near Fowler in Clark County, described a sincere appreciation for the Kansas landscape, their neighbors, and the promised opportunities of pioneer life. Heston's words, written for a worried mother and sister in Indiana, may occasionally reflect an optimism she did not feel, but attitudes like hers enabled people to persevere through drought, flood, blizzards, and grasshoppers. "The country bids fair to be a second Garden of Eden and I have no ax to grind either. . . . I have a great deal more leisure time than I used to have it dont take near the work to keep up one room that it does a big house." She never complained of loneliness, noting there were thirteen sod houses and one frame house in sight of their claim.[64]

Loneliness and dreariness also seemed to play little part in the life of teenager Emily Butcher on her family farm in Barber County, south of Pratt. From her diary in 1896: "Wed. December 2nd. Went to school; and to Hargis's for night. Thursday 3rd. Went to school. Kittie Cook stayed all night with me. Friday December 4th. Went to school; Went to the Odd Fellow's dance at Sun [City]. Danced a few sets. About 13. Got home at half past 4. Saturday December 5th. Got up at 8 and finished my dress and helped tie a quilt. Pet was over."[65] Her description of Pet's visit indicates that tying a quilt (a quick form of securing quilt top, batting, and backing) continued to be the same kind of cooperative, social activity that quilting was.

The tied comforter was just one of many nationwide changes in quilt styles that appeared in the 1880s and 1890s. After 1880, newspapers and magazines began to influence choices of pattern, technique, and color scheme. In the past, styles had changed slowly as women learned of new trends in face-to-face contact, one quilter at a time. The speed of change increased as national periodicals reached more farm families on the new rural free delivery routes and as the technology for illustrations improved, allowing readers to exchange quilt patterns across the country.

One of the first fads disseminated by ladies' periodicals was the crazy quilt, a collage of odd-shaped fabrics lavish with embroidery, which was fashionable not only in Philadelphia and Boston but also in Kansas. "I can remember the one in our pioneer home," recalled Carrie Hackett Hall, "and how sorry I felt for anyone who was too poor or too shiftless to own one." A Morton County woman who signed only her initials wrote a letter to the newspaper: "While [my husband] is gone I take care of thirteen head of cattle, two pigs, one colt and milk four cows, do my housework, make lace and crazy patch." The Missouri Heritage Quilt Project, the Nebraska Quilt History Project, and the Kansas Quilt Project recorded similar high incidences of crazy quilts. The Missouri project, which focused on nineteenth-century quilts, found that 9.68 percent of all quilts were crazy quilts; the Nebraska project, which recorded quilts made to 1940, found that 9.7 percent were in that style. Of the 1,421 quilts estimated by the KQP to have been made between 1880 and 1925, 9.3 percent were crazy quilts.[66]

Indian Fair, Jackson County, 1917.
Jules A. Bourquin Collection, Kansas
Collection, University of Kansas
Libraries.

The Kickapoo and Pottawatomie
tribes held Indian Fairs from the turn
of the century through the 1950s. This
display of entries in both "Domestic
and Fancy Work" and "Bead Work
and Curios" categories illustrates the
range of handwork done by the women
of these tribes in the early twentieth
century. The pieced, appliqued, and
crazy quilts are identical to those made
by their nonnative neighbors.

Kansas T's

The 1890s
marked many
changes in
Kansas' transi-
tion from the
frontier. The
last of the 105
counties was
organized in 1890, the year the
federal government officially declared the frontier closed. In
1893 Kansas enacted a herd law
that mandated the fencing of live-
stock. By that time Kansas was
established as the number-one
"wheat state," an achievement
rarely yielded since.

In dry circles, Kansas was considered the most progressive of
states. A state constitutional
amendment passed in 1880 prohibited the sale of liquor "except
for medical, scientific and mechanical purposes." This first
constitutional prohibition had

long been the goal of many in
the moral reform societies that
had offered spiritual, social, and
cultural events since territorial days,
when a temperance society was
organized at the Pottawatomie
Mission in 1839. "At the close of
each meeting," recalled Elise
Dubach Isely of later temperance
events, "both young and old were
urged to come to the front of the
church and sign the teetotaler's
pledge. Such an act entitled the
signer to wear the temperance in-
signia, the blue ribbon."[67] A teetotaler foreswore all spirits—
liquor, wine, and beer—rather
than merely pledging temperance, which permitted consump-
tion of wine and beer. In some
societies total abstainers placed a
T by their names on the rolls, the
custom from which the word teetotaler is probably derived.[68]

The T was a symbol for the
movement that likely inspired

Wheel fund-raiser quilt made by members of the Methodist Episcopal Church in White City, Morris County, 1896. Cottons. Collection of Beth and John Ford. Smithsonian Institution Negative 74-7893.

Nearly five hundred community members paid ten cents each to have their names inked on the spokes and twenty-five cents for the hub position in this wheel quilt, which raised money for new church carpeting. The finished quilt was presented to the pastor, the Reverend Dr. John S. Ford, and his wife, Sarah Swigart Ford. Under the central wheel is inked "Presented to Brother and Sister Ford by the Ladies of the M[ethodist] E[piscopal] Church of White City, Kans. March, 1896. God Bless You All."

A bedroom in the D. S. Harrington home, Gardner, Johnson County, 1901. Johnson County Museum System.

This wistful unnamed woman poses with a rack of fresh laundry in the basement of the Dunn home in Ottawa about 1910. The fabrics in her dress and apron and the skirts on the rack are the inexpensive cottons so popular for quilts at the time.

several quilt designs recorded in turn-of-the-century literature, such as Capital T, Imperial T, and Double T.[69] One specific reference to Kansas and its innovative prohibition law was found by the Quilts of Tennessee project, which recorded a turn-of-the-century sampler of various block designs, each labeled with a name. On a pattern of T's was inked Kansas T's, a reminder of the years when prohibition was known as the Kansas Idea.[70]

Kansas women had obtained the right to vote in municipal elections in 1887. That year Susanna M. Salter, a temperance candidate in Argonia, was elected the first woman mayor in the United States. In 1888, the Oskaloosa city council also attracted national attention when five women council members and a female mayor were voted in, resulting in a flurry of "petticoat tickets" in the state. Full suffrage remained the goal of many women, a continuous campaign that was funded in part by ladies' fairs at which portraits of Mayor Salter were sold. A three-day fair held in Topeka in 1892 served two purposes: The needlework sold both raised money for the cause and proved the point that voting in city elections had not defeminized the voters, who could still do the finest domestic fancy work.[71]

As the century turned, small-town Kansas took on its present appearance. White cottages formed neighborhoods of neat grids, varied by a few turreted mansions in the Queen Anne style that housed the prosperous who made money in cattle, agriculture, railroads, and commerce. The economy derived from practical farming and ranching rather than speculation, and the weather was generally kind with

only an occasional extreme. Kansans who had stayed congratulated themselves on perseverance, prosperity, and their position as moral beacons. Prohibition, which had been haphazardly enforced, actually began to cut down on drinking as Carry Nation earned a national reputation for smashing saloons that flouted the law. Kansas also was in the forefront in controls on smoking and gambling. Robert Smith Bader in his book *Hayseeds, Moralizers, and Methodists* characterized the state's early-twentieth-century image as a paragon of progressive thought and material success. He quoted Carl Becker, who wrote that Kansas was "no mere geographical expression, but a 'state of mind,' a religion and a philosophy in one."[72]

In 1912, an equal suffrage amendment to the constitution passed, giving women the right to vote in state elections. Topekan Martha VonOrsdol Farnsworth recorded the event in her diary: "Tues. [November] 5th. Up early, got Breakfast, but only took time to eat a wee bite and hurried away to the Polls for its Election day and we women are to make a last stand for our enfranchisement. I was at the Polling-place (2nd of 6th Ward) before daylight and handing out cards. . . . Wed 6. '*This is the day after*.' And so bright and sunny—a glorious day, and 'there is sunshine in my heart', for while I went to bed last night a *slave*, I awoke this morning a *free woman*."[73]

At the turn of the century we see quilts that reflect Kansas as a community with a strong Protestant religious network. Quilts made to raise funds for causes took on a new look; the signatures became the design. Groups,

especially church groups, organized wheel quilts for which "different people bought spokes in the wheel so their names were on the quilt. Fifty cents for the hub; 15 cents for the spokes and 25 cents for the corners" were the prices on a Wagon Wheel embroidered in red and white by the Rock Creek Brethren Ladies' Aid in 1923. Nearly seven hundred Sabetha individuals and businesses (including Weigel Tire Shop; Dr. B. M. Davenport, Osteopath; Kreitzey Bros. Bakery; and Behmeys Cash-Carry Store) were recorded on the quilt that was later auctioned at the local auction barn.[74]

The increase in Kansas-made quilts and the decrease in quilts made elsewhere and brought here between 1900 and 1924 reflects the slowing of immigration into the state. Those who did come were no longer required to bring bedding, as manufactured goods were widely available owing to the increased reach of the railroads and mail order houses. The availability of inexpensive fabrics was a factor in the increase in Kansas-made quilts; another was that quiltmaking was enjoying one of its many revivals. The growing idealization of America's colonial past, manifested as a "colonial revival" in architecture and home decorating, also called for quilts. In 1904, the magazine *House Beautiful* advised housewives to add quilts to their decor. "One of these old quilts, into which a woman of long ago put so much creative and adaptive skill, will give an air to even the most commonplace beds. It will glorify a beautiful old bed."[75] Women who had not inherited antique quilts were advised to make their own but in shades to match the new colonial decorating schemes.

KQP Ff084. Lone Star or Star of Bethlehem pieced by Joanna M. Chaney Waldron, Harper County, 1916–1917. Cottons. Collection of Maxine Halton.

Joanna Chaney donated this quilt to raise money for the Red Cross during World War I. Her granddaughter recalls that a form of an auction was held in which the auctioneer and assistants held up the quilt and the audience threw money onto the quilt. The money went for war relief, and the quilt was returned to the maker with a commendation for her patriotism.

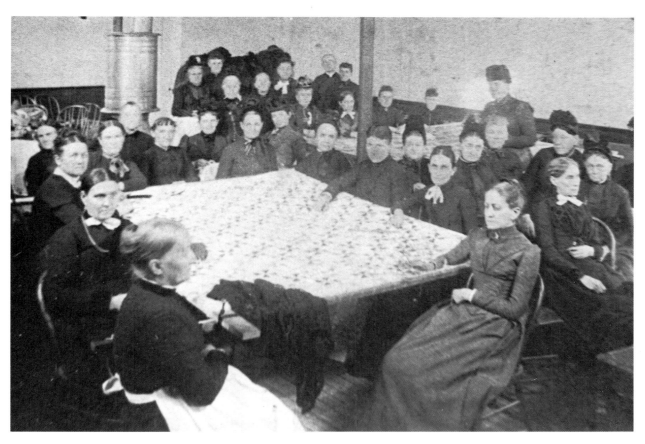

The women of the Ladies' Aid Society of the First Methodist Episcopal Church in Lawrence, about 1900. Kansas Collection, University of Kansas Libraries.

An unknown baby perched on a string quilt. 1900–1920. Courtesy of Terry Thompson.

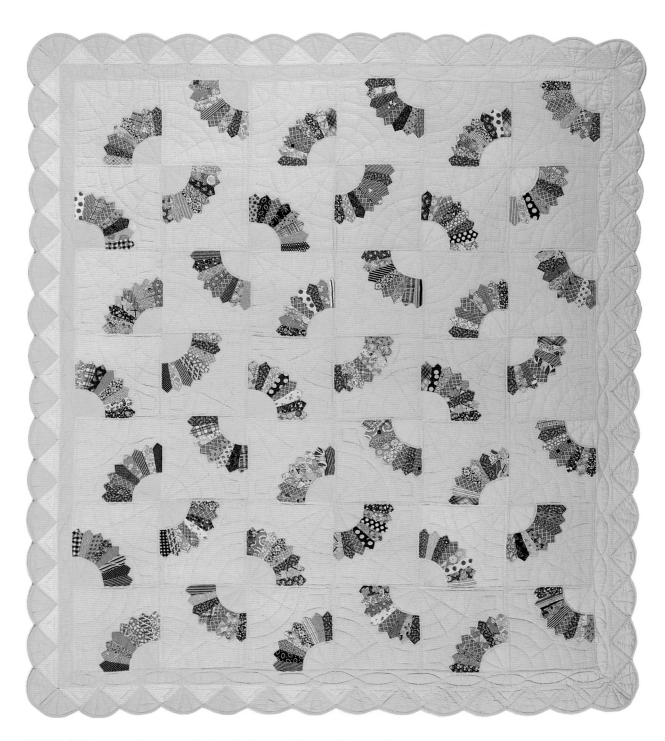

KQP Dg065. Japanese Fan, pieced by Estelle McConnell Loyd (1891–1984), quilted by Estelle and her sister, Elizabeth Mc-Connell Loyd, near Hiawatha, 1932–1935. Cottons. Collection of Mary Loyd Chadwell.

Capper's Weekly *offered a Japanese fan pattern with a "pie-wedge" border and recommended a yellow and green color scheme to complement a scrap bag of prints. Those with empty scrap bags could send a quarter for twenty-five printed cottons.*

Estelle May McConnell was born in 1891 near Baker in Brown County. During her later years she and husband Frank Loyd spent their evenings collaborating on applique kits, which often came with hundreds of numbered shapes stamped onto cotton. Daughter Mary recalls Estelle calling out which piece she needed next; her husband would sort through the yardage and cut it out for her to whip down.

Turkey red, green, and gold were not advised, nor were crazy quilts, so recently popular.

The quilts surviving from the first quarter of the twentieth century were generally rather dark, made of many scraps of print fabric, with blue and gray as predominant color schemes. Style may have been dictated by the availability of certain cheap, colorfast cotton prints, primarily in shades of blue, red, black, and white. Quilting remained rather minimal, with tying still a popular option. Applique was rare; pieced patterns were increasingly diverse as national magazines and needlework companies generated designs. To obtain patterns, magazines held quilt block contests. In the 1910s a national magazine, *People's Popular Monthly*, received entries from California to North Carolina, and two of the top three winners were from Kansas. In 1919, *Farm and Fireside* received 1,500 blocks in the mail; Mattie Whitbeck of Fredonia, Kansas, tied for second place with a traditional tulip applique.[76] Kansas quilters were beginning a tradition of national recognition that continues to the present time.

Many unquilted tops from this era remain. Numerous finished quilts recorded by the KQP were pieced between 1890 and 1925, left as tops for generations, and quilted rather recently. Today, unfinished tops have little value for some owners, who feel they should eventually be quilts (a practice conservators and historians decry because quilting through fabric over fifty years old weakens it and changes the tops' historical value). The quiltmakers who left so many tops may have valued them as they were; at least one county fair awarded prizes for "Quilt, piece top" in 1917.[77]

Changes in the division of quiltmaking labor may have contributed to the surplus of tops. The informal, cooperative quilting bee of the nineteenth century in which participants quilted each others' tops seems to have been in decline in the early twentieth century, replaced by church groups and social clubs. The KQP heard many stories of Ladies' Aid societies that specialized in quilting for others for a fee. Tops may have been set aside waiting for a little extra cash to pay the dollar or two the Ladies' Aid asked.

Leona Burroughs of Kingman told KQP interviewers that she learned to quilt as a girl with a group of twenty that met every Wednesday at the Methodist Church. Working on two quilts at a time, the group raised money to pay for a new church, charging two cents for each yard of quilting thread used.[78] In 1904 the women of the Church of the Brethren in Quinter organized a Sisters' Aid Society (to distinguish it from the Methodist Ladies' Aid). Initially, they charged a half cent per yard of quilting thread used. In 1928 they quilted forty-one tops; in 1930 they finished one hundred and enjoyed a reputation for doing beautiful quilting that "became known far and wide."[79]

One offshoot of the cooperative quilting bee was the formalized social club devoted to sewing side by side, making friendship quilts, and quilting each other's tops. The KQP recorded many quilts made by clubs like the Daisy Embroidery Club of Independence and the Willowdale Happy Hour Club of Abilene, which has met since 1915.[80]

Kansas Dust Storm

As the social fabric of America changed in the 1920s, quilts changed, too. A major influence was the change in women's dress. Clothes grew less restrictive, with shorter skirts and freer shapes, and manufacturers created new fabrics, fibers, and colors. Improvements in dye chemistry allowed mills to offer lighter, brighter cottons in their inexpensive lines, inspiring a new look in quilts that was characterized by a multicolor palette, a good deal of plain white cotton as a neutral to coordinate all the colors, and innovative patterns, such as the Butterfly and the Double Wedding Ring.

The new look in quilts was also related to more subtle changes. As urban dwellers came to dominate in America, both demographically and culturally, rural values were viewed as old-fashioned. Patchwork quilts in dark cottons and wools were linked to rural life and came to be considered old-fashioned, too. Quilts in novel designs in the lighter cottons were seen as modern and were acceptable to chic, urban women and to rural

Barbara Brackman

ELECTRIC FAN IS A MOTIF FOR QUILTS.

Letha's Electric Fan

1 SOLID BLUE

20 DIFFERENT PRINTS

4 WHITE

4 WHITE

As the churn dash was a motif for quilts 100 years ago, today the electric fan becomes conventionalized for that use. Thanks to an enthusiastic quilt fan.

(Copyright, 1938, by *The Kansas City Star*.)

Opposite: KQP Gc086. Letha's Electric Fan, pieced by Sarah Suffel Schaefer (1862–1950), Emporia, quilted by Mildred Sill, 1938–1970. Collection of Fern Stockton.

Sarah Schaefer's husband, depressed by his failing health, shot himself in 1929. Quiltmaking provided her solace after his death. She made one top for each of her 24 grandchildren, most of them from patterns printed in the Kansas City Star. *Granddaughter Fern Stockton said, "I've often thought on it, how timely it was that the Star would start printing patterns. What a godsend it was to be challenged every week with a new pattern." Sarah (right) pieced Letha's Electric Fan for Fern, who had the top quilted in the late 1960s. The pattern appeared in the* Kansas City Star, *April 2, 1938.*

women who wanted to keep up with fashionable trends. The change from dark to light quilts was abrupt; between 1922 and 1927 pastel quilts quickly replaced quilts with dark blue, gray, or maroon color schemes, developing into a nationwide craze among women of all ages, income levels, and backgrounds.

Quilts made between 1925 and 1950 account for one-third of all the quilts recorded by the KQP. Of these quilts, 257 had a date inscribed, a number large enough to plot trends. The height of the quilt fad was the period 1930 to 1936, with fifteen or more dated quilts each year during the depression years that people most commonly associate with quiltmaking. But interest had developed before the stock market crash in 1929; date-inscribed quilts increased gradually through the early 1920s, with the first burst of popularity in 1927.

Further evidence of a popular interest in quilts that year was the first of a long series of quilt pattern features in Topeka's *Capper's Weekly*. On February 12, Louise Fowler Roote, using the pen name Kate Marchbanks, initiated the column: "Since old time pieced or patchwork quilts have again stepped in the limelight, the paper had received requests for quilt block ideas."[81] The *Kansas City Star* soon followed suit with a column in September 1928 initiating three decades of quilt columns. The *Star* inspired quilters in Kansas City–area homes with weekly patterns that appeared in the Saturday evening paper and reached quilters in five states (Arkansas, Iowa, Kansas, Missouri, and Oklahoma) through a weekly farm paper. The majority of the patterns were contributed by readers

Barbara Brackman

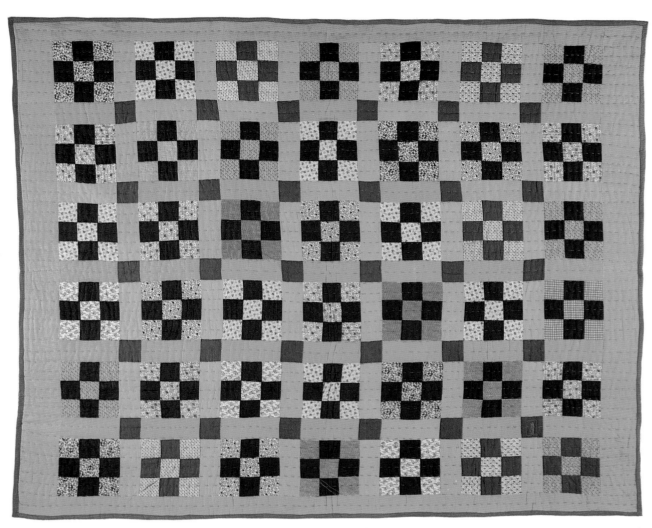

Opposite: KQP Jb017. Embroidered quilt, embroidered by Ruth Wasson Sturges (1922–   ), Peru, Chautauqua County, 1934–1937. Collection of Ruth Sturges.

Ruth's sister, Betty Wasson Nation, designed and drew the ladies' heads and sold them to friends for one or two dollars per set, a way to make extra cash during the Depression. Ruth embroidered these in 1934 when she was twelve years old; three years later she and her mother, Minnie Wasson, quilted the top in three weeks.

Above: Nine Patch, pieced and quilted by Gladys Roe, Baldwin, Douglas County, 1925–1950. Collection of Cathy Dwigans and Ray Wilber.

The unusual quilting stitch, almost a basting stitch, is done with heavy cotton. We heard it called by several names. Some called it the Depression stitch and told us it was done in the 1930s with string recycled from feedsacks. In Haysville today, it's called the Long Stitch and done with crochet cotton (see Chapter 8). We have also heard it called the Mennonite Long Stitch (presumably because the Mennonite quilting groups used it, although we found no evidence of this). Another name is the Saddle Stitch. The fabric in this nine patch is from feedsacks.

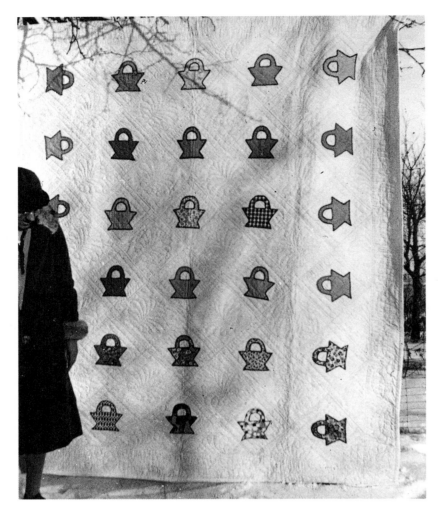

A woman identified on the back of the photo as Jennie Larson, Redding, Kansas, displays a basket quilt in a snowfall. Courtesy of Terry Thompson.

Scioto Imhoff Danner sold patterns from her home in El Dorado, Kansas; Ruby Short McKim of Independence, Missouri, and the Aunt Martha Studios in Kansas City, Missouri, had great influence through nationally syndicated designs. Kansas quiltmakers also continued to earn national reputations through contests (Rose Kretsinger and Josephine Craig are discussed in Chapter 5). Kansans, with their strong traditions of quilting in church groups and social clubs, may have been uniquely ready to offer experience, skills, and ideas to a national audience curious about an art that in other regions of the country had been considered lost for several decades.

The road to Kansas, as always, went two ways; many quilters used patterns they found in Kansas newspapers that printed syndicated columns from New York, Chicago, and Des Moines under names such as Nancy Page, Laura Wheeler, and Hope Winslow. The designers, whether they lived in Kansas City or New York, so influenced quiltmakers that it is rare to find a quilt made between 1925 and 1970 that cannot be traced to a published source.

Needlework companies influenced the look of Kansas quilts with embroidery transfers and cotton quilt blocks stamped with designs. Iron-on transfers had long been popular for pillow shams, dresser scarves, crazy quilts, and white quilts embroidered with turkey red cotton thread. (The 1871 state fair had had a prize for "best transferred embroidery.")[83] But in the 1920s, embroidered quilts enjoyed a new surge in popularity, the result both of an improvement in the colorfastness of cotton embroidery thread and of the

living in those states, with a good number sent by Kansans. Some, like Goldie Hibbs of Thayer, sent in traditional designs. Her "old pattern" was an Old Fashioned Goblet. Other Kansas quiltmakers renamed traditional designs for current events. Mrs. Alvah Ryan of Scott City contributed a star variation she called Kansas Dust Storm in 1935. Some readers designed new patterns: Roberta Christy, also of Scott City, sent the Kansas Beauty.[82]

In this quilt revival, Midwestern states from Kansas through Iowa and Missouri to Illinois moved into positions of leadership in national quiltmaking trends. This was accomplished, in part, by pattern companies.

marketing of stamped squares. Firms such as the Rainbow Quilt Block Company and Marvil Art distributed stamped blocks through five-and-ten-cent stores and by mail. Pearl Lear remembered ordering, as a teenager in the late 1920s, the blocks for an embroidered Bible history quilt from the St. Joseph, Missouri, radio station KFEQ.[84]

The KQP recorded dozens of embroidered quilts and heard many stories about their popularity, especially for friendship quilts. At a quilt day, one woman recalled that quilters preferred the new prestamped blocks to traditional pieced designs for group quilts, for two reasons. The purchased blocks cost a dime and thus had more status than a block pieced of sewing scraps. And, unlike the pieced blocks that inevitably varied, purchased blocks all finished the same size.

The 1930s are remembered everywhere as the decade of economic depression; the Dust Bowl added to the misery in Kansas and the southern plains. After years of drought and decades of pushing the soil to its limits, the first big dust storms boiled up in 1933, carrying what New Yorkers called "Kansas dirt" as far east as Buffalo. Blizzards of black grit continued regularly through 1941, when the drought finally broke. In 1937 there were seventy-two dust storms on the Great Plains, days when visibility was less than a mile. On many of those days a woman could not see her pump from her kitchen window.[85]

Again, Kansas-made quilts moved west as people gave up. During the 1930s, ten thousand farmhouses in the Great Plains were abandoned, with Kansas losing more population than any other state. Nearly half the peo-

ple in Morton County, in the southwestern corner of Kansas, moved away.[86] Families walked out the door with their clothes and bedding, leaving furniture to sit in empty houses until Jenny Lind beds, round oak tables, and mission-style dressers acquired value again in the antique markets of the 1970s.

At the beginning of the Great Depression, Carrie Hackett Hall, a dressmaker in Leavenworth for forty years, realized demand for custom-made clothing was dwindling. Her expert services were requested only for lavish weddings and formal occasions, now rare events. Looking about for a way to support herself, she noted "the whole country was 'quilt conscious.'. . . The making of quilts in the home has become astonishingly popular, even to the extent of interfering with bridge schedules and attendance at the matinee. . . . It's an ill depression that blows no good." Always flexible, in her mid-sixties she converted her interest in quilt patterns to a career as a lecturer.

She had begun collecting patterns during World War I, acquiring them here and there. During the 1920s, as more magazines and newspapers added pattern features to their needlework pages, friends clipped them for her, and soon friends of friends were passing them along. A dedicated collector, she eventually organized hundreds of designs into scrapbooks and envelopes. When the collection was in its infancy, she entertained the idea of stitching a fabric block of each, little realizing, she later wrote, "the magnitude of the undertaking." By the time she lost interest in the mid-1930s she had finished 850 pieced and appliqued blocks.[87]

The women in Hall's many

clubs asked to see her quilt block collection and soon she was traveling around the state, carrying the blocks in a suitcase tossed in the back of her automobile and giving lectures on the poetry she heard in the pattern names. Women's study clubs, rural social clubs, farm bureau clubs, literary clubs, domestic science clubs— the network of Kansas women's social life—were all interested in quilts. She occasionally designed a pattern to honor the club she addressed, drafting a Tonganoxie Nine Patch for the Ladies Association of the Congregational Church there and the Mary Tenney Gray Travel Patch for the Mary Tenney Gray Traveler's Club in Kansas City, which had been meeting since 1881. On a visit to Emporia Hall met Rose Kretsinger, and they agreed to collaborate, producing *The Romance of the Patchwork Quilt in America* in 1935. Over a half-century later the book was still in print; its popularity was due to the section featuring photos of Hall's blocks that indexed pattern names.

Although Hall made an income from quilts in a novel way, making quilts had been a common means for Kansas women to earn money. Frances Williamson of Dexter wrote a pen pal in Maine that she pieced a quilt for two dollars.[88] The 1917 Wilson County Fair premium list contained a rare acknowledgement of that fact with a prize of one dollar, their highest premium, for a "quilt entered by quilter and judged on quilting."[89] The names of such professional quilters are rarely remembered today; the line on the KQP interview form that asked about quilters was only occasionally filled in with information such as "Mrs. Stapleton charged $5 in 1929 in

KQP Jb176. Rose applique by Anna Todd McCann (1889-1963), Chautauqua County, 1942. Collection of Maxine Todd.

Anna Todd appliqued this quilt while her husband, Lou, was missing in action in Germany in 1942. Her daughter, Maxine, feels the project helped her maintain her sanity while she waited for news. Lou Todd survived the prisoner of war camp and came home, only to be killed later in an industrial accident.

We assume this quilt was from a kit or pattern, rather than an original design, but we have not yet found the pattern source.

Frankfort, Marshall County."[90]

Lurinda E. Brumbaugh, a quilter, was interviewed in 1930 in the *Globe* in Dodge City, where she had lived for thirty years after raising eight children alone in Ness County. In her later years, she earned an income quilting for others, spending three to six weeks on each quilt. Her age, eighty-seven, interested the reporter. Did it tire her to quilt? "No. I can see to do those stitches far better than I can read at length. I often work until 10 o'clock at night."[91]

Mrs. W. C. Opfer of Clay Center had been quilting for others for four years when *Capper's Farmer* interviewed her in 1931. Her quilting business had several components: She sold patterns and waxed thread (waxing a cotton sewing thread reduces its tendency to knot), she planned quilting designs and marked tops for those who wished to quilt their own, and she organized community exhibitions of modern and antique quilts. Her primary business, however, was quilting tops for others; people from several neighboring states were among her customers. "How did I get into commercial quilt making? Well—I 'put in' as the early New Englanders used to say—an embroidered quilt for myself. A bride-to-be saw it, and begged me to do two for her. Then the bride's aunt wanted a rose charmeuse [satin] quilt quilted. These three quilts seemed to establish me, as I found myself with a business from that time on. . . . I would not advise a woman to go into the quilting business with the hope of making her entire living at it. Quilting is tedious handwork, and the person who engages in it must take part of her pay in the joy of creating some-

While her husband was fighting in World War II, this unknown woman occupied her time making a quilt. The photo is dated 1942. Courtesy of Larry Schwarm.

KQP Ac063. Fence Rail pieced by Ora Holliman Cathey, embroidered by Anna Maring (1924–   ), Craig, Colorado, and Bird City, 1947–1975. Wools. Collection of Anna Maring.

Ora Cathey pieced this comforter of cuffs cut from men's trousers in the Colorado clothing store where she worked. It was a wedding gift for her niece, Anna Maring, who covered the seams with embroidery and tied it decades later.

thing of lasting beauty."[92]

Women were not the only ones earning money with quilts; the daughter of Augustus Parr of Rossville told KQP documenters that her father marked tops with quilting designs to earn extra cash for his family's Christmas presents.[93] Memories of the Depression are as diverse as earlier recollections of the pioneer era, but stories of making do, neighborly kindness, and a barter economy are common threads that run through family histories and personal memories of quilts made in these years. A Dresden Plate quilt was made in a home economics class from scraps left from the girls' dressmaking project. The teacher had bought the yardage for all of their dresses, a generosity they repaid with the quilt that was a gift to her. A Double Wedding Ring was brought to a Quilt Discovery Day by the descendants of a doctor to whom a family owed a

considerable medical bill, a debt fulfilled with quilts made from the family scrap bag.[94]

Such stories of hard times were rarely evident in the appearance of the pretty, soft quilts, a paradox discussed by Merikay Waldvogel of the Quilts of Tennessee project. She noted that the quilts of the 1930s, more than of any other time, were the product of the decorating and craft market. Magazines and pattern companies made little mention of the Depression because hard times do not sell. The quilts are cheery and light for the same reason that Depression-era movie audiences demanded escapist screwball comedies and high production musicals.[95]

The commercial influence encouraged several fad patterns, the most common being the hexagon design known as Grandmother's Flower Garden, with the Double Wedding Ring second in popularity.[96] One of the

The Vinland Grange Fair in the late 1940s. The women (left to right): Marie Howard Wiggins, Roberta Hoskinson, Bertha Weiler, Dorothy Pine Leary, Margaret Craig Deay, Berniece Gottstein, Nora Witt, unknown, Nell Deay, unknown. Courtesy of the Vinland Fair Board.

Barbara Brackman

Opposite: KQP Hc077. Cowboys appliqued and embroidered by Fern Eller (1904–ca. 1960), Greensburg, 1954 or 1955. Cottons. Collection of Twila and David Allen.

When David Allen (above, age 2 1/2, 1952) was four or five, neighbor Fern Eller made this quilt for him, embroidering the names of half a dozen neighborhood boys who fancied themselves to be cowboys. Although several cowboy figures were sold by pattern companies in the 1950s, this one seems to be unique.

early examples of the Double Wedding Ring was said by the family to have been made in 1923, when Mrs. Erwin O. Allen of Corning drew out a pattern after seeing one on display at the Free Fair in Topeka. It was the first of twenty in that pattern that she made.[97] Quilts with dates inscribed on them indicate that the Double Wedding Ring was the first pattern craze, corroborating the memories of a woman who brought in her grandmother's quilts. "She made her Wedding Ring quilts in the 1920s and her Flower Gardens in the 1930s."[98]

Kansas Star

World War II put an end to the Depression in Kansas as the prices for grain and beef rose. Air bases and factories gave new infusions of cash to the Kansas economy and attracted a new wave of immigrants. Many women kept busy during the war with quiltmaking, which sometimes provided solace to those worrying about friends and family overseas. Maudie Tinkler of Gypsum spent the war years stitching scraps less than an inch square into tiny nine patches to keep from worrying about her son in the service.[99]

Inspection of date-inscribed quilts indicates that the peak of the quiltmaking fad had passed before the attack on Pearl Harbor on December 7, 1941. (There are sixteen quilts dated 1940 and only six the following year.) The war certainly affected the craft; fabric shortages made patchwork impractical, and paper shortages made magazine patterns a luxury.

Fabric rationing inspired many

to make do with printed feedsacks, a resource most people associate primarily with the Depression but that was used through the 1950s. After the war, manufacturers of sacks hoped marketing techniques would inspire frugal women to continue to reuse fabric sacks. The 1949 state fair in Hutchinson offered prizes for "items made of the Staley print-Sax in which Staley poultry, hog and dairy feeds are packed. Suggestions: house dresses, children's and infants' dresses, men's shirts, smocks, pajamas, buffet sets, luncheon cloths, bridge sets, towels, kitchen curtains, table runners, quilts, rugs." That fair also had a category for "original designs in a quilt or spread," a class that had been instituted in the 1930s, but quilts in original designs continued to be rare.[100] The popular styles echoed the 1930s—wedding rings, flower gardens, embroidered designs, and applique kits; the major difference was a darkening of the soft colors in the cotton prints. A bride of 1952 brought to a Quilt Discovery Day a Double Wedding Ring quilt, one of a pair she had requested as a wedding present to top the twin beds in her new home, which she planned to decorate in the latest colors. The quilts had received little wear, she sheepishly explained, because the chartreuse background behind the rings of scraps quickly passed from fashion and clashed with later decorating schemes.[101] Cross-stitch embroidery quilts, made from kits with printed designs to be embroidered with colored floss, were an innovation of the 1950s, with the earliest date-inscribed example from 1956.

During the 1950s, quilting, like much else that was old, held little appeal for tastemakers who

Opposite: KQP Ea045. Necktie quilt pieced by Saloma Palestine Cox, Greensburg, 1950–1960. Silk, cotton and synthetics. Collection of Pam Washburn.

Saloma Cox's husband was characterized by the family as a "real wild man," a trader who homesteaded in the Cherokee Strip in Oklahoma before bringing Saloma to Kansas. Quiltmaking for her was a refuge in a difficult marriage, a "way to keep her sanity."

This very functional quilt represents wonderfully both the fabrics and the way quilts looked in the 1950s and 1960s.

Above: Saloma Palestine Cox.

opted for synthetic blankets, Danish modern furniture, and television consoles. President Dwight Eisenhower on the news and Matt Dillon and Miss Kitty on "Gunsmoke" gave Kansans a sense of pride in an image improved from Dust Bowl notoriety. The state had become conservative, with few traces of early radical and progressive ideas. State prohibition had fallen in 1948, and urban Kansans now outnumbered rural dwellers. Kansas, in the middle of the country, came to symbolize ideas in the middle of the political spectrum.

Many Kansans, climbing back to prosperity as a result of generous rainfall, good farm prices, scientific farming, and a broader industrial base, preferred to forget the Depression and all the make-do crafts associated with it. The KQP recorded fewer quilts dated in the 1950s than in any decade after 1920. The waning interest in traditional crafts must have been a factor in the 1960 decision at the *Kansas City Star* to discontinue the weekly quilt pattern column. Had the editors been able to view the future, they would have seen a rebound in interest in the craft. The KQP saw an increase in quiltmaking that began around 1960; the number of dated quilts in the 1960s was double that of the 1950s. One contributing factor may have been the 1961 Kansas Centennial celebration when men grew beards in the name of history and women dressed in calico costumes stitched of reproduction prints. Calicoes suited for period costumes or quilts were hard to find as polyester threatened to make cotton fabric a relic of the past. The new polyester batting gave quilts a puffy look and required less quilting. Standards for

quilting and applique that had revived in the 1930s eroded as quality cottons, quality quilting, and innovative patterns became harder to find.

During the mid-1960s, a new generation began looking to traditional crafts as a route to a simpler life with less reliance on factory-made items. Counterculture values glorifying craftsmanship, recycling, and nostalgic fashion combined to create a new interest in old quilts. Young women who discovered quilts in thrift stores and antique shops and tucked away in their mothers' linen closets taught themselves to piece and quilt, little realizing that experienced advice was available from quilting groups still meeting in churches all over the state. Once the new quiltmakers figured out the basics, they organized classes, taught others, and developed a new network.

One woman who continued the tradition of quiltmaking as a means of income was Topekan Kay McFarland, who ran a cottage industry, selling quilts made by Kansas quiltmakers. Quilts by Kay McFarland offered finished quilts "in old-fashioned calico prints" for $150. The income paid her way through law school at Washburn University, from which she graduated in 1964. She is now sitting on the Kansas Supreme Court, the first woman in that position and surely the first justice to finance a legal education through mail-order quilts.

The women's movement that began in the early 1970s also encouraged a reappraisal of traditional women's art forms and the appreciation of women's domestic contributions to society. Quilts became an important focus in feminist art, literature, and history. The American bicentennial celebration in 1976

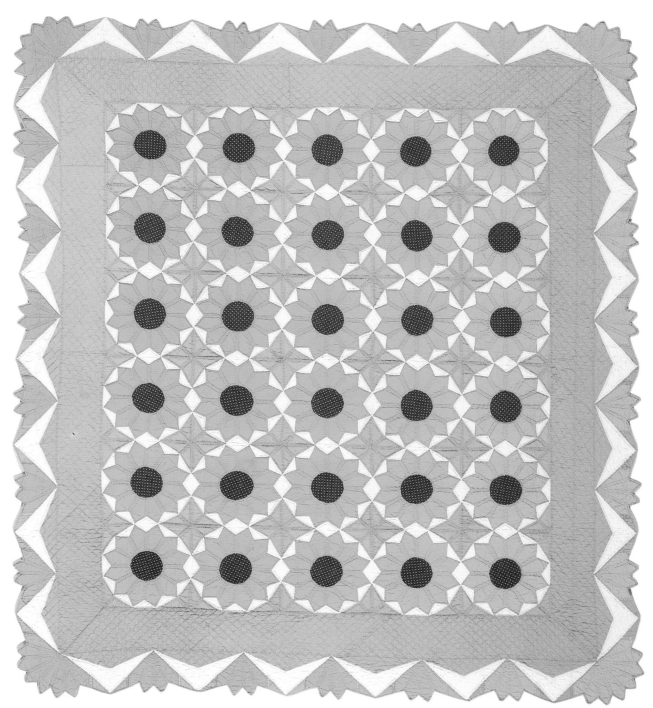

KQP Ic002. *Kansas Sunflower, pieced by Louisa Schierkalk Laverentz (1889–1977), Nashville, Kingman County, 1961. Cottons. Collection of Virginia Laverentz.*

"Lizzie" Laverentz used a pattern from Capper's Weekly *for her Kansas centennial quilt. She started collecting fabric for it in the late 1950s. She made many trips to nearby dry goods stores to find the dotted fabric necessary for the center of each sunflower.*

widened the popular interest in quilts as a link to both craftsmanship and history. Quilts made from 1975 through mid-1988 when the last Quilt Discovery Day was held accounted for 26 percent of all the quilts recorded by the KQP. Although recently made quilts have a higher chance of survival than those made earlier, this figure indicates that quiltmaking was again a craze.

Since the bicentennial, quilting professionals have widened the niches created in the 1930s, earning national reputations as prize-winning quiltmakers, designers, writers, teachers, and lecturers. Small social clubs and quilting groups have received new infusions of younger mem-

bers. The Quilters' Guild of Greater Kansas City, the first of the contemporary guilds, began meeting in 1975. In 1988, while the KQP was holding quilt days, there were thirty-five Kansas guilds, some with several hundred members, and one statewide group, the Kansas Quilters' Organization.

It is difficult to see trends when living in the midst of them, but one apparent change in recent years is the emphasis on a single woman's finishing the quilt from patchwork to binding. Women still meet socially to sew side by side, they still make cooperative friendship quilts, and church groups and professional quilters still finish other people's

Costumed quilters at a Kansas Centennial quilting bee, Hutchinson, 1961.

Louisa Schierkalk Laverentz and Henry Laverentz, 1950.

Terry Thompson, 1975 or 1976. Terry Thompson started the Quilting Bee in Kansas City in 1973. It was one of the first shops devoted to quilts and quiltmaking during the current craze. In 1978 she added a line of patterns.

tops, but most quilts made in the 1980s were made by individuals. This change in the division of labor may reflect the changes in household management in which the woman of the family now does housework without the help of servants. Hiring a woman to finish a quilt may be as old-fashioned as hiring a maid or a cook. And professional quilters are now scarce, due to the widening job market for women. The one-woman quilt of today is also an outgrowth of the emphasis on creativity and originality that developed in the 1960s and 1970s. It reflects the way teachers and magazines view the quiltmaking process. Both teach everything from fabric purchase to signature with the understanding that quiltmakers should master each step.

Quilters working since the bicentennial are quite likely to sign and date their work. Of all quilts the KQP recorded, 15.8 percent were date inscribed; of those made between 1975 and 1988, 34.8 percent were dated, a change attributable to four factors: (1) an increased awareness of quilts as historical documents that outlive their makers, (2) persistent pleas from professionals to sign quilts, (3) workshops and magazine articles on techniques for inscriptions, and (4) new pens and equipment for marking.

Another current trend is a diversity of style. National styles and trends come and go fairly quickly with new decorating colors and the influence of magazines and national teachers. Many women continue to make what are considered traditional quilts, the styles that developed in the 1920s and 1930s. Some quiltmakers, inspired by quilt history, work in colors and styles fashionable in the nineteenth

KQP Ea036. *Sampler, pieced, appliqued, and quilted by Margaret Lightner (1916–), Garden City, 1979. Cottons. Collection of Margaret Lightner.*

   The pattern is Terry Thompson's Beginning Sampler, which she designed for first-time quilters. Such a sampler of piecing and applique designs became the standard first quilt in the 1970s. Margaret Lightner was so interested in taking quilt lessons that she drove from Garden City to Liberty, Missouri, to meet with teacher Grace Pettys, who used Terry's pattern in the class on basic skills. Margaret in turn became a quilt teacher and used this pattern in her classes. We saw several quilts in Garden City that reflected her influence.

Strip quilt top, appliqued and pieced by Lena Hawkins Banks (1888–1988), 1960–1980. Cottons and synthetics. Parsons. Collection of Antonio Muñoz.

Lena Hawkins was born in Newellton, Louisiana. She married Fred Banks in 1903 and moved to Parsons, Kansas, in 1922. The Muñoz family owns three of her quilt tops. The early ones are typical pieced quilts from the 1900–1925 era—repetitive block patterns in conventional cotton calicoes of the time. This last top, made fifty years later, is of common clothing fabrics with an uncommon aesthetic. We saw only a few quilts with this combination of fabrics, side-by-side color, strip format, and casual attitude about pattern (see pp. 54 and 160 for two that share a few of those characteristics). This is the only one by an African American woman. It may be that there are far more quilts of this type out there, but they were not brought to Quilt Discovery Days. This top, in fact, was not recorded at a quilt day; Banks's friends brought for documentation the more conventional tops, recently quilted, that she made when she was younger.

Lena Banks on her one-hundredth birthday, 1988.

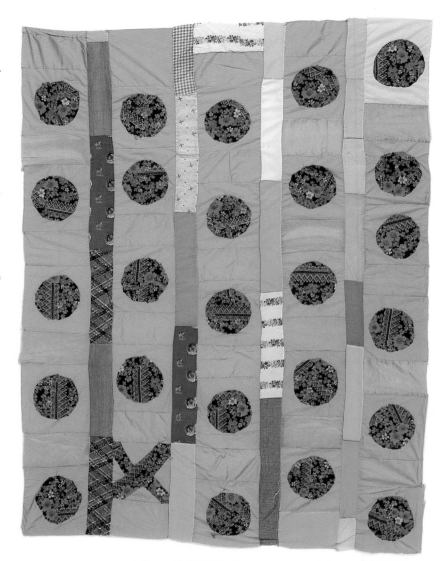

The Quilting Bee, designed, appliqued, and quilted by Elaine Darr Sparlin (b. 1915), Lenexa, Johnson County, 1984.

Elaine Sparlin (left) was inspired to design this quilt by a photo of a Lenexa quilting party. In 1976 she worked on a bicentennial quilt for the city of Lenexa, making a pictorial block of an aspect of the city's history. Since then she has made many picture-type quilts, which she calls memory quilts. "We all make memory quilts whether we call them that or not."

Sparlin was born in Missouri and learned to do patchwork at the age of five when her grandmother taught her to make a four patch. "She told me that if you could make the four patches line up, make the seams in the center meet perfectly, you could piece any kind of a quilt, and it's true." Elaine came to Kansas in 1945 with her husband, Merle, who was a firefighter at Fort Riley and later at the Olathe Naval Air Station.

This photo from the Topeka Capital-Journal, *May 24, 1987, illustrates the part that family-tree quilts are playing in events such as family reunions. Twenty-two descendants of Azro and Lucinda Hughes are gathered around the unfinished quilt which commemorates their lives and marriage. Limbs for each of the couple's fourteen children were planned. The quilt was designed and stitched by Ruth Hughes, fourth from the bottom right. Photo: Steve Wolgast. Photograph printed with permission of the* Topeka Capital-Journal.

century. And far more quilters than in the past value originality, designing their own patterns or adaptations.

In times when commercial sources are at an all-time high (in 1988 there were fifteen national magazines devoted to quilts), there is also evidence that some styles develop with little commercial input. One is the family-tree quilt, a genealogical record made to celebrate a wedding, anniversary, or reunion. Three early family-tree quilts, made between 1950 and 1976, were recorded by the KQP. They were much like friendship quilts, but instead of signatures of block makers, the patterns featured names and birthdates of all family members. Quilts with specific symbolic and pictorial designs, none of which appear to be from a commercial source, have been used to record kinships since 1976. They appear to have been inspired by a fashion for bicentennial quilts that pictured community buildings. Some family-tree quilts depict events in family history, one featured family members in silhouette, and several recorded names, birthdays, and kinship in a tree design.

The road in and out of Kansas continues, but the traffic today is not so much in quilts as in ideas. New styles, fashions, and techniques come into the state through the nationwide network of quiltmakers, and new ideas go out as today's Kansans teach, write, and design patterns. At the end of the twentieth century, Kansas, right in the middle of the contiguous United States, remains central to quiltmaking.

Notes

1. Elizabeth B. Custer, *Boots and Saddles* (1885; repr. Williamstown, Mass.: Corner House, 1969), 12–13.

2. Phoebe George Bradford, "Phoebe George Bradford Diaries," ed. W. Emerson Wilson, *Delaware History* 16 (April 1974): 11.

3. Clara Gowing, "Life among the Delaware Indians," *Kansas State Historical Society Collections* 12 (1911–1912): 185.

4. Merrill J. Mattes, *The Great Platte River Road* (Lincoln: Nebraska State Historical Society, 1969), 23.

5. Mary M. Colby, entry May 6, 1850, in Kenneth Holmes, *Covered Wagon Women: Diaries and Letters from the Western Trails*, vol. 2 (Glendale, Calif.: Arthur C. Clark Co., 1983), 48.

6. Sara T. Robinson, *Kansas: Its Interior and Exterior Life* (Boston: Crosby, Nichols & Co., 1856), 1.

7. Abigail Scott Duniway diary, in Kenneth Holmes, *Covered Wagon Women: Diaries and Letters from the Western Trails*, vol. 5 (Glendale, Calif.: Arthur C. Clark Co., 1986), 50.

8. Tamsen E. Donner, June 16, 1846, in Kenneth Holmes, *Covered Wagon Women: Diaries and Letters from the Western Trails*, vol. 1 (Glendale, Calif.: Arthur C. Clark Co., 1982), 71.

9. Susan Shelby Magoffin, *Down the Santa Fe Trail and into Mexico: The Diary of Susan Shelby Magoffin*, ed. Stella M. Drumm (Lincoln: University of Nebraska Press, 1982), 6.

10. Rebecca Ketcham, "From Ithaca to Clatsop Plains: Miss Ketcham's Journal of Travel," ed. Leo M. Kaiser and Priscilla Knuth, *Oregon Historical Quarterly* (September 1961): 251.

11. Ellen Tootle diary in Kenneth Holmes, *Covered Wagon Women: Diaries and Letters from the Western Trails*, vol. 7, (Glendale, Calif.: Arthur C. Clark Co., 1987), 63.

12. Quilt is pictured in Jean Ray Laury, *Ho for California* (New York: E. P. Dutton, 1989), 44.

13. The first nine volumes in Holmes's series contain seventy personal accounts, and there are four in Sandra Myres, ed., *Ho for California: Women's Diaries from the Huntington Library* (San Marino, Calif.: Huntington Library, 1980).

14. Myres, *Ho For California*, 133.

15. Magoffin, *Down the Santa Fe Trail*, 156.

16. Donner, in Holmes, *Covered Wagon Women*, vol. 1, 72.

17. Louisa Cooke diary, entry June 8, 1862, in Holmes, *Covered Wagon Women*, vol. 7, 31.

18. Ketcham, "From Ithaca to Clatsop Plains," *Oregon Historical Quarterly* (December 1961): 380.

19. John Mack Faragher, *Women and Men on the Overland Trail* (New Haven, Conn.: Yale University Press, 1979), 199, 83.

20. Helen Carpenter diary, entry June 3, 1857, in Myres, *Ho For California*, 100.

21. Lucy Rutledge Cooke diary, entry April 30, 1852, and April 1853, in Holmes, *Covered Wagon Women*, vol. 7, 233, 294.

22. Lucy Larcom, "Call to Kansas," in Miriam Davis Colt, *Went to Kansas* (1862; repr. Ann Arbor, Mich.: University Microfilms, 1966), 33.

23. Miriam Davis Colt, *Went to Kansas* (1862; repr. Ann Arbor, Mich.: University Microfilms, 1966), 22.

24. For more about Colt's commune, see "A Vegetarian Utopia: The Letters of John Milton Hadley 1855–56," ed. Joseph Gambone, *Kansas Historical Quarterly* 39 (Spring 1972): 65–87.

25. Colt, *Went to Kansas*, 152.

26. Hannah Anderson Ropes, *Six Months in Kansas: By a Lady* (Boston: John P. Jewett, 1856), 62.

27. *Kansas Herald of Freedom*, April 14, 1855, 1.

28. Jane Carruth, June 1856, in Glenda Riley, "Kansas Frontierswomen Viewed through Their Writings," *Kansas History: A Journal of the Central Plains* 9 (Summer 1986): 7; Clarina Nichols, letter to *Boston Evening Telegraph*, January 9, 1855.

29. Mary Tenney Gray diary, March 4 and June 4, 1857, Kansas State Historical Society.

30. Five quilt owners brought to Quilt Discovery Days quilts they believed were made in Kansas before 1865, but no corroborative genealogical proof was found for any of them. For more on the lack of quilts made in Kansas before 1880, see Chapter 3 and Barbara Brackman, "Quilts on the Kansas Frontier," *Kansas History: A Journal of the Central Plains* 13 (Spring 1990): 13–22.

31. Ropes, *Six Months in Kansas*, 197, 217, 46.

32. "D," May 25, 1855, *Lawrence, Kansas Tribune* (June 20,

1855): 1.

33. "Have Historic Quilt," *Topeka Daily Capital*, February 10, 1930.

34. Keith Melder, "Ladies Bountiful: Organized Women's Benevolence in Early 19th-Century America," *New York History* 28 (July 1967): 231–254.

35. Robinson, *Kansas*, 209, 215–216.

36. Virginia McLoughlin, ed., "Establishing a Church on the Kansas Frontier: The Letters of the Reverend O. L. Woodford and His Sister Henrietta, 1857–9," *Kansas Historical Quarterly* (Summer 1971): 185.

37. *Kansas Farmer* 1 (December 1, 1863): 170.

38. Mary Tenney Gray, undated clipping in Wyandotte County clippings, vol. 5, Kansas State Historical Society Library, 59–62.

39. "The Constitutional Convention Proceedings and Debate," *Wyandotte Daily Commercial Gazette*, July 29, 1859.

40. Catherine Wever Collins, diary, and Hallie Riley Hodder, diary, in Lillian Schlissel, *Women's Diaries of the Westward Journey* (New York: Schocken Books, 1982), 132.

41. L. T. Bodine, *Kansas Illustrated: An Accurate and Reliable Description of This Marvelous State* (Kansas City: Kansas Pacific, 1879).

42. Abbie Bright, April 18, 1871, "Diary of Abbie Bright," ed. Joseph W. Snell, *Kansas Historical Quarterly* 37 (Fall and Winter 1971): 250.

43. Howard Ruede, letter dated May 2, 1877, *Sod House Days: Letters from a Kansas Homesteader 1877–8*, ed. John Ise (Lawrence: University Press of Kansas, 1983), 66–68.

44. KQP Aa068.

45. Barbara Brackman, *Clues in the Calico: A Guide to Identifying and Dating Antique Quilts* (McLean, Va.: EPM Publications, 1989), 24–25.

46. Luna E. Warner, "The Diary of Luna E. Warner, A Kansas Teenager of the 1870s," *Kansas Historical Quarterly* 35 (Autumn 1969): 287.

47. Gowing, "Life among the Delaware Indians," 192.

48. *Abilene Chronicle*, September 15, 1870; September 22, 1870.

49. Douglas County Agricultural and Mechanical Association, *Pre-mium List* (Lawrence: n.p., 1871), 13.

50. Wilson County Fair Association, *Premium List* (Fredonia, Kans.: n.p., 1893), 34–35.

51. Virginia Gunn, "Quilts at Nineteenth-Century State and County Fairs: An Ohio Study," *Uncoverings 1988*, ed. Laurel Horton (San Francisco: American Quilt Study Group, 1989), 105–128.

52. I examined twenty-three premium lists from Kansas state and county fairs from 1863 to 1949; nine included a category for children's quilts, and seven of those had a category for "under 15."

53. Florence V. Kniseley Menninger, *Days of My Life: Memories of a Kansas Mother and Teacher* (New York: R. R. Smith, 1939), 28; Carrie A. Hall and Rose G. Kretsinger, *The Romance of the Patchwork Quilt in America* (Caldwell, Idaho: Caxton Printers, 1935), 28.

54. Pat Ferrero, Elaine Hedges, and Julie Silber, *Hearts and Hands: The Influence of Women and Quilts on American Society* (San Francisco: Quilt Digest Press, 1987), 18. Thirty quilts stitched by children younger than sixteen, made between 1890 and 1949, were noted in an examination of the records from nineteen quilt days chosen at random. The youngest child recorded was a four-year-old who began hers in 1948; two six-year-olds were described (1906 and 1929), and one seven-year-old (1929). Most children were older; the average age was 9.9 years.

55. In the 1980s, mothers again began to teach their children to quilt at a young age, possibly inspired by the flowering of quilt history publications that included historic accounts of five-year-olds learning to piece.

56. James Redpath and Richard Hinton, *Hand-book to Kansas Territory and the Rocky Mountains Gold Region* (New York: Colton, 1859).

57. Elise Dubach Isely, *Sunbonnet Days* (Caldwell, Idaho: Caxton Printers, 1935), 217.

58. Elizabeth Custer, *Tenting on the Plains* (New York: Charles L. Webster & Co., 1889), 669.

59. Anna Webber, "The Diary of Anna Webber: Early Day Teacher of Mitchell County" ed. Lila Gravatt Scrimsher, *Kansas Historical Quarterly* 38 (Autumn 1972): 335.

60. Mrs. S. T. Roach, "Memories of Frontier Days in Kansas: Barber County," *Kansas State Historical Society Collections* 17 (1926–1928): 615–616.

61. Craig Miner, *West of Wichita: Settling the High Plains of Kansas 1865-1890* (Lawrence: University Press of Kansas, 1986), 172.

62. John Ise, ed., *Sod House Days: Letters from a Kansas Homesteader 1877-8* (Lawrence: University Press of Kansas, 1983), xxxii; Glenda Riley, "Kansas Frontierswomen Viewed through Their Writings," *Kansas History: A Journal of the Central Plains* 9 (Summer 1986): 3.

63. Miner, *West of Wichita*, 154.

64. Flora Moorman Heston, "I Think I Will Like Kansas: The Letters of Flora Moorman Heston, 1885-1886," *Kansas History* 6 (Summer 1983): 70–95.

65. "Diary Account of Emily Butcher," Manuscripts Department, Kansas State Historical Society.

66. Hall and Kretsinger, *The Romance of the Patchwork Quilt*, 28; letter from "P.E.T." in Harper, Kansas, *Sentinel*, November 15, 1889, 17; Bettina Havig, "Missouri: Crossroads to Quilting," *Uncoverings 1985*, ed. Sally Garoutte (San Francisco: American Quilt Study Group, 1986), 52; Joseph Stonuey and Patricia Cox Crews, "The Nebraska Quilt History Project: Interpretations of Selected Parameters," *Uncoverings 1988*, ed. Laurel Horton (San Francisco: American Quilt Study Group, 1989), 159.

67. Isely, *Sunbonnet Days*, 210.

68. Ian R. Tyrrell, *Sobering Up: From Temperance to Prohibition in Antebellum America, 1800–1860* (Westport, Conn.: Greenwood Press, 1979), 135, 152.

69. A number of T designs are indexed in Barbara Brackman, *An Encyclopedia of Pieced Quilt Patterns* (Lawrence, Kans.: Prairie Flower Publishing, 1979–1986).

70. Merikay Waldvogel, letter to author, 1986.

71. Wilda Smith, "A Half Century of Struggle: Gaining Woman Suffrage in Kansas," *Kansas History* 4 (Summer 1981): 79.

72. Carl Becker, "Kansas," in *The Heritage of Kansas: Selected Commentaries on Past Times*, ed. Everett Rich (Lawrence: University of Kansas Press, 1960), quoted in Robert Smith Bader, *Hayseeds, Moralizers, and Methodists: The Twentieth-Cen-*

tury Image of Kansas (Lawrence: University Press of Kansas, 1988), 20.

73. Martha Farnsworth, Plains Woman: The Diary of Martha Farnsworth 1882–1922, ed. Marlene Springer and Haskell Springer (Bloomington: Indiana University Press, 1986), 216–217.

74. KQP Dc002.

75. Helen Blair, "Dower Chest Treasures," House Beautiful, February 1904, quoted in Jeannette Lasansky, "The Colonial Revival and Quilts," Pieced by Mother: Symposium Papers, ed. Jeannette Lasansky (Lewisburg, Pa.: Oral Traditions Project, 1988), 101.

76. People's Popular Monthly and Farm and Fireside (September 1919), 30.

77. Wilson County Fair Association, Premium List (Fredonia, Kans.: n.p., 1893), 28.

78. Leona Burroughs, interview with KQP researcher, Kingman, Kansas, 1988.

79. Chalmer E. Faws, Our Heritage 1886–1986 (Quinter, Kans.: Church of the Brethren, 1986), 141–143.

80. For more about social clubs, see Mary Margaret Rowen, "Group Quilting in Kansas," Kansas History: A Journal of the Central Plains 13 (Spring 1990): 23–31.

81. Capper's Weekly, February 12, 1927.

82. Kansas City Star, March 24, 1937; December 28, 1935; February 26, 1936.

83. Kansas State Agricultural Society, Premium List (Topeka: n.p., 1871), 33.

84. KQP Dd052.

85. Donald Worster, Dust Bowl: The Southern Plains in the 1930s (New York: Oxford University Press, 1979), 12–14, 49.

86. Bader, Hayseeds, Moralizers, and Methodists, 72.

87. Hall and Kretsinger, The Romance of the Patchwork Quilt, 29, 7.

88. Frances Williamson, letter dated December 10, 1886, Letters of Frances Williamson, ed. Marianne Frances Garland and Eleanor Jean Swartz (Wellington, Kans.: n. p., 1989), 27.

89. Wilson County Fair, Premium List (Fredonia, Kans.: n.p., 1917), 28.

90. KQP Cb136.

91. H.H.F., "She Knows Her Quilts," Dodge City Globe, n.d.

92. Joan Woolf, "She Sews a Fine Seam," Capper's Farmer, July 1931, 30.

93. Helen Harschaake, interview with author, Topeka, 1989.

94. KQP Fj269 and Dh050

95. Merikay Waldvogel, Soft Covers for Hard Times (Nashville, Tenn.: Rutledge Hill Press, 1990), 91.

96. The KQP recorded 559 examples of the Grandmother's Flower Garden pattern (4.4 percent of all the quilts brought to quilt days). During the 1925–1950 era, 7 percent of the quilts recorded were variations of the pattern. Of fifty-two date-inscribed examples, only three were dated before 1930 (1897, 1898, and 1904). Four examples were dated 1930; sixteen for the entire decade. The dated examples indicate that the design lost popularity after 1942. There are three dated examples in the 1950s and none in the 1960s, but the pattern enjoyed a revival in the 1970s and 1980s, when 2 percent of all the quilts recorded were in the pattern. The Double Wedding Ring was almost as popular, with 446 examples recorded over all, 3.5 percent of the total, again with most recorded in the 1925–1950 era. The earliest dated example was 1926; there were sixteen dated examples made between 1926 and 1950, three between 1950 and 1974, and another revival of interest in the 1970s. The Nebraska Quilt History Project also found Grandmother's Flower Garden to be their most popular pattern; 7.1 percent of the quilts in their sample of pre-1940 quilts were in the design. The Double Wedding Ring was second at 6.1 percent (Stonuey and Crews, "The Nebraska Quilt History Project," 161.)

97. KQP Db051.

98. KQP Cc129.

99. Maudie Tinkler, interview with author, Salina, April 2, 1991.

100. Kansas State Fair, Premium List (Hutchinson: n.p., 1949), 126, 130.

101. KQP Df172.

KQP Fb082. Applique Quilt. Catherine Johnson Cover (1830–1888), Fayette County, Pennsylvania, 1850–1880. Appliqued, reverse appliqued. Collection of Martha Jo Longhofer.

Chapter Three

Nineteenth-Century Red and Green Applique Quilts

Nancy Hornback

IN 1881, MARY ELIZABETH COVER AND GEORGE WESLEY EASTER MARRIED IN WESTERN PENNSYLVANIA AND TRAVELED BY TRAIN TO KANSAS TO HOMESTEAD NEAR ABILENE IN DICKINSON COUNTY. AMONG THE POSSESSIONS LIZZIE CARRIED ON THE JOURNEY WAS A RED AND GREEN APPLIQUE QUILT MADE BY HER MOTHER,

Catherine Johnson Cover, and presented to Lizzie for her new home in Kansas. In addition to its intended utilitarian function, the quilt served as "nonverbal communication": It was a symbol of stability, representing the bond between mother and daughter and preserving memories of the family left in the East.[1] The quilt would provide continuity between the Easters' Pennsylvania roots and yet unborn generations in Kansas.

Catherine Johnson Cover's red and green applique quilt was one of a type made prolifically in nineteenth-century America, a style that began in the mid-Atlantic region and spread along migration routes. These quilts had in common certain features: They were appliqued (defined as the technique of sewing fabric to a larger background fabric of contrasting color to form a design); the majority used a predominantly red and green color scheme against a white background; most displayed excellent workmanship and elaborate quilting; the patterns were usually floral, and their designs varied from simple to sophisticated. The vogue for these red and green quilts began about 1840, peaked at midcentury, and declined toward the end of the nineteenth century.[2]

Information on nineteenth-century red and green applique quilts is scattered and fragmen-

tary in quilt history literature. The most significant treatment of these quilts to date is contained in Ricky Clark, George W. Knepper, and Ellice Ronsheim's *Quilts in Community: Ohio's Traditions;* their findings generally corroborate those of the research results presented in this chapter.[3] Taking into account the examples of 147 such quilts in the Kansas Quilt Project, in this chapter I will argue for a wider application of design principles in determining the source of motifs for these quilts than has been suggested by any other published research. In addition to the sources of design inspiration, an examination of techniques of applique and quilting and motivations for the red and green color choice reveals these quilts to be a type distinctive from other nineteenth-century quilts.

Much has been written about nineteenth-century applique quilts, yet scant attention has been paid to the red and green feature.[4] In most instances, the observation is made that "red and green was the traditional color scheme" with little or no attempt to explain its appeal. In *American Beauties: Rose and Tulip Quilts*, Gwen Marston and Joe Cunningham do discuss the red and green color choice. Their discussion is necessarily brief since the publication is primarily intended as an instructional book for today's quiltmakers.[5] Barbara

Brackman's *Clues in the Calico* classified red, green, and white appliqued and pieced quilts by color and style and designated their period of popularity as 1830 to 1900, but also without in-depth discussion.[6] Jeannette Lasansky, in examining specific quilts from a documentation study in central Pennsylvania, described the choice of the red and green palette as "typical central Pennsylvanian."[7]

Neither the development of the red and green applique quilt as a type nor the design origins have been fully explored. Since the nineteenth-century applique quilts in the Kansas study were made in various geographical locations, an examination of their characteristics will provide a more generalized body of information and add perspective to limited regional investigations.

Such a study, which defines the characteristics of a distinctive type of quilt, is congruent with interdisciplinary scholarship that supports new approaches to history as well as new methods of investigation. Over much of the twentieth century, the scope of history has broadened from a traditional elitist perspective of writing about important people and events to include the everyday lives and activities of ordinary people in order to gain a more realistic, fuller understanding of the past.[8] With the recent expansion of women's studies scholar-

Mary Elizabeth Cover and George Wesley Easter, ca. 1880. Catherine Johnson Cover, ca. 1870. Courtesy of Martha Jo Longhofer.

ship, lives of women are now included in historical studies.

To fill the gaps and to supplement written history, material culture from earlier times is being examined in order to discover clues to the makers' values and attitudes.[9] In the absence of basic written resources on the lives of women, historian Rachel Maines has argued that needlework is an important subject for study since "the female culture is documented almost exclusively in creative forms."[10] Who were the makers of these red and green applique quilts? What socioeconomic level of society did they belong to? How did the quilts reflect the technology of the times in which they were made? What were the influences on the quiltmakers' aesthetic choices of color and design? What were the intended and unintended uses of the quilts? What does the degree of esteem in which they were held reveal about the attitudes and values of the makers and users? Since quilts can never provide direct answers to these questions, examining what E. McClung Fleming would call their "unique set of physical and aesthetic characteristics" as primary data in an interdisciplinary approach that also includes oral traditions, demographic data, and conventional history sources can yield new information and a new perspective to quilt history scholarship.[11]

Historical Background

The appearance of the red and green quilts must be considered within a context of nineteenth-century history and quilt development. Quiltmaking moved as a popular art form from the elite levels of society to the middle classes. This change was a result of early-nineteenth-century tech-

nological, social, and cultural changes that took place in progressive, interdependent stages. Evidence suggests that quilts in preindustrial America were either made or purchased and used by the well-to-do who could afford costly imported fabrics. A search through household inventories and wills in four regions of New England from the seventeenth and eighteenth centuries led quilt historian Sally Garoutte to conclude that "quilts were not common or ordinary during early colonial times . . . they were both rare and expensive."[12] In a similar study, Gloria Seaman Allen correlated the use of quilts with wealth in an examination of eighteenth- and early-nineteenth-century records from a cross section of society in Kent County, Maryland.[13] Early in the nineteenth century, America gained the technology for producing textiles, and cotton fabrics became available and affordable to the growing and relatively prosperous middle class.[14] Other consequences of industrialization, including improved communication through the periodical press, improved transportation systems, and the increased mobility of the population, affected the spread of quiltmaking's popularity.[15]

Gradual changes in the family structure of native-born whites—those who would become the emerging middle class—occurred in the wake of the Industrial Revolution, ultimately affecting nineteenth-century quiltmaking. Families less frequently worked together in the home to produce life's necessities, especially in the urban setting. Instead, men went to the workplace and women remained at home, eventually resulting in clearly defined gender-specific "spheres." Over the course of a century, society's atti-

KQP Ig084. Chintz Spread. Detail. Unknown maker, 1810–1850. Printed design cut from chintz and applied to a background fabric. Collection of Mariana Aylward.

lofty ideals, exuberance, and optimism."[18] There was a spirit of willingness to try new things. Into this atmosphere of hope, European immigrants to the United States brought with them not the skills of quiltmaking, but a love of bright color and ornamentation that may have figured into the creation of the red and green applique quilt. The inward migration of native-born Americans and new immigrants to the frontier West was a force in the dissemination of ideas, including those influencing the development of quiltmaking traditions.

By the second quarter of the nineteenth century, an increase in quiltmaking activity was a direct result of a convergence of technological, social, and cultural factors. Women could buy an abundance of cheap cotton fabrics; they were motivated by new expectations fostered by their changed social roles; they were stimulated by new ideas and influences. Overall, a democratization had taken place in quiltmaking: It had spread to broader segments of the population and was flourishing. As quiltmaking proliferated in the early nineteenth century, certain stylistic and technical changes occurred. For example, cotton became the dominant fabric for quilts.[19] Structurally, medallion and whole-cloth formats were replaced by the block style, an all-over arrangement of repeated small side-by-side square units. The stage was set for the red and green applique quilts to appear.

Techniques

The techniques of applique and quilting, both ancient arts, were brought to America primarily by British colonists. The popular method used to applique quilts in the late eighteenth and

tude toward the proper role for women shifted, and the notion of "the lady" became "the accepted ideal of femininity toward which all women could strive. It was now possible for middle-class women to aspire to that status formerly reserved for upper-class women."[16] In this prescribed role, needlework came to be viewed as an acceptable and appropriate, even ideal, activity for women of all classes, whether in rural or urban settings.

America, especially in the early nineteenth century, has been described as "a civilization in flux."[17] It was a "period of restless ferment, [characterized by]

Appliqued Quilt. Unknown maker, 1840–1880. Handed down in the family of John and Marah Evans, Belmont County, Ohio. Wichita–Sedgwick County Historical Museum.

KQP Ff140. Applique Quilt. Sarah A. Forsythe Pollock (1829–1912), Ohio, 1840–1860. Appliquéd, pieced, stuffed, stippled. Collection of Paula McFarland.

Sarah A. Forsythe Pollock. Courtesy of Heloise S. McFarland.

Vorschrift. From the permanent collection of Franklin and Marshall College, Lancaster, Pennsylvania.

Dough trough. Index of American Design; National Gallery of Art, Washington, D.C. Maker: probably Christian Seltzer or John Seltzer, 1780–1800, Dauphin County, Pennsylvania; renderer: M. Rosenshield-von-Paulin.

Nancy Hornback

early nineteenth centuries was one in which the maker cut out the realistic motifs that appeared on printed chintzes—for example, birds, flowers, or trees; she arranged the printed motifs on a background of white fabric and sewed them down.[20] By 1840, however, the makers of applique quilts had access to less costly cotton fabrics, either solid-colored or calicoes printed with small figured patterns, and were no longer restricted to using motifs already printed in expensive chintzes (see illustrations on pp. 69 and 70). This shift from the "cut-out chintz" method to "conventional applique" was fundamental to the origins of the red and green applique quilts.[21] One can speculate that, in its initial use, the ready adoption of the conventional applique technique might have been a response to early-nineteenth-century social changes. Middle-class women may have been imitating the earlier cut-out chintz quilts that had been fashionable among the upper classes.[22]

Just as the method of applique was influenced by technological and social changes, so too was the technique of quilting. Quilting served two purposes in the red and green applique quilts. First, as it did in other quilt types, it joined together the three layers of the quilt to prevent the filler from shifting. Second, it provided decorative effects that added to and complemented the applique designs. Typical of the group of 147 red and green applique quilts in the Kansas study were close, fine quilting and various degrees of elaboration in the motifs. Backgrounds were filled with different forms of grids or rows of double and triple parallel lines. In Sarah Forsythe Pollock's midcentury quilt, close back-

ground quilting gives the stuffed classical urn motif added dimension. According to family tradition, Sarah used a rose thorn to stuff her quilt from the back with cotton.[23] By far the most popular quilting motif, seen in one-third of the quilts in the study, was the feather design, either formed in wreaths or undulating and running variations.[24] Floral, clamshell, and heart motifs were also common.

Three influences appear to have affected the quilting in the red and green applique quilts. First, technology played a part. Earlier, thread had been handmade and expensive, but affordable, mass-produced cotton thread was widely available by approximately 1820, making elaborate, thread-consuming quilting more possible.[25] A second factor in quilting choices was the popularity of white backgrounds on which quilters found abundant, easy-to-mark space in which to show stitching expertise. Quilters carried over this elaborate quilting practice from earlier chintz and white-work quilt styles. In addition to the preference for a light ground, new formats, interior sashing, and alternating white blocks in the new block style encouraged this development of quilting.[26] A third factor was related to the display of expertise. The exceptionally fine quilting in the early red and green applique quilts is evidence that, by mid nineteenth century, quiltmakers were extremely proficient in needle skills. There was, after all, a priority on training young girls in basic needlework skills both at home and in special classes.[27] After industrialization, it was no longer necessary for women to spin and weave their own cloth, and clothing for men could be purchased. Ready-made

clothing for women, however, was not available until after the Civil War.[28] It is logical to assume that women became less adept at hand-sewing skills as the use of sewing machines in homes became widespread. Factory-made clothing became available for all the family, and children no longer received a thorough needlework education. The fine, close quilting diminished in relative quality and quantity in the quilts made later in the nineteenth century.

Patterns

Although the *techniques* of applique and quilting came to America primarily with the British and changed in the ways described above, *patterns* seen in the red and green applique quilts in the Kansas study suggest entirely separate cultural and geographical origins and influences. For instance, certain motifs seen again and again point to an association with traditional designs outside of England. In the late eighteenth and early nineteenth centuries, American folk art forms enjoyed a period of high popularity.[29] This movement paralleled one taking place in Europe: "This chronological coincidence . . . suggests a continental European phenomenon that affected its European fragments in the New World."[30] The influx of European immigrants to the mid-Atlantic region brought design traditions from their native countries. These traditions influenced popular decoration in the early decades of the nineteenth century in America, providing rich sources of design motifs for painting and stenciling on walls and furniture, embroidered and stenciled bedspreads, painted tinware, and other utilitarian objects.[31] Some motifs passed freely

Applique Quilt. Detail. Mary Parks Lawrence (1854–1950), near Auburn, Logan County, Kentucky, 1870. Appliqued. Wichita–Sedgwick County Historical Museum.

Nancy Hornback

from one craft form to another. One example from the culture of Germanic immigrants is the illuminated manuscript known as *fraktur-schriften*, a craft that exchanged motifs with other creative forms (see p. 72). *Fraktur* reached a peak between 1800 and 1840, putting at the disposal of craftspeople "a whole repertoire of art motifs."[32] "The motifs used were handed down from teacher to pupil, from one generation to another, and were used by all who practiced the art."[33] Another artifact form significant as a source of design motifs was the Pennsylvania German painted chest.

In an inquiry into the design origins of the red and green applique quilt, it is useful to consider two factors. First, as mentioned earlier, by 1840 quilters had moved away from the earlier medallion or whole-cloth formats to the block style with its repeated motifs. Second, the applique artist, no longer reliant on motifs printed on chintz and free to choose her own subject matter, needed design ideas. Both the use of the smaller square blocks combined with the need for new patterns provided an opportunity to experiment and invent. Where did the quiltmaker get her new patterns? Since motifs on the nineteenth-century applique quilts are similar to those found on other decorated objects of the era, it is reasonable to suppose that the ornamentation on those familiar objects in the

Mary Parks Lawrence's baby shoes, 1854. The toe of each shoe is decorated with a gold leaf design of a vase and flowers. It is interesting to think Mary was the only person who saw the design right side up, while the rest of the world saw it upside down. Collection of Marjorie Caskey.

maker's everyday household surroundings offered ideas and inspiration. Further, the standard stock of craft motifs brought by European immigrants provided the basis for the applique patterns. An analysis of designs seen on the nineteenth-century red and green applique quilts examined in the Kansas study supports this hypothesis.

In the applique quilts, symmetrical floral designs are dominant. The symmetrical motif, in fact, is part of the repertoire of many folk arts. Material culturalist Henry Glassie specified as a characteristic motif of western folk design "a bilaterally symmetrical whole, composed of three distinct units, the outside two being mirror images of each other, the central one—the focus of attention—being different but internally symmetrical."[34] Floral motifs are common in some forms of European folk art. In *The Ornament in European Folk Art*, Reinhard Peesch noted that certain fundamental floral forms were most frequently used.[35] One of these is the vase and flowers motif. Peesch described

the combination of a vase-like vessel with two slim handles, from which sprout one or more richly flowered stems. The design depends on the strict observation of axle symmetry. The two-handled vase itself is symmetrical, with the floral motif built up in the same way. The motif's most frequent form consists of a stem with three sprouting blooms when the central one with its large blossom at the top forms a definite axle, while the two on the sides, facing each other, are drawn exactly one like the other, carrying the same flowers. If the num-

ber of three is increased either in flowers or stems, an uneven number is usual as being best for achieving a symmetrical ornament with a central axis.[36]

Mary Parks Lawrence used the vase and flowers motif in the quilt she made in 1870 in Logan County, Kentucky. A two-handled urn holds a spray of tuliplike flowers; the design is bisected by the central stem and its large blossoms, which provide the axis for the symmetrically arranged smaller blossoms on either side. (See the photograph on p. 72 of the dough trough for a vase and flowers motif on a painted wooden object.)

Certain designs can be explained as variations of the vase and flowers motif. "Sprouting flowers" result when "the ornament [is] changed into a plant growing from one flower or two leaves . . . step by step sprouting new flowers or leaves."[37] In yet another variation, the place of the vase is taken by "an equally large and significant heart, when, in fact, the 'sprouting vase' becomes a 'sprouting heart.'" This motif was used on linens in brides' dowries in the late eighteenth century in Germany.[38] The unusual design on Susan Mary Howarton's quilt appears to have been an adaptation of the "sprouting heart" motif.[39]

The rosette is another basic motif often related to floral designs occurring in applique patterns that might also have had roots in folk art.[40] Historically, the rosette was achieved by two methods. The first was drawn with a compass and included either six or twelve lobes. The second type was drawn with a straightedge, forming four lines that intersected vertically, horizontally, and diagonally, produc-

ing eight pointed sections. When the periphery was rounded, an eight-leaf, flowerlike design resulted. Early folk-art historian Frances Lichten, commenting on the use of the compass and straightedge to obtain geometric decorative motifs, observed that "the folk . . . once having discovered that the radius always divides the circumference with the same invariable precision, used this simple geometric principle with much pleasure in various phases of their art."[41] Rosette-type ornaments, used in European design for several centuries as well as in decorative arts in America in the early nineteenth century, may have been the inspiration for the centers of many of the applique patterns. In the photograph on p. 79, a rosette provides the center from which other design elements radiate. Rosettes can also form the outer design elements (see the photograph on p. 80).[42] Although the rosette originated through geometric planning and the use of tools, doubtless quiltmakers, inspired by similar motifs in the ornamented objects around them, could design rosettes for quilt patterns by using simple techniques of paper folding and cutting.

Floral motifs in traditional ornamentation tend to be stiff rather than realistic or naturalistic. The artist's aim was not to accurately represent nature but rather to transform natural subjects into stylized conventions of floral pieces. The applique quiltmakers might as easily have chosen to depict flowers in asymmetrical, naturalistic, random groupings. Instead, they showed a preference for orderly motifs of symmetrical floral arrangements and repetitious geometric flower forms. The distinctive symmetrical and geometric features of the

KQP Da121. Appliqued Quilt. Probably by Mary Elizabeth Hamon Stokes, Kentucky, 1840–1880. Appliqued. Collection of Doris Drechsler.

Applique Quilt. Detail. Mary A. Turley Morgan (1854–1917), Indiana, 1869. Inscribed "Mary A. Turley 1869" in applique. Collection of Elizabeth Pett.

KQP Ja343. Applique Quilt. Detail. Susan Mary Howarton (1831–1927), 1850–1870. Appliqued. Collection of Ollideen Wright.
Susan Mary Howarton came with her family from Indiana by covered wagon in the 1870s to Stark, in Neosho County, Kansas.

KQP Ff140. Applique Quilt. Detail. Sarah A. Forsythe Pollock (1829–1912), Ohio, 1840–1860. Collection of Paula McFarland.

*Applique Quilt. Detail. Lydia Marie
Erwin Mason (1840–1916),
1860–1875. Appliqued. Collection of
Jackie Byers Frisbie.*

*Amos and Lydia Marie Erwin Mason.
Lydia was born in Ohio, married in
Illinois in 1866; the Masons moved to
Missouri in 1868 and settled in Smith
County, Kansas, in 1880. Courtesy of
Jackie Byers Frisbie.*

applique patterns are similar to those of motifs in European traditional art as well as in the Germanic culture in Pennsylvania, seen in artifacts that preceded the making of the quilts. Henry Glassie would go so far as to say they are part of "the traditional repetitive-symmetrical aesthetic" that is a universal principle of decorative folk art design.[43] This design principle is evident in red and green applique quilts throughout the nineteenth century, as illustrated by the quilt shown on p. 83, which was made by Rebecca Wilhelm in Kansas in 1895.

Color

Just as technological, social, and cultural factors affected the choices of techniques and designs in the nineteenth-century applique quilts, so too did they influence the color scheme of red and green. How can the popularity of this combination be accounted for? What led quiltmakers to begin using this particular color combination? The questions are intriguing. An explanation appears to center around the availability of reliably colorfast red and green fabrics in 1840, though further investigation may be needed.

During the span of the nineteenth century, the technology for dyeing cloth underwent rapid and complex changes. The century that began with solely natural dyes, obtained from vegetable, animal, or mineral sources since ancient times, ended with a dye industry creating synthetic dyes in chemical laboratories.[44] To determine the influence of colorfast red and green fabrics in the choice of the color scheme, however, the discussion must be narrowed to what dye technology offered in 1840: natural dyes.

In the early nineteenth century, dyers colored cottons red primarily with the root of the madder plant. Simple madder dyes offered a variety of stable shades of red. The preference of applique quiltmakers, however, was for fabrics known as "Turkey reds," which attained an even higher degree of brilliance and permanence.[45] The process of obtaining Turkey red was time-consuming and intricate; it encompassed thirteen to twenty steps, including preparation in an oil bath (hence it was sometimes termed *oil red*), and took three to four months. Dyers had used the process for centuries, but it was known only in the eastern Mediterranean countries until the 1750s, when Europeans learned the secret. Eventually the process reached England, and from there Turkey red cottons were exported to the United States.[46] American dyers did not use Turkey red commercially until after 1869 when a synthetic coloring agent was discovered and the process simplified.[47] In 1840, true Turkey reds were imported and expensive.

Green fabrics were achieved in the first half of the nineteenth century by dyeing yellow over blue or blue over yellow, using vegetable dyes. In these greens, one color or the other tended to fade out upon long-term exposure to light and washing. This accounts for the yellow-green characteristic in many early red and green applique quilts. A more satisfactory, fast green dye was developed around 1840 through a mineral-vegetable combination, by overdyeing indigo with chrome yellow.[48]

Since the madder and Turkey reds and the blue-yellow overdyed greens had been available for decades, and the quiltmakers were just beginning to use chrome greens, perhaps it was fabric availability, and not colorfastness, that was the key factor in determining the red and green color scheme. By 1840 fabrics were available in abundance to the middle-class women who had taken up quiltmaking.

If the argument that the color choice was determined solely by the availability of fabrics is accepted, a new question arises: Since the same fabrics were available in Britain, why, then, did the color scheme not catch on in popularity there until after 1850? Why was America a decade or more ahead with this phenomenon? At the time the fad for red and green was beginning in America, British quiltmakers were showing a preference for a *red and white* color scheme. In *Traditional British Quilts*, Dorothy Osler acknowledged that the vogue for red and green quilts seems to have originated in America. "These [British red and green] quilts are so directly comparable in colour and style to the 'red and green calico quilts' produced in America . . . that it seems that the British tradition was, in this case, strongly influenced from across the Atlantic."[49] According to Jonathan Platt, curator of the Colour Museum, West Yorkshire, England, "Since the availability of green dyestuffs does not seem to be the answer, I would suggest that this phenomenon could be explained in aesthetic and cultural terms."[50]

Red and green were colors popularly used in middle- and upper-class homes during the first half of the nineteenth century for drapes, walls, carpets, and table covers.[51] In addition, red and green were commonly combined for floral motifs in both European and American decorative arts of the period be-

KQP Ba008. Applique Top, 1850–1920. This unquilted top was handed down through a Nicodemus, Kansas, family. The maker might have been Mary Jane Lewis Scruggs, b. 1866 in Missouri, the daughter of ex-slaves from Kentucky. It is also possible it was made by Mary Jane Scruggs's mother, Amanda Lewis, or it could have been made by someone outside the family. Kansas Museum of History.

KQP Hc008. *Applique Quilt. Rebecca Wilhelm (b. 1837 in Ohio), Emporia, Kansas, 1895. Appliqued. Collection of Mrs. Arnold Coberly.*
   Rebecca made the quilt for the wedding of her daughter, Celia, on December 25, 1895, in Emporia.

Applique Quilt. Mary Parks Lawrence (1854–1950), Logan County, Kentucky, 1870. Hand- and machine-appliqued; hand-and machine-quilted. Wichita–Sedgwick County Historical Museum.

Mary made her quilt at age sixteen with commercially manufactured fabrics for which she traded some of her handwoven goods. She was a fifth-generation descendant of a Scotch-Irish immigrant to Pennsylvania; her family migrated from Kentucky to Sumner County, Kansas, to homestead in 1878.

Mary Parks Lawrence's daughter, Eunice, with quilt on bed behind her, ca. 1906. Courtesy of Marjorie Caskey.

Virginia Catherine (Cassie) Weddle (1885–1919), Ford County, Kansas. Courtesy of Merle Weddle.

Exhibit at Finney County, Kansas, fair, 1898. The appliqued quilt in the center was made by Eliza Holderbaum Hood, Ohio, ca. 1848. Photograph by H. L. Wolf. Courtesy of Wilene Smith.

KQP Jj084. Applique Quilt. Sarah Ellen Knowles Fisher (b. 1832), Indiana, 1850. Appliqued. Collection of Dorothy Kimbell and Pauline Trubshaw.

Sarah made her quilt at age eighteen. Sarah and her husband, Thomas, came to Kansas before 1875. Thomas had injuries from the Civil War; Sarah turned her home into a hotel in Virgil, Kansas, to support her family.

Nancy Hornback

tween 1810 and 1840. The ornamentation on stenciled and painted walls, stenciled quilts, furniture, tinware, and other household objects that still exist is proof that red and green was a popular color combination in the several decades prior to the appearance of the red and green applique quilts. It could be concluded that the technology that offered red and green fabrics in abundance made it possible for the quiltmakers to carry out what was already a popular color scheme.

Other Factors Affecting Development

With this complex historical background in mind, an analysis of the rich sample of 147 nineteenth-century red and green applique quilts documented by the Kansas Quilt Project is in order. Overall, ninety-two carry family histories telling geographical origins. Thirty-one were from Ohio, fourteen from Indiana, and ten from Illinois. Pennsylvania, Kentucky, and Kansas each accounted for six and Iowa and Tennessee for five each. Four were from Missouri. One each came from Virginia, West Virginia, Arkansas, Colorado, and Washington, D.C. Of these, only six can be verified as having been made in Kansas. Ethnic backgrounds of the makers were German, English, Scotch-Irish, Irish, and Welsh, with the sole exception of one believed to have been African American. Religious affiliations were recorded as 95 percent Protestant and 5 percent Catholic (see Appendix).[52] The histories of the makers indicate that almost all lived in either rural areas or small towns, with two exceptions: Washington, D.C., and Cincinnati, Ohio. Middle-class backgrounds are suggested by the occupations of

the quiltmakers' husbands. The majority were farmers; other named occupations included dry goods merchant, wool carder, postmaster, cabinet maker, carriage maker, and lumberman. Several were physicians in small towns. Overall, geographic origins and other biographical data provide evidence that nineteenth-century red and green applique quilts were products of primarily rural, middle-class women.

The study's six red and green applique quilts made in Kansas dated from 1879 to 1899. The state was settled after the peak popularity of the fad; in addition, several factors related to frontier life account for the small number. Although fabric had become less expensive and more accessible in the East, such was not the case on the frontier. Recalling her experiences after moving from Iowa to Franklin County, Kansas, in 1859, Mrs. D. M. Valentine wrote: "A year or two later, when our old home and marriage fineries were about exhausted, came the necessity of buying clothes, bed coverings and such. Calico was the most universal dress goods for women and small children, and it cost forty cents per yard, when cents were as hard to get as dollars were later."[53] Moreover, rustic living conditions and the rigors of frontier life were a factor in the delay of quilts' being made in the first generation or more of settlement.[54] The white backgrounds of the red and green applique quilts would have been particularly impractical for frontier quiltmaking.[55] Charlotte Stearns Pengra noted in her overland trail diary in 1853: "Those who come this journey should have their pillows covered with dark calico and sheets colored, white is not suitable."[56]

Sarah Ellen Knowles Fisher, c. 1895. Courtesy of Dorothy Kimbell.

David and Amanda Arrington Hutchins. Courtesy of Carol Hutchins Auten.

The Kansas Quilt Project documented 662 quilts that were brought to Kansas during the settlement period between 1854 and 1880, including the 147 red and green applique quilts. Obviously, people brought what was representative of the quilts in their home states, a topic addressed later in this chapter. However, the question of why so many of this quilt type were brought, coupled with their high survival rate, leads to a discussion of their functions as utilitarian, decorative, and symbolic objects. That the quiltmakers initially intended utilitarian purposes is suggested by the unusual design layouts of many of the quilts in the study. Borders on two or three sides or rows of half motifs are indications that the quilts were meant to fit specific beds or to be used on beds placed against walls. Yet, the ornamental, decorative aspects suggest more than utilitarian necessity. The applique quilts were time consuming to make and required specially purchased fabrics. Many are still in fine condition, having been well cared for by subsequent generations. Descendants of the quiltmakers testify to the esteem given them. One woman wrote, "Since [my grandparents] reared a family of nine children, this quilt would have been worn out had it not been given special care and 'saved.'"[57] It was not unusual for a red and green applique quilt to be taken out and used only on special occasions; one interviewee recalled that her mother put the quilt on the bed "only on days when the Ladies' Aid Society came."[58]

Still further functions of the quilts explain why settlers brought red and green applique quilts to their new homes in the West. Recent scholarship on frontier women suggests that, despite the necessary overlapping and blurring of the "separate spheres," notions of proper gender roles and ideals of domesticity were nevertheless retained. Former high standards of domesticity were difficult to maintain but gave meaning to lives that had been disrupted by the trauma of leaving family and community (see top right photograph on p. 85). "The cultural values of domestic ideology had a powerful appeal to female settlers . . . [offering] a sense of stability in an inherently unstable world."[59] These are issues in the scholarship on frontier women that are difficult to substantiate but logical to assume. Since red and green applique quilts were used for special occasions and may have been symbols of class aspirations, they would have provided that sense of stability.

In the first years of settlement, families were not able to have the kinds of homes they had left in the East. New homes in Kansas were often primitive cabins, dugouts, or sod houses. "Although determined women were often dismayed by the limitations of such housing, they showed tremendous creativity in coping with their crude homes, frequently turning their interiors into comfortable dwelling places that sometimes even boasted a touch of elegance . . . supplementing wooden homemade furniture with treasures from home."[60] In 1855, Hannah Anderson Ropes, after opening a trunkful of household goods from the East, wrote in a letter "and how we begin to look forward, as well as backward, to a condition of civilized housekeeping."[61]

Frontier historians John Mack Faragher and Christine Stansell spoke of "'various articles of ornament and convenience . . . commodities of women's sphere . . . [that] provided women with a psychological lifeline to their abandoned homes and communities, as well as to elements of their identities."[62] The red and green applique quilts carried to Kansas were, perhaps, one such psychological lifeline: a reminder of ideals of gentility and "true womanhood," symbolic of stability in a disrupted way of life, a link between the harsh realities of the frontier and the homes left behind.

Tracing the migration routes and settlement patterns in combination with biographical data can be valuable in shedding light on issues and trends in the red and green applique history and development. Since the Ohio Valley was the origin of many Kansas settlers, it is logical that the Kansas Quilt Project documented a large number of quilts brought to Kansas from that region as one step on a major, well-traveled migration route. It is possible that the area of the Ohio Valley was the geographical location of the greatest development of the red and green applique quilts. Or one could hypothesize as follows: first, the red and green applique quilts originated in the mid-Atlantic states; next, large numbers of immigrants moved into the Ohio Valley region at just the time the fad was beginning, approximately 1840, bringing with them the ideas for the techniques, designs, and colors of the red and green applique quilts; finally, later immigrants carried the quilts farther west to Kansas and other Western states, where rigorous frontier life delayed making more of the quilt type for another generation or so.

Evidence for such a hypothesis can be supplied by the history of the movements of the quilt-makers, that is, knowing not only where the quilts were made but also the intermediary steps in the migrations. "The most natural and common mode of advance was by relatively short removals into adjacent territory, and this repeated by succeeding generations as new lands became available."[63] Numerous examples of this migration mode were discovered in the makers' histories in the Kansas study. For instance, quiltmaker Amanda Arrington Hutchins's mother, Sarah Kyle Arrington, was born in Northumberland County, Pennsylvania, ca. 1796. Amanda was born in Montgomery County, Ohio, in 1816; in 1842, she married David Hutchins and moved to Grant County, Indiana, where she made her quilt. The quilt was brought to Kansas in 1885 by her son, Thomas J. Hutchins.[64] Another example is demonstrated by migration movements of quiltmaker Susannah Baer Boyer, born in 1798 in York County, Pennsylvania, the daughter of immigrants from Germany. In 1820, Susannah married Jacob Boyer, a wool carder and dry goods merchant; in 1834 the Boyers moved to Sandusky, Ohio. Susannah made a red and green applique quilt in 1844 before the birth of her sixth child, William Jacob Boyer, who brought the quilt with him when he settled in Pratt, Kansas, in 1904. A third example is that of quiltmaker Susan Cogel Blakely, born in 1832 in Lancaster, Pennsylvania, the daughter of Gottlieb and Barbara Dice Cogel, immigrants from Wurtemberg, Germany. Susan grew up in Cincinnati, Ohio; there, in the period before her marriage to John Blakely in 1853, she made her quilt with the help of her

mother. John and Susan made subsequent moves to Illinois, Minnesota, and Texas, finally taking up residence in Wichita, Kansas, in 1880.[65]

These samples are typical of a pattern of migration seen again and again in connection with the red and green applique quilts brought to Kansas. It is intriguing to speculate about the significance of migration to the origins and development of the quilts. Statistical and anecdotal evidence from the Kansas study supports the theory that the red and green applique quilt type reached its greatest development in the Ohio Valley states by women whose families had migrated from the mid-Atlantic region. As data become available from other state documentation projects, it may become clearer just how this occurred.

Conclusion

An examination of techniques, design, and color in nineteenth-century red and green applique quilts shows them to be a distinctive type, set apart from other nineteenth-century quilts. Various technological advances and social changes resulted in the spread of the practice of quilt-making from the upper classes to a wider portion of the population. The adoption of the conventional applique method, basic to the origins of the red and green quilts, may have provided a way for middle-class women to imitate earlier quilt styles of the elite. Use of the conventional applique technique also created a need for patterns, and floral designs in the quilts suggest the influence of traditional aesthetics. The abundance of fabrics available by 1840 made it possible for quiltmakers to carry out a color scheme that was already popular

in the culture in yet another form. Migration was a force in the rapid spread of the quilt type, and tracing the westward paths of the quiltmakers and their descendants offers new perspective on its development. The red and green applique quilts brought to Kansas were practical and decorative objects; they performed additional functions as symbols of stability, continuity, and bonding and as expressions of the ideals, hopes, and values of nineteenth-century women.

Notes

1. Kenneth L. Ames, "Material Culture as Non-Verbal Communication: A Historical Case Study," *Journal of American Culture* 3 (Winter 1980): 619, 620. There are many references in quilt history of owners who value quilts as symbols of family memories. In "Diaries and Quilts: Women's Lives on the Frontier" (unpublished manuscript, Wichita, Kans., 1990), Gayle R. Davis explored the role of quilts as "mediators between the familiar and the new" in their makers' adjustments to the plains frontier.

2. James Deetz, *In Small Things Forgotten: The Archaeology of Early American Life* (New York: Doubleday, 1977), 67. "Over time, a graph of the popularity of any cultural trait will have a single peak. Styles of artifacts . . . have small beginnings, grow in popularity until a peak is reached, and then fade away."

3. Ricky Clark, George W. Knepper, and Ellice Ronsheim, *Quilts in Community: Ohio's Traditions* (Nashville, Tenn.: Rutledge Hill Press, 1991). Several sections are devoted to the red and green floral applique style in Ohio quilts: see pp. 22–29, 81–84.

4. This chapter will bring together substantive information that has been published, leaving out more particularized types like the Baltimore album quilt.

5. Gwen Marston and Joe Cunningham, *American Beauties: Rose and Tulip Quilts* (Paducah, Ky.: American Quilter's Society, 1988), 16, 17.

6. Barbara Brackman, *Clues in the*

Calico: A Guide to Identifying and Dating Antique Quilts (McLean, Va.: EPM Publications, 1989), 141, 142, 155–157.

7. Jeannette Lasansky, "The Typical versus the Unusual: Distortions of Time," in *In the Heart of Pennsylvania: Symposium Papers*, ed. Jeanette Lasansky (Lewisburg, Pa.: Oral Traditions Project, 1986), 56.

8. Thomas J. Schlereth, "Social History Scholarship and Material Culture Research," in *Material Culture: A Research Guide*, ed. Thomas J. Schlereth (Lawrence: University Press of Kansas, 1985), 157.

9. Material culture or social history–based women's histories have proliferated. See Pat Ferrero, Elaine Hedges, and Julie Silber, *Hearts and Hands: The Influence of Women and Quilts on American Society* (San Francisco: Quilt Digest Press, 1987); Judith Reiter Weissman and Wendy Levitt, *Labors of Love: America's Textiles and Needlework, 1650–1930* (New York: Alfred A. Knopf, 1987); and Margaret Vincent, *The Ladies' Work Table: Domestic Needlework in Nineteenth-Century America* (Allentown, Pa.: Allentown Art Museum, 1988).

10. Rachel Maines, "Fancy Work: The Archaeology of Lives," in *Feminist Collage: Women in the Visual Arts*, ed. Judy Loeb (New York: Columbia University Teachers' College, 1979), 7.

11. E. McClung Fleming, "Artifact Study: A Proposed Model," *Winterthur Portfolio* 9 (1974): 158.

12. Sally Garoutte, "Early Colonial Quilts in a Bedding Context," in *Uncoverings 1980*, ed. Sally Garoutte (Mill Valley, Calif.: American Quilt Study Group, 1981), 23.

13. Gloria Seaman Allen, "Bed Coverings, Kent County, Maryland 1710–1820," in *Uncoverings 1985*, ed. Sally Garoutte (Mill Valley, Calif.: American Quilt Study Group, 1986), 59.

14. Rachel Maines, "Paradigms of Scarcity and Abundance: The Quilt as an Artifact of the Industrial Revolution," in *In the Heart of Pennsylvania: Symposium Papers*, ed. Jeannette Lasansky (Lewisburg, Pa.: Oral Traditions Project, 1986), 85.

15. Eric E. Lampard, "The Social Impact of the Industrial Revolution," in *Technology and Western Civilization*, vol. 1, ed. Melvin Kranzberg and Carroll W. Pursell, Jr.

(New York: Oxford University Press, 1967), 302, 303.

16. Gerda Lerner, "The Lady and the Mill Girl: Changes in the Status of Women in the Age of Jackson, 1800–1840," in *A Heritage of Her Own: Toward a New Social History of Women*, ed. Nancy F. Cott and Elizabeth H. Pleck (New York: Simon and Schuster, 1979), 181.

17. Edward R. Pessen, *Jacksonian America: Society, Personality and Politics* (Homewood, Ill.: Dorsey Press, 1969), 58.

18. Alice Felt Tyler, *Freedom's Ferment: Phases of American Social History to 1860* (Minneapolis: University of Minnesota Press, 1944), 2.

19. Maines, "Paradigms of Scarcity and Necessity," 84: "Cotton became in the 19th century a less costly fabric than linen or linen/wool blends for coverlets, and as the costs of print cloths and textile converting fell in the decades before the Civil War, printed cottons became the standard medium of the American quiltmaker." See also Joel Sater, "Cotton Was the Magic Fiber: Textiles and the Patchwork Quilt," in *The Patchwork Quilt* (Ephrata, Pa.: Science Press, 1981), 23–51.

20. In this context, the cut-out chintz method is discussed as a *technique* rather than as a regional or temporal quilt style.

21. Barbara Brackman used the terms *cut-out chintz* and *conventional applique* to distinguish the two methods (*Clues in the Calico*, 101, 102).

22. Dorothy Osler reached a similar conclusion about quiltmaking in Britain. She noted that "possession of quilts became a typical manifestation of [the] pressure to attain a better class position, by imitating the ways of wealthier folk." And "what started as a form of adornment for the rich and powerful became part of a traditional culture among peasants and working class communities" (*Traditional British Quilts* [London: B. T. Batsford, 1987], 104).

23. Heloise Schaefer McFarland, interview with author, Sterling, Kansas, March 4, 1988.

24. Kansas quiltmaker Lucyle Jewett (b. 1899), who learned nineteenth-century quilting skills from her Quaker mother and grandmother, attested to the versatility of the feather quilting design: "[one can] twist, turn, bend, make circles,

squares, or do halves—anything can be done with feathers." Interview with author, Halstead, Kansas, March 2, 1988.

25. Maines, "Paradigms of Scarcity and Abundance," 23.

26. Jonathan Holstein, "The American Block Quilt," in *In the Heart of Pennsylvania: Symposium Papers*, ed. Jeannette Lasansky (Lewisburg, Pa.: Oral Traditions Project, 1986), 22.

27. C. Kurt Dewhurst, Betty MacDowell, and Marsha MacDowell, *Artists in Aprons: Folk Art by American Women* (New York: E. P. Dutton, 1979), 13.

28. Claudia B. Kidwell and Margaret C. Christman, *Suiting Everyone: The Democratization of Clothing in America* (Washington, D.C.: Smithsonian Institution Press, 1974), 53.

29. Jean Lipman and Alice Winchester, *The Flowering of American Folk Art* (New York: Whitney Museum of Art, 1975), 9.

30. Scott T. Swank, "From Dumb Dutch to Folk Heroes," in *Arts of the Pennsylvania Germans* (New York: W. W. Norton, 1983), 74.

31. See Frances Lichten, *Fraktur: The Illuminated Manuscripts of the Pennsylvania Dutch* (Philadelphia: Free Library of Philadelphia, 1958); Lichten, *Folk Art Motifs of Pennsylvania* (New York: Dover Publications, 1954); Jean Lipman, *American Folk Decoration* (New York: Oxford University Press, 1951); Ellen Sabine, *American Folk Art* (Princeton: D. Van Nostrand, 1958); Nina Fletcher Little, *Country Arts in Early American Homes* (New York: E. P. Dutton, 1975).

32. Sabine, *American Folk Art*, 3.

33. Ethel Ewert Abrahams, *Frakturmalen and Schonschreiben* (North Newton, Kans.: Mennonite Press, 1980), 7.

34. Henry Glassie, "Folk Art," in *Material Culture Studies in America*, ed. Thomas J. Schlereth (Nashville, Tenn.: American Association for State and Local History, 1982), 133.

35. Reinhard Peesch, *The Ornament in European Folk Art*, trans. Ruth Michaelis-Jens and Patrick Murray (New York: Alpine Fine Arts Collection, 1982), 167. This chapter does not include all floral motifs but focuses on two of Peesch's categories, since they were the most fre-

quently reflected in the applique quilts in the Kansas study.

36. Ibid., 169, 170.

37. Ibid., 170.

38. Ibid., 171.

39. Susan Mary Howarton's descendants believed her quilt was made for her marriage. Ollideen Wright, interview with author, Thayer, Kansas, June 20, 1988.

40. Peesch, *The Ornament in European Folk Art*, 174. Peesch said "[the rosette's] name should be understood more as a metaphor than the name of a natural flower."

41. Lichten, *Folk Art Motifs of Pennsylvania*, 48.

42. Ibid., 174, 175.

43. Glassie, "Folk Art," 140. See also Henry Glassie, *The Spirit of Folk Art* (New York: Harry N. Abrams, 1989), 140–157, 165–166.

44. Joyce Storey, *The Thames and Hudson Manual of Dyes and Fabrics* (London: Thames and Hudson, 1978), 68.

45. George S. Cole, *Dictionary of Dry Goods* (1892), 250.

46. G. Schaefer, "The History of Turkey Red Dyeing," in *Ciba Review* 39 (May 1941), 1407, 1408.

47. Diane L. Fagan Affleck, *Just New from the Mills: Printed Cottons in America* (North Andover, Mass.: Museum of American Textile History, 1987), 55.

48. James M. Liles, "Dyes in American Quilts Made before 1830," in *Uncoverings 1984*, ed. Sally Garoutte (Mill Valley, Calif.: American Quilt Study Group, 1985), 35.

49. Osler, *Traditional British Quilts*, 38.

50. Letter to a friend, November 30, 1989.

51. Elisabeth Donaghy Garrett, *At Home: The American Family 1750–1870* (New York: Harry N. Abrams, 1990), 44 passim.

52. Of fifty-nine quiltmakers who reported religious affiliations, 27.5 percent indicated "Protestant" without identifying specific denominations. Among the specified denominations were fourteen Methodist, seven Presbyterian, and five Quaker. Three each were reported as Baptist, Catholic, and Lutheran. Two each were identified as Christian and Mennonite and one each as Christian Scientist, Church of Christ, United Brethren, and Seventh Day Adventist.

53. Mrs. D. M. Valentine, "Reminiscences of an American Mother on the Western Frontier," *Journal of American History* 4 (1910): 81.

54. For a more complete discussion of the lack of quilts made on the frontier, see Barbara Brackman, "Quilts on the Kansas Frontier," *Kansas History: A Journal of the Central Plains* 13 (Spring 1990): 17–19.

55. Quiltmaker Mary A. Turley (see photograph on p. 78) married Levi Morgan in Bourbon County in eastern Kansas in 1871. In 1885, the Morgans took their family of six children by covered wagon to Morton County, in the southwestern corner of Kansas, bordering Colorado and Oklahoma. Daughter Catherine recalled their arrival: "We landed on as bare a prairie claim as can be imagined." The Morgans filed on a preemption claim and built a 12 foot by 20 foot soddy. They dug and cut the sods for the walls and used wood planks for the roof, covering it with sod and dirt. "Many a night when it rained Mother would put us all on the bed and put the wagon sheet over us to keep us dry." The Morgans later built a dugout, with two rooms, wooden sides, and a shingle roof. Unpublished reminiscences of Catherine Morgan Cunningham; also *Morton County 1886–1986: Cornerstone of Kansas* (1986), 156 (this publication was compiled by members of the Morton County Historical Society).

56. Lillian Schlissel, *Women's Diaries of the Westward Journey* (New York: Schocken Books, 1982), 81.

57. Martha Jo Longhofer, letter to author, April 21, 1988.

58. Nadine Vining, interview with author, Tonganoxie, Kansas, May 27, 1988.

59. Robert L. Griswold, "Anglo Women and Domestic Ideology," in *Western Women: Their Land, Their Lives*, ed. Lillian Schlissel, Vicki L. Ruiz, and Janice Monk (Albuquerque: University of New Mexico Press, 1989), 18.

60. Glenda Riley, *The Female Frontier: A Comparative View of Women on the Prairie and the Plains* (Lawrence: University Press of Kansas, 1988), 88.

61. Hannah Anderson Ropes, *Six Months in Kansas: By a Lady* (Boston: John P. Jewett, 1856), 93, 94.

62. John Mack Faragher and Christine Stansell, "Women and Their Families on the Overland Trails," in *Portrait of America*, vol. 1, ed. Stephen B. Oates (Boston: Houghton Mifflin, 1987), 298.

63. Roy L. Butterfield, "On the American Migrations," *New York History* 38 (1957): 368.

64. Carol Auten, letter to author, October 10, 1990.

65. *Portrait and Biographical Album of Sedgwick County, Kansas* (Chicago: Chapman Brothers, 1888), 364–365.

One Patch, unfinished top, maker unknown. Pieced, cottons. Collection of Terry Thompson. Photo: Jon Blumb.

Chapter Four

Fabric and Conversation Prints

Terry Thompson and Barbara Brackman

QUILTS GROW OUT OF THE FABRIC AVAILABLE TO THE QUILTMAKERS. MANY BELIEVE THE PATCHWORK QUILT, A COLLAGE OF FABRIC SCRAPS, TO BE A PRODUCT OF SCARCITY. IN REALITY, HOWEVER, PATCHWORK RE-QUIRES AN ABUNDANCE OF FABRIC.[1] IN THIS CHAPTER WE EXAMINE THE RELATIONSHIP BETWEEN FABRICS AVAIL-able in nineteenth-century Kansas and the resulting Kansas-made quilts. The focus is on the one-patch quilt, a type of scrap quilt, and on one popular cotton fabric, the "conversation print."

The primary source of cotton fabric in nineteenth-century America was the New England mill. The findings of the KQP re-vealed no sign of home produc-tion of cotton or silk fabric and only three quilts made of home-produced linen or wool,[2] fibers that were commonly woven in American homes before the end of the Civil War. None of these quilts was made in Kansas, which was opened for white settlement about a decade before the end of that war.

Written evidence of home production of fabric in early Kansas is sparse. Martha E. Jor-dan of Shawnee County left in her reminiscences a rare recollec-tion of one family that attempted to produce wool, linen, and cot-ton during the Civil War. Their wool production was curtailed when a wolf ate their lamb after one shearing. Linen production fared no better when a storm de-stroyed the flax crop from which the fiber was to be obtained.

We raised some cotton, which we picked as fast as it was ready for ginning, and I car-ried it on horseback to a hand gin about three miles away, where I ginned it myself, then brought it home for mother to card and spin on an old-time spinning wheel. She made all our summer stock-ings and kept the family in many kinds of clothing. She made plenty of heavy cloth which we used for different purposes, one of which was heavy underskirts to make our skirts stand out. That was just before hoops came in style. . . . We also knit plenty of [wool] stockings for my brother who was in the Union army."[3]

Her description of growing, ginning, spinning, and weaving cotton in Kansas is unusual be-cause cotton has never been a popular crop in the state. The cotton gin she described is prob-ably the one owned by Joseph Pi-azzek (1834–1921), who brought it to Valley Falls during the Civil War when "the people were short of cotton batting." (The gin is now in the collection of the Kansas Museum of His-tory.) In a memoir he recalled that Kansans, cut off from eastern goods, planted small patches of cotton. "I, the only man foolish enough to invest in a cotton gin . . . made batting, wrapping it in brown paper, tied with a string and sold it to the store and oth-ers at 95 cents a pound. I think this lasted about two years after the Civil War."[4]

Another Civil War reference to cotton growing appeared in the Lawrence *State Journal* in February 1863: "A cotton gin is being set up in Lyon County. The Douglas County cotton ex-citement has spread all over the state and next year we'll talk about cotton mills."[5] The theme running through the rare descrip-tions of cotton growing in Kansas, during the Civil War and after, is the lack of mills to process the crop and the false hopes that the equipment would soon be in place.

The first state fair, held in Leavenworth in 1863, offered prizes for fabric produced in Kansas mills and homes, but pre-mium lists described wool and linen.[6] After the war, through the 1870s and 1880s, county and state fairs commonly offered prizes for Kansas-made textiles, both mill and domestic, in linen, silk, hemp, and wool. The only mention of home weaving of cot-ton was for mixed wool and cot-ton fabric, which probably had a weft of home-spun wool and a warp of factory-produced cotton yarn (presumably purchased from eastern mills). One exception was the Western States Fair held in Lawrence in 1882, which offered a premium for all-cotton fabric produced by a mill to accommo-date the cotton-growing states of Texas and Arkansas, included in this regional fair.[7]

The 1870 census reported no cotton goods manufacturers in Kansas. The nine manufacturers

This Minneapolis, Kansas, dry goods store offered a wide variety of fabric and notions to the early-twentieth-century seamstress.

of woolen goods listed may have produced fabric from Kansas-grown wool, and Kansas quilt-makers may have used fabric from these factories in their quilts. The Kansas Quilt Project heard no such family histories.[8] The few family tales about Kansas factories as sources for quilt fabric were fairly recent and involved factories that manufactured clothing from fabric made elsewhere. An Onaga woman traded milk in the 1870s for scraps from a factory that made gym shorts, and an Osawatomie quilt was pieced of scraps from a blouse manufacturer.[9] We can assume nineteenth-century quiltmakers also obtained scraps from Kansas clothing manufacturers that im-

ported cottons from the east.

The reliance of Kansas quilt-makers on fabric from eastern mills is one good reason for the dearth of quilts made here in the mid nineteenth century. Most personal reports indicate that imported fabric was scarce through the 1850s and 1860s, although advertisements and articles in early Kansas newspapers suggest that materials suitable for quilts were abundant in Lawrence, one of the largest towns. The *Kansas Herald of Freedom* in May 1855 noted that calicoes were ten to twenty cents per yard and un-bleached domestic (a white fabric suitable for quilt backs) was nine to fourteen cents per yard. In that year's run of the *Kansas*

Terry Thompson and Barbara Brackman

KQP Df125. Nine Patch, detail of a quilt top, pieced by Ida Iva Helder Pellett (1869–1944), Lawrence, Douglas County, 1890–1910. Collection of Fay Talley. Photo: Jon Blumb.

Ida Iva Helder came to Kansas in 1871 to be adopted by a Lawrence family. She and her twin, Ada Ava, were born in Freeport, Illinois, and separated when their mother died. Ada was adopted by a North Dakota family. Iva's Nine Patch contains several conversation prints; the most unusual is the dog head.

Richard and Ida Pellett, ca. 1910.

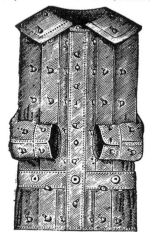

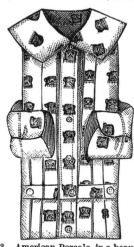

MEN'S RUBBER COATS.

366
367

ME

White Vests and Bar Coats.

A page from Bloomingdale Brothers' catalog. Courtesy of Mary Williams.

Horseshoes, symbolizing good luck and an aristocratic sport, were popular images at the end of the nineteenth century. The boy's shirt is of fabric similar to the horseshoe conversation prints. Collection of Terry Thompson.

Tribune the Hornbys and Ferrile store on the California Road advertised "every variety of Dry Goods . . . bleached and unbleached sheeting . . . prints from 8 ½ to 15 cents." Two years later, Helen Carpenter, on her way to California, shopped in Lawrence and recorded in her diary that she bought "two pairs of shoes, calico for two spencer waists, jeans for a dress skirt, needles, pins and thread and so forth," a confirmation of a good supply of fabric in the town. A few days later she was disappointed to find that the store in Riley City (near Fort Riley) "contained but little in the way of dry goods."[10]

Her complaint about Riley City is probably an accurate account of how much fabric was available beyond Lawrence. Chestina Bowker Allen, living in Pottawatomie County in 1857, was thrilled to receive a gift from a newcomer from New Hampshire who had brought "from the benevolent ladies there 20 yards of calico."[11]

Several old settlers writing their memoirs in the early twentieth century recalled trading with the Native Americans for the fabric they received as part of their regular allotment. Lucy and Annie Miller recalled trading butter and eggs to the Pottawatomie for beads and calico. "The writer used to think that one of the most beautiful dresses she ever had was a bright purple bought from the Indians."[12]

Clothing was in short supply because of the shortage of fabric. Clarina I. Howard Nichols, writing in 1869, declared that the colors of the state were what she called "parti-colors," implying that the state flag should be patchwork, to represent the patches on everyone's clothes.

Georgiana Packard, who settled near Topeka, recalled a visit from a man whose "clothes were patched past belief. He said 'they put all the patches on him and the others would have to go without.' His wife used to ravel out muslin and twist it up to make thread." She remembered that fabric was so hard to find that people wove shoddy, fabric made of raveled-out wool clothes, "which would drop to pieces if worn a little." During a drought in the early 1860s, sacks of food were given away, labeled with the name of the agent (later a U.S. senator) who handled the distribution. "Men wore clothes of sacks that held goods, and they said that 'when they were worn to shreds, there still in bold relief were the words *S. C. Pomeroy, Beans.*'" Percy Ebutt, who lived near Manhattan and Junction City in the 1870s, wrote advice to those planning to move to Kansas: "You must not care much for appearances, and be reconciled to seeing patches on your clothes, and again think yourself lucky if they are of the same colour. I have seen brown overalls with patches of flour-sacking, with the brand and description of the flour in blue letters still on."[13]

During the 1870s, as an expanding population meant an increase in towns and stores, and as the advent of the railroads made fabric more available, Kansas women in their diaries and letters began to regularly mention buying fabric. Luna Warner, a sixteen-year-old living south of Downs, went with her mother to shop in Cawker City in 1871. "Got home about 1 o'clock, bought me a pair of shoes and four kinds of pink calico." In the years 1871 and 1872 she mentioned three new homemade dresses. In Manhattan, Etta Parkinson Reynolds recorded five fabric purchases over a two-year period in her diary. "Did some trading at Mr. Purcell's. Got a lot of dimity for a dress. Didn't know what to do with it." In 1874, she bought twelve yards of calico at ten cents; in 1875, thirteen and a half yards at nine cents.[14]

Boating in Finney County. Photo: Wolf.

The little boy with the boater hat is wearing a nautical print. Courtesy of Wilene Smith.

The 1870s brought a "calico craze" all over the country as the eastern mills, recovered from the Civil War and experimenting with new industrial technology, produced millions of yards of inexpensive cotton prints that were so affordable nearly everyone could buy fabric for a new dress with regularity. The calico craze hit Kansas, too; the 1879 Lyon County Fair offered a prize for a "calico baby" and the "handsomest lady dressed in calico," and calico balls became a fashionable alternative to fancy dress balls in Topeka, Garden City, and elsewhere.[15]

The advent of the mail-order catalog meant that women living far from stores also had access to a wide variety of fabrics. Montgomery Ward's first catalog in 1872 began its list of goods with "Cotton Prints." Their 1882 catalog listed for sale the "Best Prints" manufactured by Hamilton, Cocheco, Merrimack, and other New England print works. These standard brands sold for five cents a yard, a price that offered competition to the hometown stores in Kansas and enabled many farm women and wives of working men to afford printed cottons and the clothes, furnishings, and quilts made from them. Competition increased with the Bloomingdale Brothers in 1886, followed by the Sears, Roebuck and Company catalog, which began offering fabrics in 1895. Each catalog featured "dry goods," furnishing goods, and clothing for every member of the family.[16] The abundance of calico prints is reflected in the number of Kansas-made quilts recorded in the 1875–1900 era. It is also reflected in an increase in the number of different prints used per quilt and a decrease in the size of

Terry Thompson and Barbara Brackman

each piece: Smaller pieces are more wasteful of fabric because more fabric is hidden in the seams.

One popular type of quilt in Kansas and elsewhere in these years was the one-patch quilt,[17] which is not organized into square blocks or set with lattice strips. Patterns were based upon a single template shape such as a square, triangle, diamond, hexagon, clamshell, or rectangle. The shapes, usually smaller than three inches across, were repeated over the entire top. There were often hundreds of different fabrics, usually cotton dress fabrics, which were very frequently organized into a pattern of alternating light and dark patches.

The periodicals and needle-craft manuals of the day published a number of patterns for one-patch quilts with names like Thousand Pyramids, Tumblers, Hairpin Catcher, Tumbling Blocks, Honeycomb, and Hit and Miss. One-patch quilts were popular for many reasons. They were a quick and easy way to use up leftover dressmaking scraps, and the use of a single shape simplified assembling the top. A busy housewife could sit down for a few minutes between chores, reach into her scrap basket and piece together a long strip, alternating light and dark patches. They were a wonderful showcase for the colorful and intricate calicoes, so much so that one subcategory of these dressmaker scrap quilts was the "charm quilt," in which the maker strove to include no two identical scraps of fabric.[18] Few quiltmakers succeeded in this goal, but they tried to give the illusion of a true charm quilt. One often has to look long and hard to find duplicate scraps.

Many consider quilts made of a multitude of fabric scraps to be the most ordinary of quilts, but they are valuable as records of the wide range of different cotton fabrics available to the American quiltmaker. The one-patch quilts provide a small window in which to view these interesting fabrics. One curious group of pictorial prints, identified as "conversation prints," can tell us much about popular culture, class, and societal values at the end of the nineteenth century.

Many examples of American prints from the late nineteenth century survive in fabric sample books at the Museum of American Textile History in North Andover, Massachusetts.[19] A comparison of fabrics found in Kansas quilts with the fabrics available in the sample books, particularly the conversation prints dating from 1880 to 1900, indicates that Kansas women had access to much the same fabric as women in the east.

Conversation print is a term in general use today by fabric collectors and quilt historians to describe a cotton with small, repetitive figures depicting recognizable objects other than florals. Other names used by fabric manufacturers are "conversationals" and "object prints."[20] The motifs appear in thumbnail size and show fine, delicate artwork. Designers chose simple motifs to be repeated and evenly spaced throughout the yardage, far enough apart so that each repeat is a discrete design, yet close enough to be present in the smallest swatch of fabric. This is one reason conversation prints were so popular with quiltmakers. The fabric was usually a shirting, popular for everyday shirts for men, play clothes for children, and waists (blouses), dresses, and aprons for women.

One variation featured a white background printed with figures in black, red, or blue. Many of the detailed line drawings were what manufacturers called mill engravings, shaded with lines and dots to give depth to the images of everything from horse heads and British sailors to bees and flies. A simpler version featured a white or black figure on a navy blue or red ground cotton.

Both name and images in conversation prints are related to a fashion in popular and fine art, the "conversation piece," a term first used in the eighteenth century.[21] This genre of stylized paintings depicted scenes of children, families, groups, and individuals busy at pleasurable activities, such as playing games, sharing a country stroll, fishing, or having a picnic. The sex of the children pictured can only be determined by their toys, animals, and sports since boys and girls were dressed alike in dresses, pantaloons, and skirts. Portrait artists painted boys holding toy knives, balls, guns, watches, tops, and bows and arrows or perched on rocking horses with riding crops in their hands. Girls, who were often pictured standing behind or to the sides of their brothers, were identified by their sewing thimbles, dolls, kittens, or baskets of fruit and flowers.[22] The same toys that appear in these paintings began to appear in the printed cotton fabrics of the mid nineteenth century. Both painted and woven images reflected the contemporary images of childhood in which all children were considered effeminate until the seventh birthday.

Susan Meller and Joost Elffers in their book *Textile Designs* picture conversation prints as old as 1810, although the majority of the swatches in their chapter on

The women working at the Hammond Laundry in Junction City in 1903 are wearing what the catalogs called wash fabrics, probably in shades of blue. White figures of anchors and horseshoes might be printed on such inexpensive dark cottons. Kansas Collection, University of Kansas Libraries. Photo: Joseph J. Pennell.

conversationals date from after 1880. An 1815 quilt in the collection of the Smithsonian Institution features a nautical print, a delicate white anchor on a blue-green ground. A scrap of cotton picturing a finely drawn dog head was glued in a French manual for calico printers printed in 1846.[23] The April 1863 issue of America's foremost fashion magazine, *Godey's Lady's Book*, includes an early description: "We find ourselves first among the Percales, suitable for nursery wear as well as shirting. Some are quite original in design. For instance, a white ground with tiny watches of various colors scattered over it, another with pitchers arranged to form figures, others seemingly covered with small dots, but, upon examination, these dots are in some cases, small Arabic figures, and in others letters. Others again have do-re-mi-fa arranged in diamond form. The more expensive Percales have the loveliest pearl, mode and white grounds, with the daintiest figures imaginable." Two years later *Godey's* referred to cotton goods "finished

with lovers knots, lace designs, angles, triangles, feathers, lozenges, diamonds, squares, linked rings, fox heads, bouquets, horseshoes, butterflies, bugs, birds and parallel lines."[24]

American mills in the last quarter of the nineteenth century produced a large number of such images, although later motifs were slightly larger and not as detailed as the mid-century style. *Bloomingdale Brothers' Spring and Summer Catalog* of 1886 featured ready-made boys' shirt waists, "manufactured on the premises," described as "Genuine French Percale, our own patterns, consisting of dog's heads, lion's heads, horses' heads, etc." Another description: "American Percale, in a beautiful variety of heads, birds, figures, etc."[25] The 1893 catalog from Montgomery Ward advertised shirting prints: "anchor patterns in black, pink or blue grounds, and include drums, bicycles, etc. Per yard 12 cents."[26]

The catalog descriptions and the prints used in Kansas quilts reflect a wide variety of Victorian taste that is echoed in trade cards, labels, and Currier and Ives lithographs. Trade cards, an end-of-the-century innovation, were designed as giveaways from salesmen to promote sales. The clever, colorful cards made full use of symbols and motifs that were popular trends in consumer taste, picturing horses, horseshoes, anchors and chains, kittens, puppies, children, and hot air balloons. The same symbols appeared on labels for yard goods and thread, cigar bands, and logos for medicines, cures, bitters, flour, starch, sarsaparilla, and tobacco.

Currier and Ives lithographs and similar inexpensive prints presented a picture of an age in

Terry Thompson and Barbara Brackman

which horseracing, hunting, fishing, and sporting events such as prizefighting, sailing, ice boat races, and baseball were popular pastimes. Trotting horse races drew large crowds of people to country fairs in Kansas and elsewhere. The Kentucky Derby began in 1875, and horse racing fever spread throughout America. The fashion for racing and hunting was reflected in the motifs most frequently printed in the conversation prints—horseshoes, whips, stirrups, spurs, jockey caps, and horses.

Kansans could read about the wealthy who built yacht and racing clubs. Middle-income families here and elsewhere enjoyed boating and racing small boats. Boating images were almost as popular as horse-related prints. Oars, oar locks and anchors, sails, and racing pennants are common figures in the subcategory of conversation prints called "sporty" or "sporting prints." Men's and boys' shirtings also "sported" baseball caps, hands holding bats and balls, golf clubs, bowling pins, darts, tennis rackets, bows and arrows, fish hooks and bobbers, creels and poles. After the safety bicycle, with "two wheels of the same size," replaced the precarious "high wheeler" around 1885, roadracing on bicycles became popular, special arenas with inward sloping tracks were built, and bicycles of both types appeared on prints.[27]

Women's sports included bicycling, tricycling, horseback riding, croquet, lawn tennis, and ice skating, all activities encouraging fashion change. Victorian sports enthusiasts enjoyed more freedom of movement as bustles were replaced by bicycle skirts and shirtwaists. Women and girls of all classes could show their good taste by wearing a blouse or

a dress with designs that displayed their appreciation of the pursuits of the gentry in the community. Images of more traditional female pursuits, especially sewing, were commonly depicted. Thimbles, needles, buttons, and scissors are found again and again. One Kansas woman included in her quilt a print of a kitten unrolling a spool of thread. Men's occupations were also well represented with hammers, screws, axes, knives and whetstones, bricks and trowels, fire hats and ladders. Pictures of military life appeared in the conversation prints of the 1880s: crossed swords and rifles, crest shield and arrows, groups of three arrows, rifle and powder bag, swords and fez. These images may have reflected the widening range of America's military interests or perhaps symbolized some of the secret societies and fraternal orders that reached a peak of popularity toward the end of the century.

Patriotic and political fabrics were most popular during the 1870s when the celebration of the Centennial of the United States in 1876 produced flags, liberty bells and caps on liberty

Three tennis players, identified as Jan, Bess, and Ruth, wear white "waists" that were commonly printed with mill engravings of finely detailed shirting prints. The figures could easily be conversation prints of some type, although such detail is not visible in the photograph.

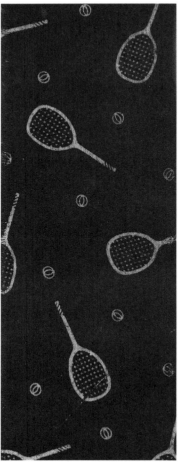

poles, eagles, and words like "Centennial" and "1776–1876." Politicians appeared in thumb-sized portraits. Opponents Ulysses Grant and Horace Greeley each had their own fabrics in 1872; in 1892 partisans could wear shirts with prints of Grover Cleveland or Benjamin Harrison. Let Us Have Peace slogans, flags and stars, muscled arms with rolled up sleeves, brooms, and roosters (the symbol of the Democrats at the time), printed as bandannas and yardage, represented the political platforms on which the candidates stood. As specific elections faded into history, the fabric went into the scrap basket only to wind up in quilts, giving the candidates a kind of immortality.

In the last quarter of the nineteenth century, Americans expressed a keen interest in the exploration of the earth as well as in astronomy and astrology. *The National Geographic Magazine* was established in 1888, giving Americans a window to the rest of the world. Conversation prints featured aspects of natural history in great detail, especially graphic depictions of birds and insects. Yard goods also included hundreds of variations of astronomical images, particularly stars and crescent moons, planets, and a scattering of spots that appears to represent the Milky Way, printed in white on shades of heavenly blue. These may represent the charting of the heavens or the public fascination with the 1910 visit of Haley's Comet.

It seems apparent from the descriptions in the fashion magazines and catalogs that most conversation prints were printed for infants' and children's wear; the most common references are to boy's clothing, as in the 1891 Montgomery Ward catalog that listed "shirting prints in figures, checks or stripes in black, blue, red or brown. Checks and stripes in cheviot effects and sporting patterns for boys' waists."[28] There appear to be more prints with masculine themes than feminine. It may be that boys under seven years of age found it easier to wear a dress if the print were fishing poles, drums and bugles, or other declarations of masculinity. Parents may have used the prints to identify male and female children in much the same way the colors pink and blue continue to differentiate gender today.

The prints undoubtedly were yardage for adults' clothing too, and they may have been used for curtains, upholstery, or other kinds of furnishings. No advertising has been found directed toward the furnishings market, and no photos of any interiors using the prints have been discovered. The manufacturers may have realized conversation prints were popular in quilts and marketed them for such a use, but no such advertising has been found. The mail-order catalogs described some fabrics as appropriate for patchwork, quilts, or comforters; in 1898 a Lawrence dry goods store advertised sale prices for "large flower pattern comfort cloth . . . only takes five widths for a comfort."[29] However, the fabrics advertised specifically for quilts do not appear to be conversation prints.

The conversation prints are rarely seen as more than a scrap of fabric in a patchwork quilt. One exception is an 1876 quilt by Amelia Tucker of Eureka, who in her Flying Geese quilt used many yards of a centennial print, purchased by her husband at the Centennial Exposition in Philadelphia.[30] Because the typical conversation prints are used as

Celestial prints and one featuring screws.

patchwork, it seems likely that they were scraps left over from home sewing. Moreover, the fact that most appear as a single, isolated piece in a scrap quilt seems to indicate that they were in short supply, which is surprising considering the wide variety of prints manufactured and their price, which was equal to other calicoes of the day. Meller and Elffers noted that conversation prints could be manufactured in short runs of 100 yards, a practice that allowed the mills to produce odd images such as insects

or bats that had no broad appeal.[31] Many of the unusual prints may therefore have been limited. It may also be that taste dictated that quiltmakers use the pictorial fabrics sparingly or that they traded scraps of conversation prints.

The prints reached their high point of detail and diversity in the last quarter of the nineteenth century. Conversation prints continued to be produced into the twentieth century, although by 1910 the mill engravings with their fine detail had become a

Boy's shirt made from a horseshoe print. Collection of Terry Thompson.

Conversation prints from the mid-twentieth century were multicolored and did not have the detail that the earlier mill engravings had. This group of patches was cut from sewing scraps by Lora Housholder Wedd (1888–1975). Granddaughter Shirlene Wedd remembers several from her clothing in the 1950s. Lora Wedd used a postcard as a pattern; scrap quilts made from rectangles were often called Postcard Quilts.

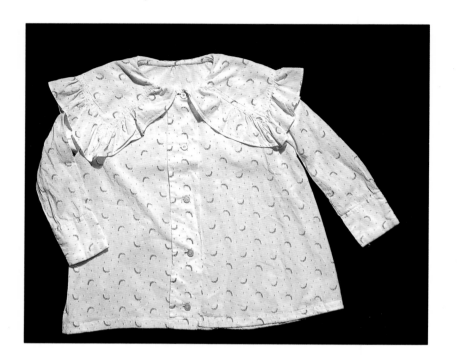

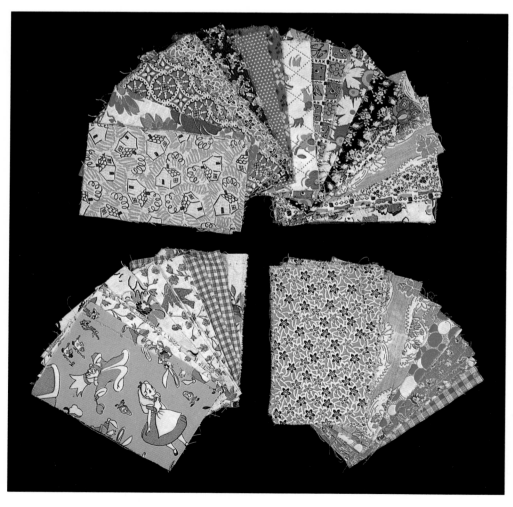

Terry Thompson and Barbara Brackman

whisper. Conversation prints with a different look were revived again in the 1920s when juvenile themes were printed in colors of bright yellow, pink, green, and blue. The emphasis was almost exclusively on nursery images that might appeal to children of either sex. Prints such as animated cartoon characters, toys, building blocks, stuffed animals, nursery rhyme characters, and farm and zoo animals continued to be popular through the 1950s. Although many scraps survive in quilts, the major purpose of these fabrics again was children's clothing. The lack of gender-specific images may reflect the more gender-specific styles in twentieth-century children's clothing.

The many conversation prints that appear in Kansas quilts from 1875 to 1900 give us a glimpse of the images popular in Victorian life. They also give us an idea of the volume of eastern goods available in the last quarter of the nineteenth century. If we use the variety of such prints as a measure, it appears that the scrapbags of many Kansas quiltmakers equaled those of their eastern sisters. The abundance of fabric was one of the dramatic changes that occurred in the few decades between statehood in 1861 and the end of the century as Kansas moved away from the frontier era.

Notes

1. Rachel Maines, "Paradigms of Scarcity and Abundance: The Quilt as an Artifact of the Industrial Revolution," in *In the Heart of Pennsylvania: Symposium Papers*, ed. Jeannette Lasansky (Lewisburg, Pa.: Oral Traditions Project, 1986), 84–88.

2. KQP Je93, Bc90, and Fj179.

3. Martha E. Jordan, "Early Life and Experiences in Kansas," *Kansas State Historical Society Collections* 17 (1926–1928), 587.

4. Joseph Piazzek, manuscript collection of the Kansas State Historical Society.

5. Lawrence *State Journal*, February 19, 1863.

6. *Kansas Farmer*, December 1, 1863, 170.

7. Western National Fair Association, *Premium List* (Lawrence, Kans.: n. p., 1882), 29.

8. Francis A. Walker, *Ninth Census: The Statistics of the Wealth and Industry of the United States* 1 (Washington, D.C.: Government Printing Office, 1872), 606.

9. KQP Dc86, Gb161.

10. "Prices Current," *Kansas Herald of Freedom*, May 26, 1855, 1; *Kansas Tribune*, advertisements from January through October 1855; Helen Carpenter, "Kansas to California," in *Ho for California: Women's Diaries from the Huntington Library*, ed. Sandra Myres (San Marino, Calif.: Huntington Library, 1980), 93, 100.

11. Ferdinand Crevecoeur, *Old Settler's Tales: Historical and Biographical Sketches of the Early Settlement* (Onaga, Kans: The Republican, 1902), 13.

12. Lucy and Annie Miller, "An Old Landmark," *Holton Recorder*, March 14, 1935.

13. Clarina I. H. Nichols, *Kansas Daily Commonwealth*, December 9, 1869; Glenda Riley, ed., "Kansas Frontiers-women Viewed through Their Writings: The Memoirs of Georgiana Packard," *Kansas History Quarterly* 9 (Winter 1986–87), 187. The S. C. Pomeroy story was also told to Ferdinand Crevecoeur by unnamed persons near Marysville (Crevecoeur, *Old Settlers' Tales*, 84; Percy Ebutt, *Emigrant Life in Kansas* [London: Swan Sonneschein and Co., 1886], 230).

14. Venola Lewis Bivans, ed., "The Diary of Luna E. Warner, A Kansas Teenager of the 1870s," *Kansas History Quarterly* 35 (Winter 1969), 286; Ellen Payne Paullin, ed., "Etta's Journal, January 2, 1874 to July 25, 1875," *Kansas History* 3 (Autumn 1980, Winter 1980).

15. *Emporia Daily News*, September 20, 1879; Barbara Oringderff, "Reflections on Southwest Kansas," undated clipping in the collection of the Kansas State Historical Society.

16. Montgomery Ward, *Catalog* 1, 1872 and 1882; Diane Fagan Affleck, *Just New from the Mills: Printed Cottons in America* (Andover, Mass.: Museum of American Textile History, 1987), 43; Sears,

Roebuck and Company, *Catalog*, 1895.

17. The name One Patch was first used for single-template designs by Ruth E. Finley in *Old Patchwork Quilts and the Women Who Made Them* (Philadelphia: J. B. Lippincott, 1929), 48.

18. Cuesta Benberry, "Charm Quilts Revisited," *Quilters Newsletter Magazine* 198 (January 1988), 30.

19. We are grateful to Diane L. Fagan Affleck at the Museum of American Textile History for her assistance.

20. Barbara Brackman, *Clues in the Calico: A Guide to Identifying and Dating Antique Quilts* (McLean, Va.: EPM Publications, 1989), 92. Susan Meller and Joost Elffers, *Textile Designs* (New York: Harry N. Abrams, 1991), 20.

21. Anita Schorsch, *Images of Childhood, an Illustrated Social History* (Pittstown, N.J.: Main Street Press, n.d.), 87.

22. Ibid., 88.

23. Meller and Elffers, *Textile Designs*, 268; Smithsonian Institution Quilt #H6680; Brackman, *Clues in the Calico*, 92.

24. *Godey's Ladies Book and Magazine* (April 1863), 404; (May 1865), 474.

25. Bloomingdale Brothers, *Catalog* (Spring/Summer 1886), 65.

26. Montgomery Ward, *Catalog* 5 (Fall/Winter 1893–1894; 1895), 14.

27. Bradley Smith, *The USA: A History in Art* (Garden City, N.Y.: Doubleday & Co., 1975), 244.

28. Montgomery Ward, *Catalog* 50 (Fall/Winter 1891–1892), 570.

29. *Lawrence Daily Journal*, September 14, 1898.

30. KQP Ji163.

31. Meller and Elffers, *Textile Designs*, 304.

Orchid Wreath. Designed and appliqued by Rose Good Kretsinger (1886–1963), Emporia, 1928–1930. Quilter unknown. Helen F. Spencer Museum of Art, University of Kansas. Gift of Mary Kretsinger.

When daughter Mary asked for an orchid quilt to match her bedroom decor, Rose Kretsinger found inspiration in an advertising card she had seen at a soda fountain. Several Emporians copied the Orchid Wreath, among them Ifie Arnold, Jennie Soden, and Lottie Whitehill.

Chapter Five

Emporia, 1925–1950: Reflections on a Community

Barbara Brackman

DURING THE SECOND QUARTER OF THE TWENTIETH CENTURY, IN THE MIDST OF THE NATIONAL FAD FOR QUILTMAKING, A GROUP OF WOMEN IN EMPORIA, KANSAS, CREATED A BODY OF QUILTS OUTSTANDING IN WORKMANSHIP AND DESIGN. BEST KNOWN OF THESE WOMEN ARE ROSE KRETSINGER, WHOSE TWELVE QUILTS are in the collection of the Spencer Museum of Art in Lawrence, Kansas, and Charlotte Jane Whitehill, whose fourteen quilts hang in the Denver Art Museum. Their work has been published around the world as ideal examples of quiltmaking in this century. To understand Kretsinger's and Whitehill's "near legendary" reputations, one must look at their quilts in the context of the times.[1]

Between 1925 and 1945, the typical American quilt was pieced of a jumble of inexpensive bright cottons, tamed with a wide expanse of white fabric. The variegated prints were splashy, featuring several contrasting colors. The 1927 Sears, Roebuck and Company catalog described them as the "new, handsome, multicolor effects" during one of the first seasons these prints were on the market.[2] Multicolor applied to the overall look of the quilt as well as to the individual fabrics. A scrap look was prized, whether the quilts were made of actual sewing scraps, recycled feedsacks, or purchased yard goods. Such quilts could also be pieced of factory cutaways like those advertised in the Emporia *Gazette* in 1930. "$2 Quilt Patches $1 . . . Four pound bundle broadcloths, ginghams, percales, plain and fancy . . . hand-selected. Large cuts . . . 5 x 7 inches."[3]

Quiltmakers found their patterns in newspapers and magazines—such as the *Kansas City Star* and Topeka's *Capper's Farmer*—or purchased them from pattern houses like Mrs. Danner's in El Dorado, Kansas, and the Aunt Martha Studios in Kansas City. Many quilters limited themselves to fad patterns—Dresden Plate, Grandmother's Flower Garden, Sunbonnet Sue, and the Double Wedding Ring. Those who wanted to invest time

GRANDMOTHER'S FAVORITE   PATTERN 1677

in an exceptional quilt might trace an applique design off the Mountain Mist batting wrapper or splurge on a kit from Bucilla or Paragon, two major designers for ready-cut patches for applique quilts. The fancy quilts from the pattern and kit companies usually featured floral motifs arranged in the fashionable medallion format, a central design framed by a border or two. Kits included all the pastel cottons needed to assemble the daffodils, iris, or pansies as well as the background yardage stamped with placement lines

and quilting designs. Patterns gave women a few more options to personalize their quilts than the kits did, but both enabled the quiltmaker to reproduce the designer's model. Any patient seamstress, even one who lacked the talent or confidence to experiment with original designs, could make an eye-catching quilt. The nature of the quilt craze, and the many patterns and kits it spawned, created a predictable product, a quality that Rose Kretsinger criticized in the early thirties: "Women are depending more upon the printed pattern sheet to save time and labor. These having been used time and again often become very tiresome."[4]

The most distinctive of the Kretsinger and Whitehill quilts are the original designs—Whitehill's Kansas Pattern and Rose Kretsinger's Orchid Wreath— that cannot be traced to patterns or kits available from the pattern companies of the day. Such original designs are a minority; most are creative interpretations of traditional designs, nineteenth-century applique patterns redrawn for a more formal, sophisticated balance. But even the patterns obtained from commercial sources show creativity in the way design elements are rearranged and borders redrafted to provide strong, symmetrical frames for quilts that looked as good on a wall as a bed.

Peter Pan Park. Designed, appliqued and quilted by Ruth Adams Lee (1893–1965), Emporia, 1930–1940. Collection of the Rinker family.

William Allen White donated Peter Pan Park to the city of Emporia in memory of his daughter, Mary. Ruth Lee often took her daughter, Loretta, to play near the lagoon and worked on this quilt while she watched her. The design, like four other applique quilts by Lee, is original. Loretta Lee Rinker recalled that Ruth Lee and Rose Kretsinger occasionally worked on quilts together. Lee was probably inspired by Kretsinger's original design work to try her hand at one-of-a-kind applique.

The Whitehill and Kretsinger quilts are distinctive enough that the Kansas Quilt Project set a goal to determine whether Emporia was a unique quiltmaking community or merely the best documented of several Kansas towns where masterful quilts were made between 1925 and 1950. The Quilt Discovery Days with which we blanketed the state would, we theorized, give us many more leads to seamstresses in other towns whose work was equally distinctive. We intended to conduct follow-up research on exceptional applique quilts not traceable to kits or patterns to determine the sources of the designs and whether the maker had produced a substantial body of such work the way Kretsinger and Whitehill did.

Our analysis of the data on quilts brought to quilt days, however, was disappointing. Of the more than 13,000 quilts recorded by the KQP, approximately one-third were made between 1925 and 1950, giving us a substantial sample of quilts from the target era. We found few applique quilts not traceable to commercial patterns or kits. We discovered few individuals with substantial bodies of exceptionally fine applique work in those years, few who designed even one original pattern, and no evidence of any other communities with more than one quiltmaker approaching the quality of Whitehill and Kretsinger. We were led back to Emporia, where we conducted follow-up research. Through interviews and period newspapers, we identified thirteen women and one man with ties to Emporia who made exceptional applique quilts during the 1925–1950 period.[5] We interviewed relatives of twelve of these individuals. A comparison of their quilts to those made elsewhere and an examination of their social networks led us to hypothesize that some Emporia quiltmakers developed a community aesthetic with standards for design, craftsmanship, and originality that differed from those of their peers in Kansas and the rest of the country.

Emporia between 1925 and 1950 can be compared to other areas where quiltmakers have produced a cluster of unusual quilts. The best known of these is Baltimore, where women of the 1840s and 1850s made masterful album quilts. The origins of the Baltimore style are mysterious; many of the long-ago makers remain anonymous, and too many quilts are divorced from family and community histories. Emporia offered an opportunity to examine the social context that contributed to the exceptional quilts. Because the Emporia quilts were created fairly recently, many living family members recall their making. Quiltmaking in Emporia was also well documented in the press of the day. Thus, oral history and published accounts gave us an opportunity to understand the dynamics of the quiltmaking community there, an opportunity that may be of use in understanding quiltmaking in earlier communities.

In her 1980 catalog of album quilts made in pre–Civil War Baltimore, Dena Katzenberg summarized three possible explanations for the exceptional community aesthetic that developed there. She theorized that (1) one talented individual might have made them all, (2) one individual influenced a group of seamstresses, and/or (3) a spirit of competition motivated a group.[6] We can apply her theories on the Baltimore quiltmaking community in the 1840s and 1850s to Emporia eighty years later.

The first theory, that the Baltimore quilts were the handiwork of an individual, possibly a seamstress named Mary Evans,[7] is an idea that has been discounted by Elly Sienkiewicz, whose evidence suggested that no single person could have stitched so many complex designs in the span of years the style was in fashion.[8] In Emporia, where the makers are well documented, there is no possibility that one individual made the group of quilts despite their occasional identical fabrics, similar workmanship, and creative design.

It seems more likely that Katzenberg's second explanation for the Baltimore quilts, that an individual might have "effected a design revolution" and by "her example and precepts encouraged the development of a more refined and elegant style," is the case.[9] In Baltimore, Katzenberg theorized that the influential individual was Achsah Wilkins; in Emporia, the individual was Rose Kretsinger. Katzenberg's third explanation for the excellence of the Baltimore blocks, an "inherent spirit of competition," is also probably a factor in the Emporia phenomenon.[10] Katzenberg painted a complex picture of Baltimore society in the pre–Civil War decades, noting the importance of the Methodist Church and local fraternal organizations to the lives of the women associated with the quilts and to the look of the quilts. The Baltimore quilts owe much to the context of the city and the times. Did the development of the Emporia quilts owe anything to the city? It would seem that the city's relative wealth during the 1920s and even into the Great Depression, its position as a cultural center,

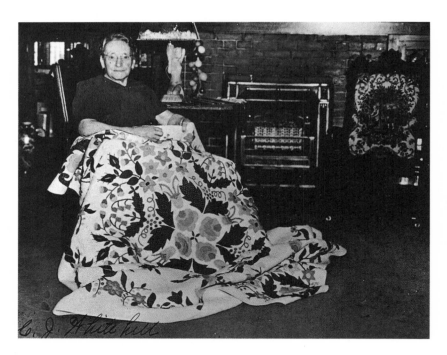

Charlotte Jane Whitehill (1866–1964) working on a Garden quilt, ca. 1940.

Whitehill's version of the Garden is different from either Rose Kretsinger's or Josephine Craig's. Whether she finished this quilt and where it is now are unanswered questions. In the early 1940s she moved to Denver and later gave her quilts to the Denver Art Museum; this is one of two she made that she did not donate.

its complex network of women's clubs, and the influence of an unusual newspaper may have had more than a subtle effect on the quiltmaking community.

Emporia, located on the Neosho River in east central Kansas, was founded in 1857, three years after Kansas was established as a territory. The city received its name from the Greek word for *marketplace*. The name was an accurate prophecy of the commercial success eventually derived from the railroads: the Atchison, Topeka and Santa Fe line and the Missouri, Kansas and Texas (the "Katy") line that shipped beef fattened on the Kansas bluestem grass in the nearby Flint Hills eastward to urban markets. Emporia, however, was more than a cowtown or a railroad junction; it was the "Athens of Kansas." The nickname was bestowed by William Allen White, Emporia's resident sage and editor of the *Gazette*. He created a national image of his hometown as *the* small town, the antithesis of urban, industrial

New York City. The town became a national symbol of front porch, main street values. In 1930, with a population of about 13,500, two local colleges, thirty-one churches, six hotels, an internationally known newspaper, and the largest Women's City Club in the state, Emporians were confident they deserved the praise of such famous visitors as writer William Dean Howells, who said, "I do not know any pleasanter place to visit in the world."[11]

In 1920, White had described Emporia as a town with a "fairly equitable distribution of wealth,"[12] but it was not the truly egalitarian society White liked to portray. There was an upper class for whom he edited his paper—the "best people of the city," he called them in his first editorial.[13] The *Gazette* gave many more column inches to the bridge clubs, committee meetings, and vacations of the wives and daughters of the town's "more prominent citizens"—the bankers, ranchers, and mill owners—than to the activities of women related to automobile salesmen or railroad workers.[14] However, the social lives of these women occasionally intersected in clubs like those devoted to gardening, associations so popular that *Life* magazine featured Emporia's garden clubs in a 1956 issue.[15]

The women from the upper and middle classes of Emporia joined their peers all over America in rediscovering quilts in the late 1920s. They began to view quiltmaking as a pastime that made the most of their needlework skills, creativity, and good taste. This was a new perspective, changed from the beginning of the century when quiltmaking was considered the province of

The Tomato Flower, appliqued by Charlotte Jane Whitehill (1866–1964), Emporia, 1931. Quilter unknown. Denver Art Museum.

Hallmarks of the Emporia style include precision drafting of a traditional nineteenth-century applique design, elegant quilting, period and reproduction calicoes, and a sophisticated, symmetrical border. This is one of two quilts belonging to Emporia's Martindale family that Whitehill reproduced. Rose Kretsinger's hand seems apparent in the border, but whether she was actually involved in the design is unknown.

poor rural homemakers who sewed patchwork for economy and tied comforters for bedding. Many of the Emporia women newly attracted to making quilts did not need them; they could buy bedspreads and blankets at Newman's or Poole's Dry Goods on Commercial Street; at Emery, Bird and Thayer Department Store in Kansas City; or at Marshall Field in Chicago. Economy was no incentive. They had the time to spend hours stitching intricate applique flowers and to take the train to Topeka or Lawrence to look at antique quilts. They had the money to buy Cloth of Gold and Pastoral Cloth, the expensive cottons sold specifically for applique. And when they couldn't find a fast color to suit them, they sent to London for a better line of cotton.[16]

The new fashionableness of quilts grew from a fascination with "colonial" antiques, inspired by a nostalgia for an imagined American past coupled with a developing pride in American arts and crafts. The colonial revival dictated maple bedsteads, Windsor chairs, rag rugs, and patchwork quilts in bedrooms across the country. Magazines advised homemakers to dig antique family quilts out of the trunks in the attic and encouraged those who hadn't inherited any to make their own heirlooms. The trendsetters advocated a return to old-fashioned standards for needlework, emphasizing the applique work and fancy quilting that had fallen from fashion during the late nineteenth century as the sewing machine moved into the American home. They gave instructions for updating old patterns with new color schemes, a change summarized in the Nancy Cabot quilting column from the

Chicago Tribune: In the "early days . . . only strong colors were available. . . . A 20th century quiltmaker would undoubtedly prefer dainty pastel shades."[17] Ruby McKim, a Kansas City designer, gave specific suggestions—lavender, blue, yellow, and orange—for a traditional wreath design that a nineteenth-century quilter would have made up in bright red and green.[18]

The new fashionableness of quilts crossed economic lines, influencing the choices of the rural poor women who had been making quilts all along. Although they might not be able to afford the kits, patterns, and expensive cottons, they were quick to adapt the new color schemes and designs to their practical quilts.

Charlotte Jane Cline Whitehill (1866–1964) was an Emporian who responded to the quilt craze. She had been raised with quilts made by her mother in Wisconsin at the time of the Civil War. Presumably, Lottie learned the usual needlework skills as a child, but she had no interest in making quilts until 1929. At that time she was a district manager for an insurance company, a position she may have inherited from her husband. She had been a widow for four years when she turned to quiltmaking to fill her evenings, beginning with the Ohio Rose design, a traditional applique block that was published in *Needlecraft Magazine* in 1925.[19] Whitehill made at least thirty-six quilt tops between 1929 and 1945, all of them fancy needlework rather than everyday utility quilts. As she became more involved in the art, she looked beyond the contemporary commercial market for her designs, drawing from old quilts, museum pieces, and heirlooms owned by Emporia families.

Her major inspiration appears to have been Rose Kretsinger. Whitehill's first quilt was probably a copy of an earlier Kretsinger version of the same *Needlecraft* design. She later made several copies of Kretsinger's original patterns. Even in her redrafting of antique quilts, she owed a debt to Kretsinger, who often did the same. Such a link to Kretsinger was observed again and again in the network of Emporia quiltmaking.

Rose Francis Good (1886–1963) was born in Hope, Kansas, southeast of Abilene. Her father, Milton Good, had been a partner in Good & Eisenhower, a dry goods store. Shortly before Rose's birth he sold his share to David Eisenhower, and when the new baby was a few weeks old Milton and Anna Gleissner Good returned to Abilene. David Eisenhower, who could not make the store profitable, eventually moved to Texas, where he and his wife, Ida, added a son, Dwight David Eisenhower, to their family.[20] Milton Good tried several other business ventures in Abilene during the financially unstable 1890s. When Rose was in her teens the family moved to Kansas City, Missouri. She received a degree in design from the Art Institute of Chicago in 1908. After a year studying in Europe she returned to Chicago, where she designed jewelry until she retired from commercial art in 1915 to move to Emporia and marry widower William Kretsinger, an attorney and rancher. In 1926 she clipped the *Needlecraft Magazine* pattern for the Ohio Rose, deciding to make her first quilt to decorate a bedroom with a recently inherited antique bed. Quiltmaking initially served as a form of therapy, too; she found handwork consoling after

Pennsylvania Beauty or Pennsylvania Garden, appliquéd by Rose Good Kretsinger (1886–1963), Emporia, 1930–1945. Unfinished top. Helen F. Spencer Museum of Art, University of Kansas. Gift of Mary Kretsinger. Photo: Jon Blumb.

*   This unfinished top was recently donated to the Spencer Museum by Mary Kretsinger, Rose Kretsinger's daughter. Rose finished only one quilt after 1932, possibly because of illness. A threaded needle is still in place.*

Right: Rose Good Kretsinger with Mary, 1915. Courtesy of Mary Kretsinger.

Opposite: Morning Glory. Appliqued by Ifie Espey Arnold (1870–1945), Emporia, Kansas. 1927–1945. Quilter unknown. Collection of the Helen F. Spencer Museum of Art, University of Kansas. Photo: Jon Blumb.

Ifie (Eye-fee) Arnold (above) made a pair of *Morning Glory* quilts for her daughter, Iras Arnold Armour, whose monogram is on each. The feather quilting is a Kretsinger trademark, and the family believes that Kretsinger helped in the design. The central lattice and flower resemble an appliqued and embroidered coverlet designed by Elisabeth May Blondel for *McCall's Needlework* magazine about 1927. The strong art nouveau border has a distinctive Emporia look.

Ifie and Frank Arnold were friends of the Kretsingers, so close that the Arnolds had a cat named Kretsy that Rose had given them. Arnold's granddaughter Carrie Humphreys remembers the two women planning quilts, although she has no memories of any actual quilting in the Arnold home. She recalls Ifie as an artistic woman who loved handwork. She was active in numerous clubs, among them the Daughters of the American Revolution and the Garden Club.

Ifie Arnold was born in Bushnell, Illinois; soon after her birth her mother died, and her father moved to western Kansas. She lived with her grand-mother until she was sixteen, when she traveled to Ashland, Kansas, to visit her father. There she met Frank Arnold and married him in 1888. They homesteaded a claim and stayed through the drought of the 1890s, raised two sons and two daughters, prospered in the cattle business, and moved to Emporia in 1914. There Frank Arnold founded a bank, the Commercial National Bank and Trust.

Ifie left three other quilts besides this pair of *Morning Glories*; the Spencer Museum also has her copy of Kretsinger's *Orchid Wreath*.

Emporia, 1925-1950: Reflections on a Community

A quilting pattern hand drawn by Rose Kretsinger. Helen F. Spencer Museum of Art, University of Kansas. Gift of Mary Kretsinger. Photo: Jon Blumb.

Ifie Arnold and Rose Kretsinger found inspiration in this McCall's *design (middle right).*

Charles and Emily Bigler (bottom right), 1937.

Emily Smith Bigler was born in Hartford, southeast of Emporia. Her mother died when she was young, leaving her to help care for her brothers. She married a farmer, Charlie Bigler, with whom she had ten children. During the 1930s they lived on land near Hartford that they rented from the Kretsingers. Daughter Dollie remembers that the pattern for the Indiana Wreath came from Rose Kretsinger, who was a friend as well as a landlady. Emily personalized her version with a few changes.

Emily Bigler was a professional quilter who quilted for others in her home. Dollie does not believe she ever quilted for Rose Kretsinger, but the friends may have quilted together in a group sponsored by the Extension Homemakers Unit. Emily Bigler's daughter remembers her as a cheerful woman who loved company and keeping busy. She made about twenty quilts; the Indiana Wreath is recalled as the nicest. Two others were pictured *in* The Romance of the Patchwork Quilt in America *by Carrie Hall and Rose Kretsinger.*

KQP Gc073. Indiana Wreath appliqued and quilted by Emily Smith Bigler (1879–1957), Hartford, 1932. Collection of Dollie Colglazier.

    A mid-nineteenth-century version of the Indiana Wreath appeared in Marie Webster's 1915 book Quilts: Their Story and How to Make Them *(New York: Doubleday, Page, and Co.), where it was described as a "most beautiful example of the American quilt at its best." Several Emporia women, including Kretsinger, Craig, and Whitehill, were inspired to make a copy. About 1936 McCall's published a pattern, but the Emporia examples predate the commercial pattern.*

Emily Bigler's quilting patterns.

Hannah Haynes Headlee with her brother, Clif Haynes, and niece, Pauline. 1912. Courtesy of the Shirer family.

losing her mother in an automobile accident.[21]

Kretsinger became interested in reproducing old designs when her housemaid showed her fragments of two brides' quilts the family believed had been damaged in the Chicago fire. In each she copied the basic block but added a fresh palette of bright colors, balanced the composition, and framed it with the borders that would become her trademark. Thereafter, she borrowed antique quilts from friends and neighbors, clipped photos from magazines, and traveled to the Thayer Museum in Lawrence to find designs she could adapt for the quilts she hoped would be equal to their heavily quilted museum pieces. Kretsinger's unique combination of old-fashioned standards and modern design earned her local and national fame as she won prizes in contests from the Lyon County Fair to New York City. The Kansas City Art Institute mounted an exhibit of her quilts in the early 1930s, and her national reputation grew with the 1935 book she cowrote with Carrie Hall, *The Romance of the Patchwork Quilt in America*.[22] In 1949, *Farm Journal* magazine sold two of her designs, the only full-size patterns she published.[23]

Rose Kretsinger had no formal pattern business with printed designs, but daughter Mary recalls she was glad to draw designs for friends and strangers, charging $2.00 to $3.50 for full-sized applique and quilting patterns and including a color index card with twenty or more swatches of fabric attached.[24] Despite one incident when she considered suing a seamstress who copied her Orchid Wreath when it was on display in Kansas City,[25] she is most often recalled as generous with

*Iris, designed and appliqued by Hannah Haynes Headlee
(1866–1943), Topeka, 1935–1940. Quilter unknown.
Kansas State Historical Society/Kansas Museum of History.*

Members of Hannah Headlee's family characterize her
as having a "one-track mind" about applique in the last fifteen years of her life, when she finished seven quilts and the
borders for an eighth. She was known as "the artist in the
family," teaching water color and china painting in
Topeka.

The Iris, her masterpiece, reflects a watercolorist's love of
transparent, clear colors and a sophisticated eye in the choice
of complementary red-violets and yellow-greens. For the lush
iris blooms she found nine shades of violet cotton and dyed
the tenth herself. After her first Grandmother's Flower Garden she drew her own applique designs, inspired by
Kretsinger, says her family. Her debt to Kretsinger's Orchid
Wreath is apparent in this quilt.

Hannah Haynes was born in Topeka five years after
Kansas statehood. She supported herself primarily through
her art lessons and married three times. She is remembered
as the first woman in Topeka to own a bicycle. In 1914 she
chaperoned her niece, Pauline, to the New York School of
Fine and Applied Art, where she paid their living expenses
with china painting.

Unlike Emporia artists, Hannah Headlee did not enter
contests; the family believes she knew exhibiting her quilts at
fairs would encourage copies and she loved being an original. She did, however, judge at least one contest. In 1934 she
and two others awarded Josephine Craig's Garden quilt the
first prize in a national contest sponsored by Capper's.

Although Hannah Headlee did not live in Emporia, she
shopped for fabric there and was acquainted with several of
the Emporia quiltmakers, most importantly Rose Kretsinger,
who gave her artistic ambitions new direction in fabric.

The Garden, appliqued and quilted by Josephine (Josie) Hunter Craig (1874–1954), Emporia, 1933. Collection of Dr. and Mrs. Paul R. Carpenter.

In her 1929 book, Old Patchwork Quilts and the Women Who Made Them *(Philadelphia: J. B. Lippincott), Ruth Finley pictured an 1857 version of this Garden medallion, enthusing that it was the "acme of the branch of the art." Like the Indiana Wreath, it became a standard of excellence for Emporia's quiltmakers. Josie Craig won numerous prizes with this version. The* Gazette *told readers of her ribbons won in national contests in Topeka, New York, and Massachusetts.*

Josie Craig's quiltmaking community paralleled that of Rose Kretsinger, but she was a farm wife rather than a city socialite. She was apparently not a member of the Garden Club or the other organizations to which Rose Kretsinger, Ifie Arnold, Jennie Soden, and other well-to-do women belonged. Craig's circle included Elizabeth Goering and Maud Leatherberry, who collaborated on the pattern and quilting for this quilt. Each made her own Garden, but the locations of the other two are unknown.

her designs and with her time and fabric as well. Mary remembers her spending hours helping someone with the placement of an applique, finding the best spot for the butterflies in an Orchid Wreath, and donating a piece of her favorite gingham, ordered from Marshall Field, when she felt nothing else would do in that particular spot.[26]

Kretsinger's willingness to share was integral to the Emporia look. Had she been aloof and affronted when asked for her original pattern, her influence would have been far more limited. Ifie Arnold was a close friend whose family has credited Kretsinger as the source for her designs.[27] Margaret Soden, daughter of another Kretsinger friend, Jennie Soden, believes that Kretsinger was the primary influence on her mother's applique quilts.[28] Stephen and Hulda Rich, a husband/wife team of quiltmakers who had a quilt published with Kretsinger's in the 1949 *Farm Journal* article, lived across the street from Kretsinger. Their granddaughter, Elsie Wells, remembers a cooperative and competitive relationship between the neighbors.[29]

Emily Bigler of Hartford, fifteen miles from Emporia, made an Indiana Wreath in 1932, one of the few such complex applique quilts recorded at a Quilt Discovery Day. Bigler's link to nearby Emporia and its quilting community was obscure until Mary Kretsinger mentioned that Rose Kretsinger rented land to the Biglers and became a friend, regularly driving to Hartford to quilt in a group and undoubtedly sharing her views on design and craftsmanship as well as her pattern for the Indiana Wreath.[30]

Rose Kretsinger was also a creative influence on Hannah

Josephine Craig (center) with daughters Lois and Eleanor, two of her four children.

Haynes Headlee, who lived in Topeka but traveled to Emporia to buy fabric. Her family credits Kretsinger as a direct inspiration for two of Headlee's seven original designs.[31] Unlike others who asked Kretsinger for a pattern they might copy, Headlee was inspired by Kretsinger's originality to attempt her own pattern drafting.

Ruth Lee of Emporia also designed original patterns for five applique quilts. Her daughter, Loretta Rinker, recalled that

Barbara Brackman

Opposite: Forget Me Not or Old Fashioned Valentine. Designed, appliqued, and quilted by Ruth Lee (1893–1965), Emporia, 1930–1936. Collection of the Rinker family.

Ruth Lee (above) was born in Nebraska; her family moved to the Blue Stem Prairie near Americus when she was three years old. She often told daughter Loretta about the trip to Kansas and how she tumbled from the wagon, rolling under a wheel with no serious consequences. She came to Emporia after her marriage to Roy Lee, a salesman who sold everything from coffee to Hupmobiles during his career.

She had two children, Loretta and Roland. Her son died of scarlet fever when he was five, and she later made an appliqued angel quilt to mourn his death.

Ruth Lee had a reputation as an avid gardener and an excellent seamstress, adding to the family income by tailoring furs for Emporia's well-to-do women. As the Great Depression narrowed her list of customers, Lee turned to remaking men's suits into women's. She did a good business cutting down suits with worn spots, holes, and an old-fashioned style, turning them into chic women's clothing for a fraction of the price of a new suit. In 1936 Ruth Lee swept the category for original design at the state fairs with this quilt.

Ruth Lee and Rose Kretsinger belonged to the same garden club and occasionally quilted together. Although she does not credit Kretsinger as a direct inspiration for her mother's quilts, she notes the similarity in design elements: "You can tell these two gals knew each other."[32]

Not every unusual Emporia quilt can be linked to Kretsinger. She may have had little direct effect on the work of Josephine Craig. Few quiltmakers recall Josephine Craig today, but her name appeared each fall in the *Gazette* during the fair season. In 1932, Emporians were invited to view her Indiana Wreath in a window display at Poole's Dry Goods after it had swept the prizes at both the Topeka and Hutchinson state fairs.[33] Like Kretsinger, Craig sought prizes in competitions beyond Kansas. Her ultimate award was a first-place ribbon at the Eastern States Exposition at Storrowton, Massachusetts, one of the first national quilt contests.

Craig seems to have had her own network of quilting friends with no personal link to Kretsinger, but the two national prize winners were surely aware of each other's work as they competed against each other. Today, most people recall the quiltmakers as women whose competitive spirits were tempered by the good manners and restraint expected of their sex at the time. But competition, no matter how politely disguised, was an important factor in the Emporia quiltmaking community. Kretsinger's competitive nature is apparent in her choice of the Garden design for her last quilt. Her Calendula won second prize in a 1943 *Woman's Day* magazine contest, bested by a Garden Quilt made by a Seattle

woman, Pine Eisefeller. On the magazine picture of Eisefeller's quilt Kretsinger wrote the terse criticism, "bad design," and soon after began work on her own version of the pattern she called Paradise Garden, which won first prize in the 1945 Kansas Fair. She was proud enough of her prizes to keep a running list of them on the flyleaf of her copy of Marie Webster's book, *Quilts: Their Story and How to Make Them.* A 1946 *Gazette* article noted she had a box containing thirty first-place ribbons, six sweepstakes ribbons, and one second-place ribbon.[34]

That sense of competition was shared by other Emporia quiltmakers, who also left their children boxes full of prize ribbons. Local and statewide quilt contests were regular features of the yearly calendar. The contest sponsored by the Women's City Club during their annual Fall Frolic may have been as competitive as the Lyon County fairs of the 1920s and 1930s, which are still talked about as being so cutthroat that quiltmakers kept their entries secret until the judging so rivals could not enter copies.[35] Emporia quilters often swept the state fairs during the second quarter of this century (Kansas held one state fair in Topeka and one in Hutchinson for many years). In 1936, for example, Josephine Craig, Ruth Lee, Elizabeth Goering, and Maud Leatherberry won the top prizes in both fairs, a triumph that could not have gone unnoticed by quilters from Topeka, Atwood, or Hutchinson. New statewide quilt contests were organized in response to the popularity of quilts, and Emporians won prizes sponsored by department stores like Crosby's in Topeka and magazines such as

Capper's Farmer and the *Household*.

Through it all the *Gazette* faithfully printed quilt news under headlines such as "Lyon County Sewing Wins Honors at State Fair in Hutchinson";[36] "Emporia Woman Wins a Second National Prize with One Quilt";[37] and the periodic headline "Emporia Gets In" that noted hometown achievements in many fields. The *Gazette*'s long dedication to publishing "locals," news about Emporia and Lyon County residents, made victories even sweeter and may have heightened the spirit of competition that generated the Emporia quilt phenomenon.[38]

The secrecy dictated by competition extended beyond the annual fair entries. Stories still circulate about how quilting patterns were guarded. Many of the Emporia women hired professional quilters, a traditional division of labor that was far more common before World War II than since. Some applique artists marked their quilt tops with their own trademark quilting designs before they sent them off to the professional quilters. They did not want their templates in the hands of the quilters, who might copy them for use on the quilts of other clients, but "of course the quilters just traced them off."[39]

Finishing or quilting the quilts was frequently a cooperative enterprise. Some of the Emporia women quilted in groups, working on each other's quilts in a traditional quilting bee. Josephine Craig and her friends quilted together, and Stephen Rich helped quilt at least one of his wife Hulda's quilts.

Emporians tell many stories of professional quilters finishing the exceptional applique tops but few

recall any names, an injustice, as the quilting as well as the applique elevates these quilts above the average. Bill Kretsinger recalled going with his mother to Eskridge and Burdick to pick up quilts;[40] Mary Kretsinger remembered a woman in Cedarvale.[41] Margaret Soden recalled her mother driving in the country with the hired man to take her tops to the quilters and to discuss the patterns.[42] Lottie Whitehill recorded that she sent some of hers as far away as Chicago to be finished.[43]

Kretsinger is said to have quilted with a group in Hartford and with the garden club, so it may be that she did some of her own quilting, but her quilts, as well as her children's recollections, indicate that she used different professional quilters over the years. The quilting stitches vary from quilt to quilt, ranging from eight to eleven per inch, but there is much consistency within each of her quilts. This consistency is a desirable characteristic and one that motivated women looking for the best quilting to avoid church groups whose stitch size and regularity might vary. The best work was thought to be that of a skilled individual. Emily Bigler was such a professional quilter. She may have worked for the other applique artists.

Grandma Fannie Moon is often suggested as a candidate for one of the mystery quilters. In 1937, the *Gazette* printed a story about her, noting "she has quilted many quilts for other women, too, and could be busy all the time at this work, but she likes to take her time, refuses to be hurried. . . . She enjoys making the tiny stitches and watching the feather and scroll, hearts and rounds and compass, and other

designs, grow under her skillful fingers."[44]

The Fowler sisters, Eugenia and Grace, were professional quilters who are also mentioned as having a hand in quilting the prizewinning quilts. The quilters mentioned were among the many professionals working at the time in the city and on surrounding farms. Ellen Fleenor Clouse, who lived in nearby Americus, was written up in the *Gazette* for the feat of having quilted 148 quilts between 1931 and 1938.[45]

The names of the quilters were also well guarded, since a good needlewoman who could take direction would soon be overscheduled if everyone knew of her skills. Friendships cooled at the discovery of a so-called friend's quilt in the frame of one's own best quilter.[46] Such secrecy is a major reason the quilters have received so little credit for their part in producing these masterpiece quilts.

The spirit of competition that was so strong in Emporia encourages excellence in a community. Prizewinners are a model for the public, some of whom will be inspired to copy the design and some of whom will decide to compete for the same public approval. Competition alone, however is not enough. The most important factor seems to be an innovative individual like Rose Kretsinger who serves as a model, generating novel ideas and establishing high standards. The innovative individual may be competitive, but it is more important that she or he be cooperative. She must be willing to share her ideas through formal teaching or informal methods such as the hand-drawn patterns and one-to-one assistance that Rose Kretsinger offered. With her talent, training, generosity and competitive nature, she was at the heart of the Emporia phenomenon.

Notes

1. Thomas K. Woodard and Blanche Greenstein, *Twentieth Century Quilts: 1900–1950* (New York: E. P. Dutton, 1988), 25. Kretsinger's Paradise Garden was chosen as the frontispiece for this book.

2. Sears, Roebuck and Company, *Catalog* (1927), 244.

3. Racy Company (St. Louis) advertisement in *Emporia Gazette*, September 14, 1930.

4. Carrie A. Hall and Rose G. Kretsinger, *The Romance of the Patchwork Quilt in America* (Caldwell, Idaho: Caxton Printers, 1935), 61.

5. The quiltmakers: Ifie Arnold, Emily Bigler, Bertha Brickell, Mayme Buck, Josephine Craig, Elizabeth Goering, Hannah Headlee, Rose Kretsinger, Maud Leatherberry, Ruth Lee, Hulda and Stephen Rich, Jennie Soden, and Charlotte Whitehill.

6. Dena S. Katzenberg, *Baltimore Album Quilts* (Baltimore: Baltimore Museum of Art, 1980).

7. Ibid., 61–63. The theory about a single maker, possibly named Mary Evans, was first suggested by William Rush Dunton, Jr., whose papers are in the collection of the Baltimore Museum of Art.

8. Elly Sienkiewicz, "The Marketing of Mary Evans," *Uncoverings 1989*, ed. Laurel Horton (San Francisco: The American Quilt Study Group, 1990), 7–37.

9. Katzenberg, *Baltimore Album Quilts*, 64.

10. Ibid., 15. Katzenberg attributed the theory of a spirit of competition generating the excellence of the album quilts to Myron Orlofsky and Patsy Orlofsky, *Quilts in America* (New York: McGraw-Hill, 1974), 239.

11. William Allen White, *Forty Years on Main Street*, ed. Russell Fitzgibbon (New York: Farrar & Rinehart, 1937), 245.

12. William Allen White, *The New Republic*, May 12, 1920, 348–349, quoted in Sally Foreman Griffith, *Home Town News: William Allen White and the Emporia Gazette* (New York: Oxford University Press, 1989), 234.

13. Griffith, *Home Town News*, 32.

14. Tracing Emporia social life is facilitated by the thoroughness of the *Gazette* in recording everything from quilting prizes to garden club meetings and by the diligence of Lulu Gilson, an Emporia resident who clipped such articles for an encyclopedic set of scrapbooks filed by family name. The Gilson scrapbooks are in the collection of the Lyon County Historical Society.

15. "The Beautiful Flowering of Emporia, Kan.," *Life* (July 30, 1956), 81–86.

16. Margaret Soden, interview with author, Emporia, January 13, 1988.

17. "Nancy Cabot," *The Chicago Tribune*, July 16, 1933.

18. Ruby Short McKim, *101 Quilt Patterns* (Independence, Mo.: McKim Studios, 1938), 77.

19. *Needlecraft, The Home Arts Magazine* (Spring 1925).

20. Thomas Branigar, "No Villains—No Heroes: The David Eisenhower–Milton Good Controversy," *Kansas History* 15, 3 (Autumn 1992): 168–179.

21. Mary Kretsinger, letter to Joyce Gross, August 18, 1973.

22. Hall and Kretsinger, *The Romance of the Patchwork Quilt in America*.

23. Reba Marshall, "Blue Ribbon Quilts," *Farm Journal and Farmer Wife* 73 (February 1949), 34, 35.

24. "Rose Kretsinger: Applique Artist," *Quilters Newsletter Magazine* (December 1977), 25; Mary Kretsinger letter to Joyce Gross, August 18, 1973.

25. Helen M. Ericson, "Rose G. Kretsinger, Artist and Quiltmaker," *Nimble Needle Treasures* (Winter 1973), 26.

26. Mary Kretsinger, interview with author, January 13, 1988.

27. Kretsinger is credited with designing the Arnold quilts listed in the computerized catalog of the Helen F. Spencer Museum of Art, University of Kansas, Lawrence. The quilts are numbered 84.43, 84.44a, and 84.44b.

28. Margaret Soden, interview with author, Emporia, January 13, 1988.

29. Elsie R. Wells, letter to author, August 18, 1987.

30. Mary Kretsinger, interview with author, Emporia, January 13, 1988.

31. Marie Shirer, "My Great-Great Aunt Made Quilts," *Quilters Newsletter Magazine* (February 1980), 13.

32. Loretta Rinker, interview with author.

33. *Emporia Gazette*, November 1, 1932.

34. Ibid., September 20, 1946.

35. Helen Ericson, an Emporia quiltmaker and quilt historian, has written that the entries in the Lyon County Fairs of the 1920s and 1930s were "very competitive and secretive." Ericson, "Rose G. Kretsinger," 26.

36. *Emporia Gazette*, September 19, 1933.

37. Ibid., September 21, 1936.

38. The *Gazette* printed much county and city news to create a sense of community and to solicit readers, a policy explained by an employee, who advised William Allen White "[If we publish] 'Mrs. Smith had a quilting and Mrs. Brown and Black were there' . . . Smith, Brown and Black will take a paper." William Allen White, *The Autobiography of William Allen White* (New York: Macmillan, 1946), 3. For a discussion of William Allen White's and the *Gazette*'s emphasis on local news, see Griffith, *Home Town News*, 74, 75, 160–164, 218–223.

39. Helen Ericson, interview with author, Emporia, 1979.

40. Bill Kretsinger, interview with Sue Sielert, Emporia.

41. Mary Kretsinger, interview with author, Emporia, January 13, 1988.

42. Margaret Soden, interview with author, Emporia, January 13, 1988.

43. Lydia Roberts Dunham, "Denver Art Museum Quilt Collection," *Denver Art Museum Winter Quarterly*, 1963.

44. *Emporia Gazette*, July 14, 1937.

45. Ibid., May 9, 1938.

46. Margaret Soden, interview with author, Emporia, January 13, 1988.

Triple Irish Chain with applique, by Katharina Schrag Wedel (1865–1944),
rural Moundridge, McPherson County, begun in 1880. Cotton.
KM 87.167.1. Kauffman Museum, Bethel College, North Newton, Kansas.
This quilt has only two layers—the front (the piecing and applique are done both by hand and by machine)
and the backing, a green and red floral robe print. The quilting is done by machine in diagonal lines
through the yellow squares in the chain. The backing is folded to the front to form the binding.
The floral blocks are not identical. The stems of the plants are machine stitched with a dark green thread;
the same thread was used to machine applique the leaves and flowers.

Chapter Six

The Developing Mennonite Quilting Tradition: A History of Culture and Faith

Sara Reimer Farley

KANSAS IS A STATE WITH MANY QUILTING COMMUNITIES. THE MENNONITES, WHO ARE CONCENTRATED PRIMARILY IN THE CENTRAL PART OF THE STATE, ARE SUCH A COMMUNITY, ONE THAT IS BOUND BY BOTH RELIGIOUS AND ETHNIC TIES. THE MENNONITES' ADHERENCE TO THEIR FAITH AND ITS VALUES, PARTICULARLY A charity that seeks to serve both the spiritual and material needs of people, is evident even in their quilts. These quilts, often scrap quilts, are frequently made as part of a missionary effort, either to be sent to the mission field or to raise funds for missions. Those who have studied the Mennonite quilts in Kansas have noted their beauty, their characteristics, and the values they represent.[1] Such examinations, although essential, leave other questions unanswered.

First, how did the Mennonite immigrant women learn to quilt? Quilts such as the Triple Irish Chain by Katharina Schrag Wedel, which was begun only six years after the family immigrated to Kansas, raise additional questions: Were such early quilts the continuation of a European tradition? If so, what did their European counterparts look like? If not, did the Mennonite women have the necessary skills before they came to this country so that they could so quickly adopt a new custom? If they learned here, who were their teachers? And what effect did the origins of their quiltmaking tradition have on the styles of quilts made here in Kansas? Is there, for example, a distinctive Kansas Mennonite quilt? References to other early quilts, made for missions, raise an additional question: What role did the Mennonite church play in the development

of the quilting tradition in Kansas, particularly in the late 1800s and the early 1900s? To answer these questions, I will focus on several groups of Mennonites who came directly to Kansas from Russia around 1874. They represent the two largest denominations: the General Conference Mennonites, whose heritage is either Dutch or Swiss, and the Mennonite Brethren. All of these immigrants were part of a mass migration in which entire congregations and extended families traveled together. They came to the plains of Kansas from the steppes of Russia, seeking religious and economic freedom and personal liberty. They brought with them farming skills, an ability to "make do" and to adapt to their new environment, and a strong sense of identity that connected them to their roots in lands other than Russia: They identified themselves as Plattdeutsch (that is, Low German), Swiss Mennonites, or German-Russian. Most important, they brought a deep abiding faith in God.

European History of the Mennonites

In order to understand the development of their quilting tradition, it is necessary to know something of the social history and the heterogeneous nature of the people we call Mennonites. *Mennonite* is an umbrella term

used to refer to a number of different but related groups. Although these groups share deep Anabaptist roots, the experiences and traditions of each small denomination vary. In all, ten different branches of Mennonite denominations (including the Amish) are present in Kansas.[2]

The Mennonites trace their religious heritage back to the Anabaptists in Europe during the early sixteenth century. The early priests and lay reformers who led the Protestant Reformation were concerned with several issues: the state's authority in church matters, baptism as a voluntary and conscious decision to join the church, and the restoration of the church to a total commitment to the Christian ideals of the New Testament. Among the Anabaptists there were, however, disagreements. The Mennonites, whose name derives from one of the organizers in Holland— Menno Simons—represent one faction in the larger Anabaptist movement. In spite of the fact that the Mennonites rejected Roman Catholic doctrine, they were persecuted by other Protestant groups for their refusal to take oaths or to bear arms and for their rejection of infant baptism (Luther advocated baptism of children). The Calvinists, in particular, attacked the Mennonites for these beliefs.

For their uncompromising beliefs, the Mennonites were se-

Indigo aprons of printed fabric. The apron on the left is typical of those brought by the Mennonite immigrants to the plains states. The apron on the right, with the addition of the mustard yellow color, is a more unusual example of the block-printed fabric. KM 6547.1 and KM 6508.11. Kauffman Museum, Bethel College, North Newton, Kansas.

Embroidery dye stamps. These dye stamps were brought from Berdyansk, South Russia, by the Cornelius Jansen family in 1873 and were donated to the Kauffman Museum as part of a collection of items from the dowry chest of Anna Jansen. KM 90.33.1 Kauffman Museum, Bethel College, North Newton, Kansas.

verely persecuted in both Switzerland and Holland. To escape, they developed a pattern of moving to a new region, often at the invitation of a ruler. In each new region (the Palatinate or France for the Swiss Mennonites and Prussia for the Dutch Mennonites), they would ask for and enjoy religious tolerance for a time. During the time the Mennonites resided in these different areas, they would adopt certain of that country's customs, including German dialects, agricultural practices, and textile arts.

Some of these adoptions were not well received by all of the Mennonites, a situation that produced splintering groups across the centuries as the Mennonites struggled with the ideal of remaining separate from the world and yet actively witnessing for Christ. Jacob Amman, leader of one such breakaway group, wanted stricter discipline within the church and more separation from the world. His followers, who became known as the Amish, came to the United States by a different path and generally at an earlier time than did the other Swiss Anabaptists.[3]

Eventually, persecution endured by both the Swiss and Dutch Mennonites, restrictive land practices, and the threat of required military service for the Dutch Germans in Prussia caused many of the Mennonites to move again in the late 1700s and early 1800s. Some chose America, coming to Pennsylvania. Others moved east across Europe. The Swiss Mennonites from the Palatinate established themselves in Volhynia, which was annexed from Poland by Russia in 1793. The Dutch Mennonites migrated from Prussia to settle in two large colonies in South Russia, Chortitza and Molotschna.[4] They

were once again promised freedom to practice their religion, to establish their own schools and teach their children German, and to remain exempt from military obligations.

Although the Dutch and Swiss Mennonites sought a life that would be separated from the world, they were not entirely isolated. Even though they retained their German language while living for nearly a century in Russia, they had contact with Russians and with other religious groups as well. The settlements they established were a network of small villages and towns. Much of their trading could be done among themselves, but they also traveled to larger Russian cities to market. Closer to home, they had contact with people of other ethnic and religious backgrounds who lived in their villages. The cloth they used is a good example of this contact.

The Mennonites raised flax and hemp and sheep for wool. Although the Swiss Mennonites, in particular, were adept at weaving (a skill they had been allowed to practice in southern Germany), the thread was sometimes taken to a non-Mennonite weaver. Weaving was well developed in Volhynia and other regions of South Russia in the late nineteenth century. Typically, the resulting fabric was block printed in a variety of floral patterns or in geometric patterns that were either evenly spaced or grouped in bands. The colors were usually monochrome, the favorites being blue, black, or brown. Occasionally a combination of two or three colors was used.[5] Numerous examples of these fabrics came to the United States with the Mennonite immigrants; the aprons shown on p. 128 are an example. Some tools used in the

making of fabric were also brought to the United States, as shown on p. 128.

The Mennonites did not adapt to the Russian culture to a great degree, however, and the differences in social customs and religious beliefs as well as the Russian nationalists' growing jealousy of the Mennonites' increasing wealth created friction. Then, in 1870, Czar Alexander II's plans to unify his country through such measures as establishing Russian as the language of education, abolishing military exemptions, and restoring Russian Orthodox Christianity posed a direct threat to the Mennonites' survival. The Swiss Mennonites in Volhynia banded together with the Dutch Germans of the Chortitza and Molotschna colonies to appeal the mandate. When that appeal was denied, they began looking for a new home.

Emigration to Kansas

The Canadian government and the railroad companies in the United States actively sought to woo these people, advertising in German and sending representatives to Europe. For those who chose the prairie states of the United States, the railroads played a significant role because they offered free freight, which helped many of the poorer Mennonites meet the ticket price of $80.00.[6] Some of the Mennonites were able to borrow money from a mutual aid society formed by the emigrants,[7] and others were helped by those Mennonites who had come to the United States earlier. This assistance is well documented in articles that appeared in the *Herald of Truth*, a Mennonite English-language monthly published in Indiana. In all, from 1873 to 1883, about

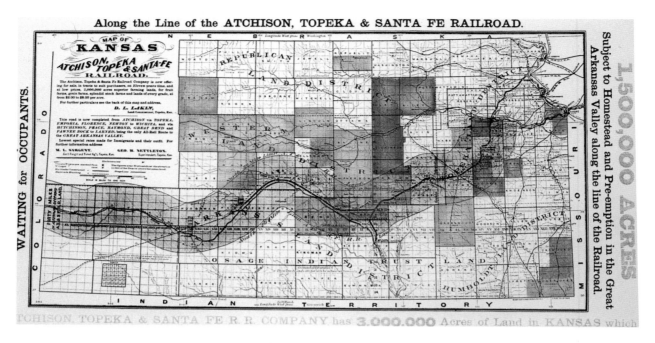

Along the Line of the ATCHISON, TOPEKA & SANTA FE RAILROAD.

Map of Kansas, 1905. The colored areas show areas of settlement by various ethnic groups. The orange represents German immigrants.

eighteen thousand Mennonites emigrated from Russia, with ten thousand coming to Kansas, Nebraska, Minnesota, and the Dakotas.[8] Those who settled in Kansas were attracted, in large part, by the promise of cheap land, $2.50 to $3.00 an acre.[9]

The pattern had repeated itself. When the Mennonites felt threatened, America beckoned, and they came. Some of the Mennonite colonies in Russia had been wealthier than others, but all faced a rather harsh reality when they arrived. They were once again in a country where they did not share a language and where the winters were cold. That first winter many Mennonites lived in immigrant houses provided by the railroads. Others stayed in free houses and sheds.[10] The Dutch Germans who had been living in West Prussia settled around Hillsboro; other Dutch Germans from the Molotschna and Chortitza colonies made their way to the Goessel and Inman areas after stopping briefly in Topeka. The Swiss Germans followed the rail-

road line from New York to Peabody and Halstead before traveling by wagon to the Moundridge area.

The Mennonites brought few material possessions, as a rule, because they had to sell many of their personal belongings when they sold their houses and land.[11] They did bring such necessary items as clothing and bedding. When possible they also packed cherished clocks, Bibles, devotional books, songbooks, *frakturs*,[12] and some fine needlework. Because they were not sure what would be available to them, various seeds for fruit trees, like apricots and mulberries, and for such crops as Turkey Red wheat were also included.

One of the concerns of these new immigrants was simply enduring the winter. Some of the groups arrived in the summer, but others came in the fall with little time to prepare for the cold winter. John F. Funk, editor of the *Herald of Truth*, described the plight of some Polish Mennonites who had settled in Canton township, McPherson

County, in an 1875 letter to Amos Herr of the Pennsylvania Aid Committee: "They have neither chair, bedsteads, nor floors. They are without stoves and have no fuel; and are insufficiently dressed. It was a cold, cloudy, dreary day, and it was very windy; I can tell you it was a hard sight to see them, even the women and children walking about in low slippers without stockings, and the children with hands and face purple on account of the cold blast. Many of the children were lying or sitting on their beds of pallets made of a straw sack laid on the floorless earth in their huts, and covered themselves with featherbeds to keep comfortable as there was neither stove nor fire."[13]

These Polish immigrants were the poorest, and their plight—typified here by the lack of bedding and adequate clothing—was not the general rule. Noble Prentis, a Kansas journalist, found a different situation when he visited a Mennonite settlement near Newton and noted the stack of bedding, which was piled high when not in use and covered with a "calico 'spread.' The top of the high, narrow pile resembled in shape a coffin," he said, "and conveyed the unpleasant impression to the visitor that he had arrived just in time for a funeral."[14] W. J. Groat described a visit to a Mennonite community at Gnadenau near Hillsboro. The house-barn was an A-frame and the furniture was primarily bedding, "of which they seem to have an abundant supply and of the warmest materials."[15]

The Questions of When and How

Could any of this bedding have been quilts? The references here and elsewhere are not spe-cific. Katharine Nickel, in her fictionalized account of one family's trek in *Seed from the Ukraine*, was more detailed. She imagined that the mothers packed crazy patch comforts, embroidered and tied to add both color and warmth to the cold gray Russian winter nights. In addition, she depicted bolts of gingham, unbleached muslin, ticking, calico, flannel, woolen cloth, mull, and paisley as well as buttons, silk braid, and lace.[16] But how realistic is this picture? Certainly, as already mentioned, in South Russia the Mennonites had access to a variety of fabrics: homespun cloth and the calico, broadcloth, and about twenty types of linen that were available at market in South Russia. Additionally, Mennonite colonies were involved in the silk industry.[17] However, the limited amount of personal belongings that each family could bring with them probably meant that other items, including wheat seed, would have preempted bolts of fabric. For each adult's ticket, only twenty cubic feet of freight-free passage was allowed.[18] Perhaps all these immigrant women could bring was the knowledge of comforts and quilts, knowledge that they could put to use once they arrived.

Many quilt researchers would disagree with such a possibility because they believe that patchwork—that is, pieced work, including the crazy quilt—is an American tradition. Patchwork and quilting, separately, are ancient arts. It is the combination of these two traditions that is often attributed to American pioneer women by general quilt historians. Those who study Mennonite quiltmaking have also commonly assumed that Mennonites learned to quilt after their arrival in North America.

Tomlonson asserted this, although she offered no evidence for her conclusion. She suggested that the Mennonite women who immigrated to Kansas in the 1870s learned to quilt from their English-speaking neighbors sometime after the turn of the century.[19] Kaufman and Clark noted that the first extant Mennonite quilts in eastern Ohio were made fifty or more years after the Mennonites' arrival.[20] In a discussion of the traditional arts of the Mennonite émigrés in the Waterloo Region, Ontario, Patterson concluded that both the Swiss Germans and the Dutch Germans who migrated to Canada learned to quilt in the New World.[21]

Linguistic evidence, a lack of physical evidence of quilting, and the recollections of immigrants who learned here do lead to the conclusion that the German-Russian Mennonite women learned to quilt in Kansas, although not in the time frame that Tomlonson has suggested nor in the time frame typical for other groups of Mennonites. Still a collected record of that evidence is warranted to verify the assumptions of the various researchers, to document the origins of the quiltmaking of these German-Russian Mennonites, and to explain the influences that have affected its development.

Without a doubt, these German-Russian Mennonite women were skilled in textile arts. When they emigrated in the 1870s, they valued textiles not only for their material value but also because activities related to the production of cloth were part of the social structure in the family and the community. For instance, in South Russia when spinning was done at home, the father might read or tell a story to the women

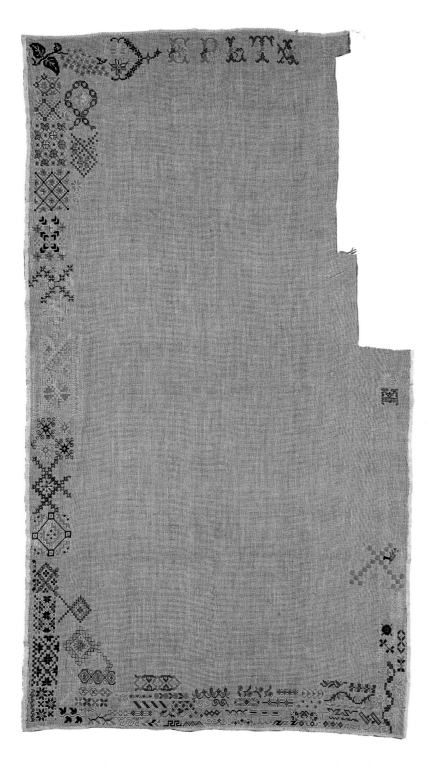

Sampler by Elisabeth Neumann Penner (1879–1955), Grossweide, Molotschna, South Russia, ca. 1895. Cotton on linen. Contains more than seventy-five different border patterns for cross-stitch and satin stitch. KM 87.129.1. Kauffman Museum, Bethel College, North Newton, Kansas.

as they worked. Other times the spinning was a social occasion, with girls getting together on a winter night and the boys coming to entertain.[22] These spinning parties sound very similar, in fact, to the quilting bees that were popular among the Kansas Mennonites earlier in this century.

A wide variety of trades, industries, and professions in the Mennonite villages were related to the textile arts, including spinning-wheel makers, cloth dyers, button makers, hatters, tailors, and seamstresses.[23] Each village had its tailors, who in the Swiss Mennonite villages were often Jews.[24] By the late 1800s some of these tailor shops had sewing machines. Women who worked as seamstresses in homes might first attend the Mädchenschule (a girls' finishing school) at Chortitza, perfecting their skill by taking sewing classes that lasted for three months.[25] Once the skills were learned, a seamstress would move from household to household during the day doing all the sewing each family anticipated they would need for a year.[26]

When the Mennonites immigrated to Kansas, they brought the various techniques they had learned in their migrations through Europe. The lace and embroidery work adorning bed linens were a sign of personal wealth in South Russia because of the luxury of time they represented. In Russia, as in other parts of Europe, featherbeds were commonly used. The featherbeds generally had a muslin casing and then an outer covering made of a beautiful, white embossed fabric.[27]

The influence of the Ukraine can be seen in some of the samplers brought by the Mennonites from South Russia. Elisabeth Neumann Penner of Grossweide,

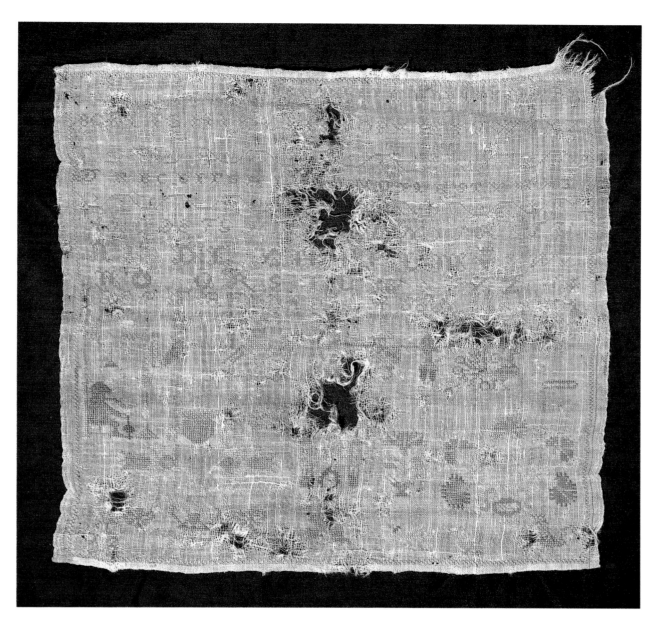

Sampler by Gertruda Clasen, inscribed 1820. Silk on wool. The maker was a member of a Mennonite community in the Vistula Delta (near today's Gdansk and Elblag, Poland). The Dutch influence can be seen in the cross-stitch motifs. KM 88.168.1. Courtesy of Kauffman Museum, Bethel College, North Newton, Kansas.

Molotschna colony, completed a
cotton on linen sampler showing
more than seventy-five patterns
(p. 132). The predominantly
geometric patterns are done in
red, blue, and black, favored colors of the Ukrainian region. The
threads are probably colored with
vegetable dye.[28] The Mennonite
girls in the Ukraine also used embroidery stitches to decorate their
blouses, as did the Russian girls
living in the surrounding areas.[29]
Embroidery skills were not
learned by the Mennonites in the
Ukraine, however, but rather
were brought with them to
South Russia. The Dutch influence can be seen in a silk on wool
sampler made by Gertruda
Clasen (p. 133). Many of the
motifs in this sampler have religious significance that is common throughout Europe. Two of
the motifs, however, are strongly
identified with the Dutch: the
figures carrying a stick laden with
grapes, which represents the Bib-
lical story of the spies who went
to Canaan to see the land they
had been promised, and the
monkey spinning thread.[30]

Perhaps if a tradition of pieced

work existed in the Ukraine, the
Mennonites in South Russia
would have learned it as well, an
opportunity that would not necessarily have been available to the
Mennonites who came directly to
the United States from Switzerland and South Germany. I have
found a brief reference to a
patchwork tradition in the
Ukraine. Twentieth-century artist
Sonia Terk Delaunay was born in
the Ukraine in 1885. She and her
husband made a significant con-
tribution to the development of
modern art; the incorporation of
abstract art into everyday life is
partially due to her influence.[31]
Sonia—a painter and a designer
of fabrics, tapestries, stage sets,
and furniture—began her experi-
ments with color by making "a
patchwork blanket composed of
bits of fabric like those [she] had
seen in the houses of the Russian
peasants." Two years later she
was making dresses, "sewn," as
she wrote, "with small pieces of
fabric that formed patches of
color."[32]

There are a few Mennonite
bedcoverings—generally pieced,
but without quilting—that are
said to have been brought from
South Russia, though none has
been satisfactorily documented.
In other cases, because the ob-
server is recording his or her
memories some years after the
events in question, it is difficult
to say whether the word *quilt* is
used intentionally to identify a
three-layered covering. For example, Cornelius Wall detailed
the death and burial of his young
son Arthur (April 14, 1922) in
Batum, a port on the Black Sea,
as the family was making its escape from Russia. He wrote that
Arthur was buried in his cradle,
"covered . . . with his baby
quilt."[33] His daughter, Mary
Wall Wiens, described the cover-

ing somewhat differently. She recalled that her mother used the baby's diapers for the burial cloths, scalloping the edges and decorating them with cut work.[34]

There is evidence of early quiltmaking by the Mennonites in Kansas, although the time frame seems remarkably short if indeed they had no previous connection with a quilting tradition. Katharina Schrag Wedel, the daughter of Swiss Mennonite parents, was born in Volhynia, Russia, in 1865. The Jacob and Katharina Stucky Schrag family then emigrated with other members of their Mennonite congregation to the United States in 1874 and homesteaded near present-day Moundridge. According to the family, Katharina began a Triple Irish Chain quilt in 1880 (see p. 126), a date that places the quilt a mere six years after her family's arrival in McPherson County, Kansas, rather than after the turn of the century as Tomlonson suggested as a probable time when these immigrants began making quilts.[35]

The quilt contains both piecing and applique, done both by hand and machine. Set in between the "chains" are floral designs, perhaps strawberries, in a sunburst. The stems are machine stitched; the borders on one side are also machine stitched, and it is machine quilted. The quilt is made of only two layers; there is no batting. The backing is a robe print, a fabric popular in the last quarter of the nineteenth century. The quilt is not typical: The lack of batting and the machine quilting may suggest the maker's unfamiliarity with quilts. The question arises of who taught the Mennonites to quilt.

There were quilts in the area where the Mennonites settled. Mrs. J. C. Stockham, a non-Mennonite who found land in McPherson County in 1874, said that she was "extremely busy after [we] moved to [our] homestead. There were quilts on the beds to shake every morning and above the rough straw or husk ticks were the feather beds, which were turned every morning."[36] Mrs. Stockham lived in Jackson township, about five miles east of McPherson. However, the Kansas Quilt Project uncovered a quilt much closer to Katharina Schrag's Moundridge home, a quilt of the same Triple Irish Chain pattern with an appliqued border rather than applique throughout the quilt (see p. 136). This quilt was made by Drusilla Showalter Cole in 1876 for her husband, Thornton C. J. Cole, according to the family. Both quilts are made of four plain cotton fabrics. The Cole quilt is green, yellow, brown, and white; the Schrag quilt green, yellow, red, and white. Both quilts are also unusual in their combination of floral applique with the Triple Irish Chain pattern. The Cole quilt also features both hand and machine work: The Irish Chain is hand appliqued, but the applique vine in the borders is done on the machine with what appears to be beige thread.

Drusilla and Thornton Cole came to McPherson County in 1872 to the place where the town of Moundridge now stands and gave the community forty acres for a townsite. The Coles were in Kansas before the Mennonites and before the grasshoppers. When the grasshoppers came, Thornton and his hired hand ran up and down the rows of their garden, shaking quilts to drive the grasshoppers away.[37] Drusilla later made sauerkraut to share with their neighbors so that no one would go hungry. It seems reasonable that people with such concern for their neighbors would have been willing to teach the immigrants a new skill or—if quilting was a skill the Mennonites knew—would have used quilts to bridge the culture and language gaps.

The Cole family and the Jacob Schrag family lived within three miles of each other, so it is certainly possible that the young Katharina could have been guided by Drusilla Showalter Cole.[38] The relationship between families existed through several generations. Not only did Katharina's future husband, Peter H. Wedel (the son of John J. and Maria Wedel), grow up a half mile from the Coles but also Katharina and Peter's daughter, Selinde, was a friend of Drusilla's granddaughter, who lived with her grandparents.[39]

At least in this instance it is possible that among their "English" (non–German speaking) neighbors the Mennonites could have found a teacher willing to demonstrate quiltmaking. Was this a typical situation? Perhaps the answer lies in how eager the Mennonites were to isolate themselves. Some visitors to the early Mennonite settlements, particularly Gnadenau and Alexanderwohl, noted that the Dutch German settlers were trying to reconstruct the Russian village plan, with its houses lining the village streets and the farmland radiating out. The effect of such an arrangement would be to increase the isolation of the Mennonites. The Mennonites quickly abandoned the plan, however, instead adopting one in which three or four houses were clustered together where farms joined. This was necessary because the land available to the

Sara Reimer Farley

KQP Df051, Triple Irish Chain, by Drusilla Showalter Cole (1847–1918), Moundridge, McPherson County, inscribed 1876. Cotton. Collection of Jacinta M. Davis.

This brown, green, gold, and off-white quilt with its floral applique borders was made as a gift for Drusilla's husband, Thornton C. J. Cole, according to the family. The inscription ("D. C. to T. C.") is quilted in the lower right corner of the quilt, along with a heart and diamond. The date 1876 is quilted between the vine and leaf in the same corner. The quilt was to be part of a pair; the matching top has not been quilted.

Drusilla Showalter Cole, ca. 1870.

Mennonites was not always in one large area.[40] Noble Prentis suggested that confusion over taxes on the commonly owned village plots also contributed to the demise of the earlier living arrangement.[41] The choice of settling in rural rather than urban areas did help the Mennonites retain their language and sense of identity.

Still they were not entirely separated from other cultures. Of the many stories relating to the Mennonite encounters with North American culture, one from Ontario, Canada, deals specifically with quilts. Its significance lies in the fact that what had been part of the everyday experiences in South Russia for this family who emigrated to Ontario had also been part of the everyday experience of these German-Russian Mennonites who came directly to Kansas: Theirs is a shared history. In 1873, Cornelius Jansen, a merchant and Prussian consul, was exiled from Russia because he had been circulating pamphlets urging the Mennonites to emigrate. He and his family left Berdyansk, South Russia, for their first temporary home in North America, in Berlin (now Kitchener), Ontario, Canada. They stayed in a small, four-room house situated behind the Jacob Schanz home. Two of Jansen's daughters kept diaries. Margarete, the eldest, noted such events as their first home-cooked meal, the day they finally had beds to sleep on, and the tasks that occupied their days. Sewing was an oft-mentioned chore. On September 29, 1873, she noted that they spent a rainy afternoon sewing at the home of the Schanzes. On October 16 she reported that her sisters Anna and Helena were taking sewing lessons from some English-speaking girls. Whether these two younger girls had sewn before their arrival in Canada is not clear, but Margarete and her mother had done needlework of various kinds in Berdyansk. Margarete's 1866 diary had referred to their sewing machine and needlework.[42]

On February 19, 1874, Margarete noted that four girls (perhaps including her sister Anna) went down to the Detweiler place to help Harriet with the quilting. On Wednesday, February 25, 1874, she knitted gloves while Susanne Schanz cut several patches for a quilt. In both of these entries, Margarete uses the word *quilt*. There is no special marking (i.e., the word is not underlined or enclosed in quotation marks); the English word stands alone in an otherwise German entry and is, therefore, noteworthy. The word *quilt* does not appear in the German language until the middle of the 1960s, according to Professor Almuth Schröder of the University of Bremen.[43] Other authors writing in German in the late 1800s or early 1900s do use quotation marks around the word *quilt* or change the typeface, indicating that the word is borrowed.[44] So the use of an English word in Margarete's entries seems to reinforce the idea that quilting was not a known skill; otherwise, one might expect Margarete to use the equivalent term in her native German. However, Margarete had acquired enough English while in Russia, perhaps by reading the English publications her father had ordered for the children, to use other English words occasionally in her diaries. For example, when talking of a frequent visitor, a Mrs. Zohrab, Margarete uses the title *Mrs.* instead of the more common Ger-

Jansen family on the porch of their home in Berdyansk, South Russia, ca. 1870. Back row (left to right): Peter, Anna von Riesen (Helena's sister), Cornelius, Jr., Helena von Riesen (mother), Cornelius (father), Margarete. Front row (left to right): Anna, John, Helena. Mennonite Library and Archives, Bethel College, North Newton, Kansas.

man *Frau*.[45] So it is possible that Margarete's use of the English word *quilt* does not signal her first awareness of a quilt. Her sister Anna also spoke of the quilting done by neighbors. In a diary entry dated April 7, 1874, Anna said that she "went over [toward evening] to see how the quilt [was] coming." Anna used the word *Decke*, which can be translated as cover or quilt. In this context it seems clear that a quilt, rather than a cover, is intended.[46] The linguistic evidence here is mixed, but the entries do suggest that even a first contact with quilting could have been made shortly after the family's arrival.

The establishment of German schools in Kansas during the winters of 1874 and 1875 underscores the Mennonites' determination to educate their children in German and the Bible, as they had done in Russia. However, education also opened the door to American culture. By 1876 Mennonites began taking the county teachers' exam, and by 1877, within two or three years of their arrival, the first Mennonite names began appearing on school board records.[47] Passing the exams presupposes familiarity with English. At a November 1877 meeting of Mennonite teachers, schools were urged to teach English so that the communities of Mennonites would be able to preserve their interests and to witness to their neighbors.[48]

All this suggests that fairly early contact with English neighbors could have taken place. Still, it may seem surprising that these Kansas Mennonites would so quickly take up the quilting tradition when there was such a lapse of time before other groups of Mennonites in other places began making quilts. For instance, the earliest documented quilts for the Amish and Amish-Mennonite immigrants who settled in Ohio in 1819 and 1831 were made between 1875 and 1900; that is, fifty or more years after their immigration.[49] These settlers had lived in Switzerland longer than had the Swiss Germans of Kansas and had retained the customs of that land; there is evidence of this in the style of house they built in Ohio: a "chalet" architecture, gabled and half-timbered.

By contrast, within six years we had a Mennonite quilt (the Triple Irish Chain made by Katharina Schrag Wedel), and within sixteen years the Mennonites at Ebenfeld Mennonite Brethren Church, rural Hillsboro in Marion County, began holding auctions at which they sold quilts and other items to raise money for church work.[50] The records for this mission sale, held in November 1889, show the buyers, the items purchased, and the cost. There are no descriptions, just the word *Dekke*. Dr. Solomon Loewen, who is a noted authority on the church's history, has translated this word to mean *quilt* in both a history of the church and also in family records.[51] The prices paid for the "covers" sold that first year suggest that they were not all equally valued. The bidders paid 50 cents, 70 cents, $2.40, and $4.60 for these items. A difference in size might account for the difference in price, but so would a difference in technique: The two lower prices are nearly equivalent with the price (75 cents) a Hillsboro store paid for comforts made by Helen Jost Koop in the 1890s and the early 1900s, although Helen was paid primarily for her labor; the store provided the fabric.[52]

The disparity of time elapsing between the arrival of the Kansas and Ohio Mennonites and the production of their first quilts can be explained in several ways. The first explanation—that the earliest-made quilts in Ohio might not have been preserved or might not yet have been discovered—does not seem likely; numerous examples of non-Mennonite quilts from the early 1800s are common in Ohio.[53] There is also evidence that other Mennonite women who settled in other eastern states did produce quilts fairly soon after their arrival. A feathered star quilt (KQP Fg061; see page 140) made by Barbara Schowalter Strohm Kramer, who immigrated to Iowa in 1853 and moved to Summerfield, Illinois, in 1856 eventually was brought to Kansas and duplicated by Barbara Kramer's great-granddaughter Gertrude Haury (KQP Fg067). Documenters at the Quilt Discovery Day at which these two quilts appeared estimated that the Kramer quilt was made during the third quarter of the nineteenth century. That would put its making very close to the time of immigration. Its design, an unlikely choice for a first-time quilter, and its execution show the skill of its maker.

A second explanation is that the community in Ohio may have remained more isolated than the Mennonites in Kansas. This certainly seems a logical possibility. The Amish in Ohio were part of the group who had chosen to follow Jacob Amman, and the issues that led to the split in Europe would also have contributed to the traditionally plain, simple, secluded life-style they brought to America. It is not likely that the church elders would have encouraged their schools to teach English within four years of their

arrival as the Kansas Mennonites did. The Ordnungsbrief, the church's written regulations, had an even more direct effect on the development of the Amish quilting tradition: Amish women were prohibited from using speckled, striped, or flowered cloth.[54]

Another possible explanation for the difference in the groups in Kansas and Ohio is that the immigrants came to the United States at different times, following different paths. Neither group would have brought a quilting tradition from Germany.[55] The innumerable migrations of the Mennonites throughout Europe, however, may have been more likely to bring them into contact with the scattered traditions of piecework. By the mid eighteenth century, when the major Amish emigration from Europe was virtually completed, pieced work did not represent a preference for bed coverings in Europe. As noted earlier, verified examples of patchwork from South Russia have not been found among the Kansas Mennonites either.

Most probably the pattern of settlement played the largest role. Eve Wheatcroft Granick noted a similar disparity in the dates of settlement and the production of the first quilts made by the Amish in Pennsylvania and Ohio. In general, the farther west the immigrants came, the shorter the time before the first quilts were produced. Granick also concluded, based on estate records, that Pennsylvania Mennonites began making pieced quilts thirty or forty years before the Pennsylvania Amish.[56]

Characteristics and Individual Styles

The quilts of the Mennonite women look very much like the

140
Sara Reimer Farley

KQP Fg061, Feathered Star, by Barbara Schowalter Strohm Kramer (1823–1900), 1850–1875. Cotton. Collection of Helen Rupp.

This quilt and a duplicate (KQP Fg067) made by great-granddaughter Gertrude Haury (1907–   ) ca. 1932 in Hutchinson are similar in coloring and quilting motifs. The quilt by Kramer is red and white; the Haury quilt is pink and white. Both quilts have outline, cable, and wreath quilting motifs; the Kramer quilt also has butterflies. With ten to eleven stitches per inch, the Haury quilt was awarded first prize in 1934 and 1935 at the Kansas State Fair in Hutchinson, Kansas.

Barbara Schowalter Strohm Kramer, (above) date unknown.

quilts of the "English" quilters who lived around them and for a very good reason: the fabric choices and the design sources were the same. Unlike the Amish, whose quilts have a distinctive style, the Mennonites were guided more by what kind of fabric was available than by church dicta. The early, everyday quilts were often of dark fabric scraps, including suit samples. Clerks at various general stores often had access to such samples and either made quilts themselves or gave the samples to someone else to use.

An unusual comfort (see p. 142) made by these economical means was designed by Helen Jost Koop of Hillsboro. Born in 1866 in Prangenau, Russia, to Peter and Adelgunda Suderman Jost, Helen settled in Marion County with her family in 1875. She was a seamstress, sewing for her own family as well as helping the neighbors. During the early 1900s she made comforts for the Schaeffler Store in Hillsboro from yard goods the store provided. For each comfort she was paid seventy-five cents. Her daughter Lena later worked as a clerk for Shaefflers and brought home wool suit samples for her mother. To use these samples, Helen Jost Koop designed a patch with appliques made of felt. Even with help from her daughters, the comfort took years to finish because of the amount of applique and embroidery required. Although the family knows of no connection Helen would have had with Mennonites in the eastern United States, this comfort resembles "cookie cutter" quilts made in Pennsylvania.[57]

Helen's contributions as a quiltmaker were far reaching. She became a baptized member of the Krimmer Mennonite Brethren Church in 1881 and worked in many church-related projects. In addition to the quilt she made each year for the church mission sale, she also belonged to a mission group at church that made bandages, mended clothes, tied comforts, and quilted. Some of the quilts and comforts made by this group were sent back to Russia during the turbulent years surrounding the 1905 Russian Revolution.

Quilts of cottons or wool scraps filled with cotton or wool batting were common among the Mennonites. Most of the small Mennonite communities had general stores that carried a wide variety of dry goods typical of fabric used in quilts made from 1880 on. Wool for batting was readily available in both the Dutch and Swiss Mennonite communities, although the batting itself was not always produced locally. Helen Jost Koop often used cotton for batting when she made comforts because, according to her daughter, it was cheaper and easier to use than wool.

The Mennonites did have some fancier materials available to them, including silk from a silk factory they operated near Peabody, Kansas, between 1887 and 1897. A crazy quilt (KQP Fa013), ca. 1890, by Elizabeth Ediger Suderman includes some of this Peabody silk (Elizabeth's husband, Herman W. Suderman, was one of the operators of the factory). This quilt also includes scraps of velvets, moirés, twills, brocades, and plain weaves, some of wool and cotton.

Most of the documented Mennonite quilts made between 1880 and 1900, as exemplified by the quilt made by Katharina Schrag Wedel, show the color

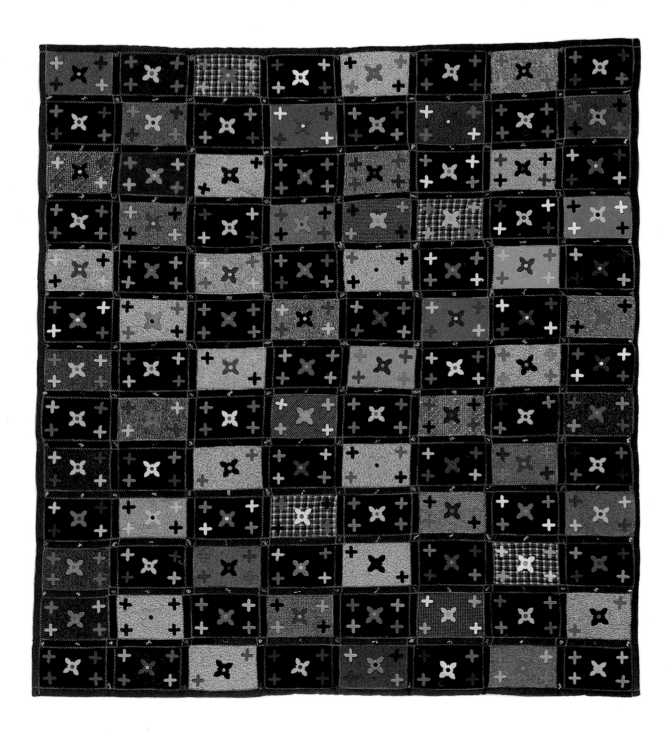

KQP Fc070, *applique comfort, by Helen Jost Koop (1866–1932), Hillsboro, Marion County. 1915–1920. Wool with felt applique (top); cotton flannel (backing). Collection of Roy L. Warkentin.*

Susie Esau, the quiltmaker's daughter, recalls that her mother said of this comfort that they would put "everything into this quilt that [they] know and then call it done."

Sara Reimer Farley

palette popular during that time. Red, in particular, seemed to be a favorite.[58] Several of these old quilts have printed backing fabric, which was also typical between 1880 and 1910.

It is difficult to label one technique or one pattern as typical of the Mennonite quilters in Kansas. Some researchers have suggested that the whole cloth, or plain quilt, is emblematic.[59] Patterson, in her study of Swiss and Dutch Mennonites in Canada, concluded that whole-cloth quilts were the style of the Dutch Mennonites there but that they would use an embroidered quilt as their top quilt if they did not have a plain quilt. Furthermore, these Dutch Mennonites divided up the labor at their church sewing circles, with the poorer quilters completing the patchwork quilts and the superior quilters stitching the whole-cloth quilts.[60]

However, the quilts brought for documentation through the KQP do not support this, nor do other Mennonite quilts I have found during my research. The project lists 295 quilts by Mennonites, but that number is not a good reflection of the number of quilts made by this group. Many Mennonite quiltmakers reportedly made fifty to two hundred quilts during their lifetimes. Many of these quilts were made for their families, but a large number were also supplied for mission work. Whether the sampling we saw is a good one is therefore difficult to ascertain. People were asked to bring their quilts—all of their quilts. In reality, people brought only a fraction of the quilts they owned. This self-selecting process often suggests what the owners valued and what they thought well preserved enough to warrant documentation.

Family of Helen Jost and Peter Koop, ca. 1898. Front row (left to right): Anna, Sarah, Mary. Back row: Henry, Helen Jost (mother), Pete, Peter (father), John, and Lena. Lena and her mother were the principal makers of the applique comfort (KQP Fc070). Helen Jost Koop, an excellent seamstress, made the dresses worn by the girls and herself. Her brother, Peter Jost, a tailor, made the suits that the boys and father are wearing.

Some communities, most notably Hillsboro, valued whole-cloth quilts. Often they were considered "Sunday" quilts, wedding quilts, or special baby quilts. In other words, these quilts were likely to be highly valued and to be saved. Dutch Mennonite Helena Peters Ewert has ten whole-cloth quilts documented. In fact, her quilts represent about one-half of all the Mennonite whole-cloth quilts found in the KQP. The other whole-cloth quilts were also made by Dutch Mennonites. Still, pieced quilts outnumber all other quilts made both by the Swiss Mennonites (who seldom make whole-cloth quilts) and by the Dutch Mennonites. Ewert's daughter reported that they also used pieced quilts, although the quilts were considered for everyday usage.

Whole-cloth quilts may be more correctly described as the style of a particular quilter or of a particular community. Helena Peters was born in a Mennonite community in Bingham Lake, Minnesota. In 1913, at the age of thirty-two, she married Gerhard Ewert, a widower with nine children, and moved to Hills-

boro. Ten years later, when her husband became a semi-invalid, Helena had to structure her life around her husband's care. She began quilting about this time as a diversion, according to one of her stepdaughters-in-law.[61] She was a prolific quilter, making approximately one hundred quilts for her extended family in addition to those she made for pay.

Helena's whole-cloth quilts are typically a medallion style: a central design bordered by one or more repetitive patterns like a grid or clamshells. Sometimes her whole-cloth quilts had one or more interior borders, again emphasizing the central medallion. These whole-cloth quilts, in particular those with a second color

used for interior borders, resemble the plain quilts made by the Ohio Amish and pictured in *Quilts in Community: Ohio's Traditions*.[62] Some of her quilts had a single outer border in a second color. The medallion set was also common in applique quilts made by Mennonite and non-Mennonite quiltmakers during the 1920s and 1930s;[63] in fact, applique patterns may have been one source of her quilting patterns.

Helena was a particular quilter, in part because she thought that since she was being paid she was obligated to provide a consistently fine piece of work. In her own quilts she also worked toward excellence. If others worked on a quilt, she could not maintain quality. Helena also disliked gossiping around the quilting frame. Her solution to both problems was the same: She assigned one of the poorer quilters to read scripture or poetry. She might also greet a visitor whose quilting skills were not up to par with, "Oh, my fingers are tired, let's just sit and visit."[64]

Often the process of making a whole-cloth quilt was shared among a number of individuals, with each person contributing her specialty. Although Helena Peters Ewert is recognized as the quilter of many whole-cloth quilts, she did not mark the quilting designs herself; the marking was done by her stepdaughter, Marie Ewert Regier. The two women often collaborated on the choice of designs; Marie marked the quilts for Helena, usually with a waterlily, rose, or cattail pattern. These patterns may have been ordered or acquired through friends.[65] If Helena finished the quilt's edging, she preferred to use a bias binding. However, if the customer wanted a crocheted-edge,

KQP Fc017, whole-cloth quilt, by Helena Peters Ewert (1881–1962), Hillsboro, Marion County. 1940–1941. Cotton. Colors: pale yellow, with light green backing. Collection of Ethel Ewert Abrahams.

The motifs in this quilt—particularly the spider web, water lily, and cattails—were typical of Ewert's work. The quilt was marked by Marie Ewert Regier, Ethel's half-sister. This quilt was placed in a cedar chest and given to Helena's daughter, Ethel, for her high school graduation in 1941.

Helena Peters Ewert, ca. 1960.

she recommended that her sister, Maria Peters Peters, do the crocheting. Anna Calem made a business of completing the hemstitching that was required before the crocheting could be done.[66] A crocheted edge does appear on a number of the quilts documented but certainly not on a majority of even the whole-cloth quilts. Perhaps baby quilts made in this style were most likely to have such a decorative edging.

The preference for whole-cloth quilts seems to have been strongest among the Dutch Mennonites in Hillsboro, Hesston, and Inman. But even in these communities, other quilters also had distinctive styles. Anna Schmidt Sperling of rural Inman was known for her fine applique in a church group that generally did pieced work. Anna was the daughter of Peter and Anna Ratzlaff Schmidt, immigrants from Franztal in the Molotschna Colony. As a young girl, Anna learned to quilt through the church mission sewing circle. Although she made crazy quilts for use at home, using wool from their sheep for batting, her specialty was applique. In fact, she appliqued various motifs on her aprons and on throw rugs in addition to her quilts. She had a talent for design and an eye for color. A spectacular example of her work is a rose applique made from her adaptation of a McCall Kaumagraph transfer pattern for curtains (see p. 146). This was a favorite pattern, one she later duplicated in a summer spread. The colors used in the quilt pictured, particularly the shades of peach, are also part of her trademark. She liked the feel and finish of cotton sateen, most often selecting solid rather than printed fabrics. Her other sources of quilt patterns included coloring books

Marking patterns used by Marie Ewert Regier (1899–1982) for the quilts she marked for Helena Peters Ewert, her stepmother. Collection of Georgie Ann Regier Schmidt.

Marie (left) opened her dining room table, inserted a plate of heavy glass into the opening, and placed a lamp underneath in order to do the markings. The lamp was necessary if she marked dark fabric. Working in her spare time, Marie could mark a full-size quilt in two weeks. If necessary, she could complete the marking in a week, working afternoons and evenings.

146
Sara Reimer Farley

Opposite: KQP Fd058, floral applique, by Anna Schmidt Sperling (1888–1959), Inman, McPherson County. 1937. Cotton sateen. Collection of Anne Colvin.

Although this quilt has remained in the family, many of Anna Schmidt Sperling's quilts were made to be auctioned at the Mission Relief Sale at Hoffnungsau Church, rural Inman, or to be donated to the Hopi Indians in Arizona. Her donations to the Hopi Indians included quilt tops or quilt blocks for them to finish in addition to completed quilts. Her pattern of choice for these donations was a water lily applique.

Anna Schmidt Sperling, Elizabeth Sperling Voth, Agatha Ediger Reimer, and Marie Voth Schmidt, (above) graduation photo, 1905. Their graduation project was to make a dress. Anna's features applique at the neck.

and patterns printed on the wrappers around batting marketed by Mountain Mist. The prairie points on the rose quilt pictured also represent a favored finish.[67]

Clearly a skillful seamstress by age seventeen, Anna Schmidt Sperling and two of her future sisters-in-law, along with another good friend, took what was probably a six-week session at a sewing school in Moundridge, Kansas.[68] They made beautiful dresses for a graduation project. Later one of these sisters-in-law, Elizabeth Voth, frequently joined Anna to quilt.

Many of the Mennonite quiltmakers in the first half of this century got pattern ideas from such publications as the *Kansas City Star* and *Capper's Weekly*. The Amish, on the other hand, seemed to have chosen conserva-

tive patterns that did not conform to popular fads of the late nineteenth and early twentieth centuries.[69] The Mennonites did not necessarily order patterns but were often able to draft their own patterns by looking at pictures. Since many of the patterns used were variations of the nine-patch or four-patch block or a one patch of either squares or rectangles, drafting a pattern would not have been too difficult. Nearly 40 percent of pieced quilts documented through the KQP as made by Mennonites before 1960 were made in these basic patterns.

Quilting has become closely associated with the Mennonites and is now so much a part of their culture that its origins cannot be clearly seen. Today's quilters often learned as children from their mothers. Lydia Kauf-

Mission Circle, First Mennonite Church of Hillsboro, taken between 1908 and 1912, in front of the Kopper home. Mennonite Library and Archives, Bethel College, North Newton, Kansas.

man Goering recalls how fascinated she was, watching as her mother sat on the floor piecing together the tiny scraps of fabric: "What my mother did, I did, too."[70] They remember their mothers and grandmothers quilting on large wooden frames (tied to the backs of chairs or resting on sawhorses). Others remember quilting bees held when relatives who lived a distance away came for a visit or when friends just wanted to get together to share their work and time. The importance of family is evident in their quilts. One can see the family ties in the whole-cloth quilts of Helena Peters Ewert, in which the various aspects of the quiltmaking process were assumed by different members of a family. Elsewhere the lines of responsibility are more blurred. The women might all get together one day to cut pieces for a quilt and return

later to quilt the top after it was put together by one person.[71] This sharing included the trading of patterns as well as the techniques of quiltmaking.

Learning in these situations was informal, but its significance cannot be denied. It is possible to take many of the family genealogies and to chart through several generations a great number of quilters whose skills and generosity were well known. One family group, for example, includes Katharina Schrag Wedel, Ida J. C. Gehring Stucky (a niece by marriage), Asta Wedel Goering (a daughter), and Elma Goering Goering (a granddaughter). The sharing of patterns can be seen in their work: Asta Goering and her daughter, Elma, often worked together on quilts, sharing patterns for blocks and borders. They also shared techniques; Elma pieced a Grandmother's Flower Garden on the machine as her mother had done. These three quilters of the second and third generations all made quilts for charity in addition to the quilts they made for their families. Although Ida Stucky did not make quilts with a church mission society, her quilts or comforts were frequently given to people in the community who were in need.

Evidence of the Church's Influence on Quiltmaking

No matter where the first quilts by these Mennonites were made, there was and is a strong link between the church and quilting. In Europe, the church had been a major influence in the life-style of the Mennonites. In the United States, too, the church's influence can be seen in subtle and overt ways. The first Mennonite mission society officially organized in Kansas was the society at the First Mennonite Church at Halstead. The members of this church arrived in Kansas in 1874 through 1875, but many of them had come from Summerfield, Illinois. While in Illinois, these Mennonites had continued the tradition of a women's society and a children's society brought with them from Schleswig-Holstein, Germany. In 1881 or 1882, the Naehverein (women's sewing society) at Halstead provided bedding—possibly quilts and comforts—for an Indian Mission in Oklahoma where the school had been destroyed by fire.[72] This was probably one of the first major projects for this society, which was then newly organized, after having met informally for a time.[73]

The Russian Mennonites had also done missionary work in Russia, the women forming missionary sewing societies as early

as 1853.[74] So it was natural that the formation of mission societies came about rather quickly in this country. In the late fall of 1888, a women's sewing society was organized at the West Zion Mennonite Church in Moundridge.[75] The Alexanderwohl Missionary Society was formed in 1891 as a means to support a mission in Oklahoma by providing garments, bedding, and monetary gifts.[76] Other sewing societies were also formed during the late 1800s and the early 1900s. The *Bundesbote*, a General Conference Mennonite publication, listed seven sewing societies in 1889 and fourteen in 1891. The *Mennonite Year Book* of 1898 lists thirty-five such societies in the General Conference, eleven of them in Kansas.[77] These societies believed that in their handwork they might in some small way help to further their religious work. Their aim was to prove themselves, as van der Smissen says, "humble servants not only in the missionary cause but especially in the round of daily duties in [their] homes."[78]

At first they met in homes, often along with visiting missionaries who provided a rallying point for the women of the church. The organization was informal, but sewing and quilting were the usual occupations. While the women worked, scripture or devotional studies would be read. When the groups became too large to meet in homes and when the churches had added a basement or dining hall to the original structure, the societies moved into the churches.[79] Gradually, additional sewing societies might be organized in a church to assist the original society with its mission work, or they might be organized to include a younger group of women. In her

history of the mission societies, van der Smissen wrote that the girls in the Halstead children's society would meet one afternoon a month to sew, and during the summer they would meet for a day to quilt. As these young girls learned skill with the needle, they would listen to missionary stories. Similar children's societies were also established in Moundridge and Hillsboro.[80]

Sometimes the children's group would work in conjunction with the senior society in producing a quilt. One of the quilts (KQP Fc045) documented in Hillsboro was the result of just such an effort. The Helping Hands Mission Society, a group of girls twelve to fifteen years old, embroidered the quilt blocks in 1937; the Senior Ladies' Mission Society then quilted the top so that it could be sold at the mission bazaar in the basement of the First Mennonite Church, Hillsboro.[81]

The type of mission work already described is certainly not unique to Mennonites; Chapter 8 indicates how common such sewing societies are. A more distinctive example of the fund-raising effort supported by the mission societies is the Mennonite Central Committee (MCC) Relief Sale, which is held yearly in fifty different countries and in many sites across North America, including Hutchinson, Kansas. These various MCC sales have raised a significant amount of money for relief projects, such as the Mennonite Disaster Service, a cultural exchange program, and educational programs in developing countries that (like the Peace Corps) work to help communities become self-sustaining. The Kansas sale, which attracts thousands of Mennonites and non-Mennonites, is generally sched-

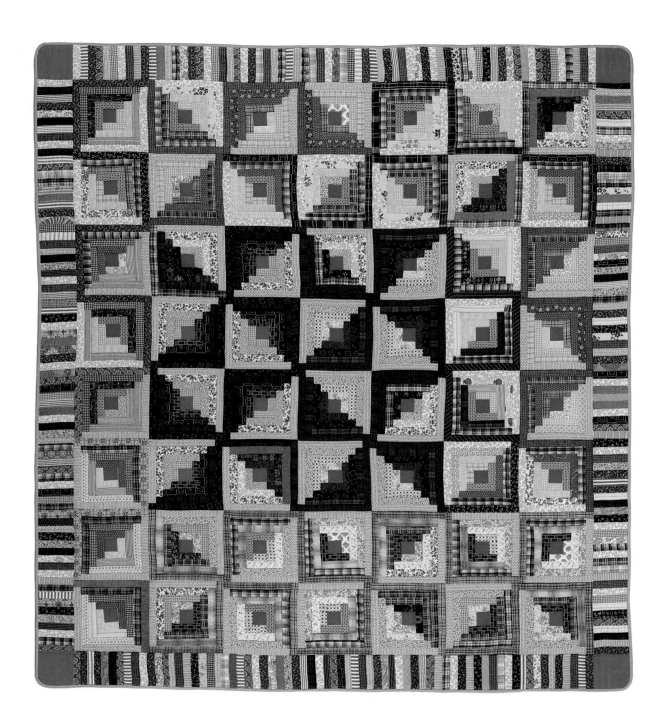

Sara Reimer Farley

Opposite: Pinwheel Log Cabin, by Sara Stucky Daum, McPherson, McPherson County, 1982. Cotton. Collection of Sara Stucky Daum.

This quilt exemplifies a number of the characteristics attributed to Mennonite quilts. An example of frugality, the quilt is made from the scrap bag of Emilie Goering Stucky, Sara's mother. The pattern chosen is simple to construct, but the arrangement of colors is nevertheless striking. The top was quilted at a Work-and-Play Camp at Camp Mennoscah, a Mennonite church camp near Kingman. This camp meeting, held yearly for women and men over sixty years of age in the Western District Conference of the General Conference, is an opportunity for these people to work on a project as a community. The men do maintenance at the church camp grounds while the women quilt. The completed quilt is then sold at the Mennonite Relief sale sponsored by the Mennonite Central Committee each year in Hutchinson. This quilt, too, was sold at auction—it was purchased by the maker because her youngest brother, Willard, upon seeing the scraps of his mother's dresses and aprons, said, "We can't give it up." So Sara bought her own quilt back!

Jacob and Sara Stucky Daum, 1986.

uled for the second week of April. Situated at the Kansas State Fairgrounds since 1971, the sale has various booths (including crafts donated by Mennonites, crafts sold for craft collectives from developing countries, and ethnic food) in addition to the auctions.

The centerpiece of the sale is, of course, the quilt auction; receipts from it total approximately $100,000, one-fourth of all goods sold. Pieced, applique, and whole-cloth quilts are donated by church groups of the various Kansas Mennonite denominations and by individuals from Kansas and other states. Current trends among the Mennonites are evident in this sale. Pieced quilts dominate the donated quilts; whole-cloth quilts represent a much smaller portion (in 1990 only 21 of the 154 quilts were whole-cloth; 115 were pieced). The Mennonites do take advantage of the preprinted fabric, although this fabric is used more often in comforts than in quilts. Approximately 150 to 170 quilts are sold each year in addition to comforts, wallhangings, and afghans.

These MCC sales are a recent phenomenon and stem from similar sales conducted at earlier dates by individual churches. In this area of Kansas the earliest sale was the one held in 1889, at Ebenfeld Mennonite Brethren, rural Hillsboro. Other churches like Hoffnungsau, rural Inman, and Eden Mennonite, rural Moundridge, also had sales.[82] The women in these churches were and are living out the Mennonite conviction that it is not enough to believe in Christ but that one's faith must be a living commitment that results in service to both spiritual and material needs of people. That their faith

was a way of life is demonstrated as well in the process of their quiltmaking, from the choice of pattern to the quilting itself. For example, Sara Stucky Daum embroidered her family's favorite Bible verses on a quilt she made in the late 1930s. Quilters also chose patterns with religious names: Joseph's Coat, Star of Bethlehem, Rose of Sharon, Jacob's Ladder, Crosses. In choosing these patterns, Mennonites were not, of course, unique, for these were popular patterns among quilters of other ethnic and religious backgrounds.

The Mennonite women would use their quilting time—both at church and at home—to reflect on God and to study the scripture. The tradition of listening to scripture or devotions while doing needlework was common from their evenings of spinning in Russia and from the informal meetings of a church's sewing society. Individual quiltmakers followed this practice as well.

Those individual quilters who made quilts at home often donated them to missions or to church sales. Some of these quilters preferred to do their quilting as a solitary occupation or perhaps as a family endeavor. One of the many Mennonite women who made mission quilts, Lydia Kaufman Goering, remembers the emphasis on practicality. The quilts must be durable, but in order to make large numbers, they must also be of simple enough design so that a limited amount of time was required. She remembers that for these quilts many different scraps were used and the material was cut into simple shapes, often squares, that could easily be pieced together on the machine and then quilted or tied.[83] Other quilters

KQP Fa051, Kansas, attributed to Maria Preheim Graber (1842–1929), Moundridge, McPherson County, 1890–1925. Cotton.

The pattern appeared in Hearth & Home *magazine ca. 1910, contributed by a reader who called herself Sunflower Sue. This pieced quilt, now faded red and brown, is well worn. Whether its maker chose the pattern for its name is not known, but Kansas did provide a welcome home for these German-Russian immigrants in the 1870s.*

Sara Reimer Farley

might have their favorite patterns, like Rail Fence, which they could vary by changing the dominant colors or the size of the block. Because they were repeating the pattern, the patchwork could be done quickly.

Since 1874, when these German-Russians immigrated to Kansas soil seeking freedom to live their faith, their churches have helped to shape the quiltmaking tradition. If some of the women first learned quiltmaking from their neighbors, they passed this instruction along through the mission sewing societies. The many quilts made by the Kansas Mennonites as part of a mission effort either to further church work at home or in the mission field clearly represent an ideology that emphasizes attending to the material as well as the spiritual needs of people.

Conclusion

This study has not exhausted the material available on Mennonite quiltmakers nor has it provided definitive answers for all of the questions with which it began. The linguistic evidence cited, the absence of authenticated quilts brought from Russia, and the memories of some immigrants or their daughters that quilting was not known in Russia all point to Kansas as the place where these German-Russian Mennonite women learned to quilt. Additional material as yet uncovered in letters or diaries, held in old trunks, or captured in stories of Russia handed down to younger generations may provide new leads. This study represents a basis for future investigations and underscores the significance of the church to the continuing development of the Mennonite quilting tradition.

Notes

1. Judy Schroeder Tomlonson, *Mennonite Quilts and Pieces* (Intercourse, Pa.: Good Books, 1985); Sondra B. Koontz and Kay Stine Morse, "Kansas Mennonite Quiltmakers," MLA-MS-V33, Mennonite Library and Archives, Bethel College, North Newton, Kansas, 1986. Hereafter referred to as MLA.

2. The Mennonite denominations include General Conference Mennonites; Mennonite Brethren; Church of God in Christ, Mennonite (Holdeman); Mennonite Church; Conservative Mennonite; Brethren in Christ; Beachy Amish; Evangelical Mennonite; Fellowship of Evangelical Bible Church; and Old Order Amish (*Mennonite Yearbook Directory, 1990–1991* [Scottsdale, Pa.: Mennonite Publishing House, 1990], 22–23). With the exception of the Old Order Amish (not listed in the *Yearbook*), the denominations are arranged here according to the number of congregations in Kansas.

3. A good history of the movements of the Swiss Mennonites is Martin H. Schrag, *The European History of the Swiss Mennonites from Volhynia* (North Newton, Kans.: Mennonite Press, 1974).

4. The name for this region is somewhat problematic. Except for places where my sources have specifically used the name Ukraine, I have chosen to use South Russia. However, when discussing regional textile traditions, I have consistently used Ukraine because that is the clearest reference for those regional traditions.

5. Lesia Danchenko, comp., *Folk Art from the Ukraine*, trans. Arthur Shkarovsky-Raffe (Leningrad: Aurora Art Publishers, 1982), 28–29.

6. Schrag, *The European History of the Swiss Mennonites from Volhynia*, 81.

7. Melvin Gingerich, "Alexanderwohl 'Schnurbuch,'" *Mennonite Life* 1 (January 1946): 45–48.

8. Melvin Gingerich, "The Reactions of the Russian Mennonite Immigrants of the 1870's to the American Frontier," *Mennonite Quarterly Review* 34 (April 1960): 137.

9. Albert Gaeddert, *Centennial History of Hoffnungsau Mennonite Church* (North Newton, Kans.: Mennonite Press, n.d.), 36, 39. According to Keith L. Bryant, Jr., the average price in 1874–1875 for Santa Fe

lands was higher—$5.59 per acre (*History of the Atchison, Topeka & Santa Fe Railway* [Lincoln: University of Nebraska Press, 1974], 69). The price the Mennonites paid was significantly lower. Elder Dietrich Gaeddert's "Application for Land" dated 1874 shows a price of $1.65 per acre, MLA-MS-7 (Dietrich Gaeddert collection), MLA. The family records of Jacob Schrag note a price of $2.50: Ed G. Kaufman, comp., *The Jacob Schrag Family Record 1836–1974* (North Newton, Kans.: Bethel College, 1974), 24.

10. P. P. Wedel, *A Short History of the Swiss Mennonites (Schweizer-Mennoniten) Who Migrated from Wolhynien, Russia to America and Settled in Kansas in 1874*, trans. Mr. and Mrs. Benj. B. J. Goering (n.p., 1960), 58.

11. Ibid., 40. The sale of household items by later immigrants as well is recalled by Kroeker, who noted: "Our sewing machines and clocks having passed from father to son, everything heavy such as books we read and loved, had all to be left to make room for refuges [sic]" (N. J. Kroeker, *First Mennonite Villages in Russia, 1789–1943* [Vancouver, B.C.: N. J. Kroeker, 1981]), 234.

12. A combination of calligraphy and illumination practiced by the Dutch German Mennonites in Europe.

13. Cited by David V. Wiebe, *They Seek a Country: A Survey of Mennonite Migrations with Special Reference to Kansas and Gnadenau* (Hillsboro, Kans.: The Mennonite Brethren Publishing House, 1959), 79.

14. Noble L. Prentis, "The Mennonites at Home," *Kansas Miscellanies* (Topeka: Kansas Publishing House, 1889), 151.

15. Wiebe, *They Seek a Country*, 153–154.

16. Katharine Nickel, *Seed from the Ukraine* (New York: Pageant Press, 1952), 16, 98.

17. P. P. Wedel, *A Short History of the Swiss Mennonites*, 24–25. Types of material available in the Ukraine during the 1800s are described in Danchenko, *Folk Art from the Ukraine*, 28. The Mennonite silk industry is discussed by M. S. Harder, "A Pioneer Educator—Johann Cornies," *Mennonite Life* 3 (October 1948): 6. Kroeker, *First Mennonite Villages in Russia*, 104, noted that

by 1840 the silk industry had become a positive economic factor for the Mennonites, and he described the mechanization of the spinning process. Silk was also produced by individuals. In the early 1900s, Agnes Dueck Wall (1894–1973), a professional seamstress of Blumenort, Molotschna, raised silkworms, unraveling the threads from the cocoons for spinning. After dying the thread, Agnes used it for knitting and crocheting. Mary Wall Wiens, interview with author, Hillsboro, Kansas, August 25, 1988.

18. Abe J. Unruh, *The Helpless Poles* (Grabill, Ind.: Courier Printing Co., 1973), 103.

19. Tomlonson, *Mennonite Quilts and Pieces*, 8.

20. Stanley A. Kaufman with Ricky Clark, *Germanic Folk Culture in Eastern Ohio* (Walnut Creek, Ohio: German Culture Museum, 1986), 2, 32.

21. This conclusion was based on interviews with the descendants of the émigrés. Nancy Lou Patterson, *Swiss-German and Dutch-German Mennonite Traditional Art in the Waterloo Region, Ontario*, National Museum of Man Mercury Series, no. 27 (Ottawa: National Museums of Canada, 1979), 37, 41.

22. P. P. Wedel, *A Short History of the Swiss Mennonites*, 30–31.

23. Kroeker, *First Mennonite Villages in Russia*, 102–104.

24. P. P. Wedel, *A Short History of the Swiss Mennonites*, 24–25.

25. Kroeker, *First Mennonite Villages in Russia*, 106–107.

26. Wiens interview. Agnes Dueck Wall, Mary's mother, was a seamstress trained in Hauptstadt, Ukraine, between 1910 and 1915.

27. Ibid.

28. Alexander and Barbara Pronin, *Russian Folk Art* (New York: A. S. Barnes, 1975), 150.

29. Walter Quiring, "Cultural Interactions among the Mennonites in Russia," *Mennonite Life* 24 (April 1969): 64.

30. Rachel K. Pannabecker, Collections Manager, Kauffman Museum, interview with author, North Newton, Kansas, March 4, 1988. She directed me to two sources: M. G. A. Schipper van Lottum, *Over Merklappen Gesproken: De Geschiedenis van de Nederlandse Merklap Vooral Belicht Vanuit Noord-Holland* (Amsterdam: Wereldbibliotheek,

1980); and Alberta Meulenbelt-Nieuwburg, comp., *Embroidery Motifs from Old Dutch Samplers*, trans. Patricia Wardle and Gillian Downing (New York: Charles Scribner's Sons, 1974).

31. Karen Peterson and J. J. Wilson, *Women Artists: Recognition and Reappraisal from the Early Middle Ages to the Twentieth Century* (New York: Harper and Row, 1976), 112.

32. Sonia and Robert Delaunay, *The New Art of Color: The Writings of Robert and Sonia Delaunay*, ed. Arthur A. Cohen, trans. David Shapiro and Arthur A. Cohen (New York: The Viking Press, 1978), 198, 210.

33. Cornelius and Agnes Wall, *As We Remember* (Hillsboro, Kans.: Mennonite Brethren Publishing House, 1979), 41.

34. Wiens interview, August 25, 1988.

35. Rachel K. Pannabecker, Collections Manager, Kauffman Museum, letter to author, February 17, 1988; Tomlonson, *Mennonite Quilts and Pieces*, 8.

36. Edna Nyquist, *Pioneer Life and Lore of McPherson County, Kansas* (McPherson, Kans.: Democrat-Opinion Press, 1932), 116.

37. Woman's Kansas Day Club, *Homesteaders and Other Early-Day Kansans*, vol. 2 (January 1978), 41–42; Moundridge Centennial Committee, *Century One: History of Moundridge, Kansas, 1887–1987* (Newton, Kans.: Mennonite Press, 1987), 248–249. Drusilla Cole's obituary underscored her contributions to the community (*Moundridge Journal*, February 14, 1918).

38. Drusilla Cole's granddaughter, Grace Newcom Kutnink, remembers that her grandmother often quilted. She quilted alone, with a group of women from the Methodist Church, and at quilting bees in her home with neighbors and friends. Grace Newcom Kutnink, interview with author, Moundridge, Kansas, March 27, 1991.

39. Elma Goering Goering, interview with author, Moundridge, Kansas, October 27, 1988.

40. Henry King, "A Mennonite Village in Kansas in 1879," *Scribner's Monthly* 19 (November 1879): 135. King described the long line of houses and compared it to the more random placement of houses employed by other homesteaders. C. B.

Schmidt, in addition to illustrating the Mennonite settlements, also pointed out the inconvenience that resulted from following the Russian pattern. *Die Deutschen Ansiedlungen in Süd West Kansas auf den Länderein der Atchison, Topeka und Santa Fe Eisenbahngesellschaft* (Halstead, Kans.: Westlichen Publikations Gesellschaft, 1878), 11, 14, 26.

41. Noble L. Prentis, "A Day with the Mennonites," *Kansas Miscellanies* (Topeka: Kansas Publishing House, 1889), 159.

42. Margarete Jansen, *Tagebuch* [Diary], February 21, 1866, MLA-MS-30 (Cornelius Jansen collection), MLA.

43. Almuth Schröder, *Textilarbelt und Unterricht*, vol. 1 (February 1987): 20.

44. The word *quilt* is given a German verb ending, but is still enclosed in quotation marks in Hillegonda v[an] d[er] Smissen, *The History of Our Missionary Societies* (n.p., n.d.), 29–30. *Die Abendschule*, a German-language newspaper published in St. Louis, consistently changed its typeface for the word *quilt* and English names of quilts (cf. April 6 and June 29, 1899).

45. Gustav E. Reimer and G. R. Gaeddert, *Exiled by the Czar: Cornelius Jansen and the Great Mennonite Migration, 1874* (Newton, Kans.: Mennonite Publication Office, 1956), 171. Margarete Jansen's diary entries for January 19 and 21, 1866, among others, include the use of the English title.

46. Anna Jansen, *Tagebuch eines alten Fräuleins* [Diary], MLA-MS-30 (Cornelius Jansen Collection), MLA.

47. H. P. Peters, *History and Development of Education among the Mennonites* (Hillsboro, Kans.: n.p., 1925), 25–30. A teacher taking the county exam did not always know English; H. R. Voth, who had some English training, would sometimes act as an interpreter. Cited by David A. Haury, *Prairie People: A History of the Western District Conference* (Newton, Kans.: Faith and Life Press, 1981), 82–84.

48. Haury, *Prairie People*, 482; P. J. Wedel, "Beginning of Secondary Education in Kansas," *Mennonite Life* 3 (October 1948): 14–15.

49. Kaufman and Clark, *Germanic Folk Culture in Eastern Ohio*, 6–7, 21.

50. Mission and Sunday School

records of the Ebenfeld Mennonite Brethren Church, Jacob Loewen, Jr., treasurer, Center for Mennonite Brethren Studies, Tabor College, Hillsboro, Kansas.

51. See *The Ebenfeld Church in Action, 1876–1976* (Hillsboro, Kans.: n.p., 1976), 16; and Solomon Leppke Loewen, *History and Genealogy of the Jacob Loewen Family* (Hillsboro, Kans.: Multi Business Press, 1983), 107–108. It should be noted that the German word *Decke* is rather ambiguous. It denotes a covering, but the items called by this name can range from a comforter to a quilt to a fancy bed covering or even to a table covering or rug.

52. Susie Esau, interview with author, Hillsboro, Kansas, October 18, 1988.

53. Numerous examples of quilts made in the first half of the nineteenth century are shown in Ricky Clark, George W. Knepper, and Ellice Ronsheim, *Quilts in Community: Ohio's Traditions* (Nashville: Rutledge Hill Press, 1991).

54. Kaufman and Clark, *Germanic Folk Culture in Eastern Ohio*, 21–22. Eve Wheatcroft Granick pointed out that quiltmaking was probably more affected by the "unwritten portion of the *Ordnung*. . . . Rather than rules, these are generally held perceptions about the proper way to make a quilt" (*The Amish Quilt* [Intercourse, Pa.: Good Books, 1989], 15).

55. Many researchers have pointed to the absence of such a tradition, combining quilting and piecing, in Germany; see Schnuppe von Gwinner, *The History of the Patchwork Quilt: Origins, Traditions and Symbols of a Textile Art* (Westchester, Pa.: Schiffer Publishing, 1988). Others have pointed to the strong influence of the U.S. communities where German immigrants settled as evidence that quilting was learned here; see Barbara Brackman, "The Strip Tradition in European-American Quilts," *The Clarion* 14 (Fall 1989): 41–51. The absence of quilts in inventories of the early Amish and Pennsylvania Dutch settlers was noted by Granick, *The Amish Quilt*, 29–32, and by Alan G. Keyser, "Beds, Bedding, Bedsteads, and Sleep," *Pieced by Mother: Symposium Papers*, ed. Jeannette Lasansky (Lewisburg, Pa.: Oral Traditions Project, 1988), 23-32.

56. Granick, *The Amish Quilt*, 36–37, 39.

57. Esau interview. The date given at this interview conflicts with information supplied at the Quilt Discovery Day in Hillsboro. The information originally submitted attributes this quilt to the early 1890s with scraps from tailor Peter Jost, a brother to the maker. The ca. 1915–1920 date is more likely, however, because Susie remembers seeing her mother work on the quilt when she (Susie) came home from school. Susie Esau (1902–   ) was the youngest of the eight children.

58. For information on dating quilts by prints, dyes, style, and pattern, see Barbara Brackman, "Dating Old Quilts," *Quilters Newsletter Magazine* (September, October, November-December 1984, January, February, March 1985). I became aware of this source through a training session on quilt documentation taught by Dorothy Cozart, Wichita, Kansas, February 7, 1987.

59. Sondra Koontz and Kay Morse, "The Mennonite Central Committee Relief Sale," paper presented at the Kansas Quilt Project Symposium, Topeka, July 9, 1988.

60. Patterson, *Swiss-German and Dutch-German Mennonite Traditional Art*, 148.

61. Ethel Ewert Abrahams, interview with author, Hillsboro, Kansas, July 25, 1988.

62. Clark, Knepper, and Ronsheim, *Quilts in Community*, 35, 42.

63. Barbara Brackman, *Clues in the Calico: A Guide to Identifying and Dating Antique Quilts* (McLean, Va.: EPM Publications, 1989), 126.

64. Abrahams interview.

65. Georgie Ann Regier Schmidt, letter to author, March 20, 1991.

66. Abrahams interview.

67. Irene Thiessen, interview with author, Inman, Kansas, June 30, 1988.

68. Goessel, Kansas, was first identified as the site of this school in an interview with Thiessen, June 30, 1988. However, Thiessen later reported that the daughter of Elizabeth Sperling Voth remembered her mother naming Moundridge as the location. Moundridge is much closer and therefore a more likely site. Irene Thiessen, letter to author, March 22, 1991.

69. Granick, *The Amish Quilt*, 31, 76.

70. Lydia Kaufman Goering, interview with author, Moundridge, Kansas, June 30, 1988.

71. These family get-togethers were described in interviews with Ethel Ewert Abrahams, Hillsboro, Kansas, July 25, 1988; Sara Stucky Daum and Linda Stucky Oberst, McPherson, Kansas, July 22, 1988; Elma Goering Goering, Moundridge, Kansas, October 27, 1988; and Esther J. Stucky and Susan Good, Peabody, Kansas, August 10, 1989.

72. Smissen, *The History of Our Missionary Societies*, 20.

73. C. E. Krehbiel, "Historical Sketch: First Mennonite Church, Halstead, Kansas," *Mennonite Weekly Review*, May 5, 1925, 3–4, 57.

74. Harley J. Stucky, *A Century of Russian Mennonite History in America: A Study of Cultural Interactions* (North Newton, Kans.: Mennonite Press, 1973), 10, 14.

75. Moundridge Centennial Committee, *Century One*, 152.

76. Smissen, *The History of Our Missionary Societies*, 17.

77. *Mennonite Year Book and Almanac for 1898*, 22. Smissen cited the figures from the *Bundesbote*, although I have not been able to verify them.

78. Smissen, *The History of Our Missionary Societies*, 19.

79. Gladys V. Goering, *Women in Search of Mission* (Newton, Kans.: Faith and Life Press, 1980), 103–105.

80. Smissen, *The History of Our Missionary Societies*, 29–30.

81. Kansas Quilt Project, April 25, 1987, Kansas State Historical Society, Topeka, Kansas.

82. Irene Thiessen, interview with author, Inman, Kansas, June 30, 1988.

83. Lydia Kaufman Goering, interview with author, Moundridge, Kansas, June 30, 1988.

Georgia Patton of Kansas City.

Chapter Seven

African American Quiltmaking Traditions: Some Assumptions Reviewed

Jennie A. Chinn

LIKE OTHER STATES, KANSAS HAS A RICH HERITAGE OF AFRICAN AMERICAN QUILTMAKING. BLACK WOMEN BROUGHT WITH THEM TO KANSAS NOT ONLY THEIR QUILTS BUT THEIR KNOWLEDGE AND SKILLS, WHICH THEY PASSED ON FROM MOTHER TO DAUGHTER AND NEIGHBOR TO NEIGHBOR. WHAT WE SEE IN KANSAS AMONG African American quiltmakers is the result of an unbroken tradition transmitted through time and space. Black quiltmakers have not been immune to the popular trends in quiltmaking, however, so quilts made in the African American neighborhoods and communities of Kansas are produced by the same process as found among other ethnic groups, resulting in a diversity of styles and aesthetics.

Research on African American Quiltmaking

Since 1970 there has been a growing interest in the art of African American quiltmaking. Credit must be given to early researchers such as Roland Freeman, Gladys-Marie Fry, Eli Leon, Robert Ferris Thompson, John Vlach, and Maude Wahlman, who pioneered the study of African American quiltmaking traditions. The main point shared by these authors is that the quilts reflect a common African American style, thought by some to be distinguished by its improvisational nature and often linked to African textiles through perceived aesthetic similarities. The conclusions reached to date concerning African American quiltmaking traditions, however, have been based on rather limited data. As further research brings more information to light, we must question whether some scholars, in their haste to celebrate the African American quilting tradition, have drawn understandable but erroneous conclusions.

Quilt historian Cuesta Benberry has called on scholars to broaden their view of African American quiltmaking traditions. In an article in *American Quilter*, Benberry wrote, "There was a rush to judgement, and the findings were extrapolated to have wider meaning than the evidence would support."[1] Nowhere is this more apparent than in the attempts made to establish the characteristics of a single African American quiltmaking style. Even though it is recognized that there is a wide range of acceptable behavior within any given group,[2] researchers in general often find themselves looking for absolutes in human behavior. This is a natural desire, as most of us find such set solutions to be more satisfying than the seemingly amorphous behaviors that we often encounter. In searching for like behaviors, however, researchers are often guilty of ignoring data that does not fit the perceived pattern. A danger also exists in viewing groups or communities as if they are homogeneous. In other words, the assumption is frequently made that all members of the group conform equally to a similar cultural standard. The answers generated from such research are then used to make historical and social generalizations.

This is not to say that patterns of human behavior do not exist. However, before generalizations are completed an exhaustive study of the evidence at hand must be made so that research results can be tested on a comparative basis. It is important that the case not be overstated or that universal judgments not be made when the data examined apply to a much smaller sphere. It is also crucial that exceptions to the rule be noted and included as part of the conclusions.

Such problems of oversimplification are often found within the literature of quiltmaking. Because this is partly the result of a limited amount of data, efforts such as the Kansas Quilt Project have been designed to add large quantities of information to the data base. Other problems arise from the fact that for too long we have studied only the objects themselves—the quilts—to gain insights. Although these objects are of great importance, they are not the only information at hand. Other primary source materials, such as diaries, census records, and oral histories, must be woven together to reveal a more-balanced view of quiltmaking traditions.

All of these issues become even more complex when dealing with aesthetics.[3] Aesthetic principles are based on taste. Individual tastes are influenced by many factors, and when dealing with aesthetics it must be remembered that there are always at least two sides to any question. The quilt-maker has her own aesthetic response to her work that guides her choice of such elements as fabric and design. Her own taste upon which the aesthetic response is based is derived from her value system, which in turn is developed from her varying roles and identities. These identities are in turn linked to memberships in various communities. Among these would be ethnic, religious, occupational, generational, and familial communities. However, the audience—the viewer or user of the quilt—also has an aesthetic response. These two responses are never exactly the same, although they can be similar.

Folklorists often speak of the "community aesthetic" that guides the work of folk artists. The idea is that the community within which the artist works sets the aesthetic guidelines, and the artist makes creative choices within those boundaries. Therefore the process and the work produced are understandable to all of those who share the same community value system. If an individual cannot understand the aesthetic choices made in the creation of a quilt, then it often means that he or she is standing on the outside looking in, trying to impose his or her own aesthetic values and guidelines on the piece of work. Sometimes a misunderstanding results either in a dislike of the work or in an enthusiasm that is based on the outsider's taste rather than on the tastes of the community. Folklorists maintain that if a quiltmaker is working within a particular community tradition, her quilts should be judged within the standards set by the community aesthetic.

All of the above issues are especially relevant in reviewing the scholarship concerning the work of African American quiltmakers. There have been at least four major assumptions about African American quiltmaking traditions: (1) the assumption that quilts made by African Americans can be detected by a physical examination of the object alone, (2) the assumption of cultural homogeneity, (3) the assumption of African origins, and (4) the assumption that the elements of one culture can remain unaffected by exposure to other cultures.

Folklorist John Vlach was an early researcher of African American textile traditions. In his work, *The Afro-American Tradition in Decorative Arts*, Vlach stated, "It is because of the continued existence of African ideas in America that Afro-American traditions continue to flourish. . . . Material artifacts—like verbal and musical creations—are based on ideas, an African idea may motivate the making of an object which itself is perceived as Anglo-American. Objects which are describably African starkly and directly assert themselves as black creations. Where Afro-American influences are of a stylistic nature, the impact of black traditions is more subtle."[4] It was Vlach's premise that in quilting we see Euro-American objects transformed by African design patterns. Like other researchers, he divided African American quilts into two categories based on the techniques of applique and strip piecing.

As is the case with researchers that followed Vlach, he based much of his discussion of applique quilts on two story quilts made by Harriet Powers, who was born into slavery in Georgia

in 1837. Her two story quilts survive in major museums in the United States.[5] For some, Mrs. Powers's quilts can be linked stylistically to the tapestries made by the Fon people of Abomey, the ancient capital of Dahomey, West Africa. Vlach also saw a possible link between the work of Mrs. Powers and that of West African artisans, but he was careful to qualify his statements.

The applique techniques used by Mrs. Powers are generally similar to methods known both in Europe and Africa. Textiles in Europe have been decorated with appliqued designs since the medieval period and have been reported from Africa since the seventeenth century. . . .
Hence, there are two simultaneous sources of support for Mrs. Powers' creative effort. Born in Georgia in 1837, Mrs. Powers would necessarily have received her heritage of Africa by example (the source of which is unknown) or by verbal description. Mrs. Powers' ancestors apparently arrived in Georgia late in the eighteenth or early in the nineteenth century. By that time most slaves were being imported from the Congo-Angola region, although a steady trickle were still entering from West Africa. This is important because the African traditions of appliqued textiles are practiced only by groups from that part of the continent. The presence of West African slaves in Georgia makes it possible, then, to link Mrs. Powers' quilts to African aesthetic systems.[6]

Perhaps the key word in Vlach's statement is "possible," when he referred to the link between the quilts of Mrs. Powers and the African aesthetic systems. Vlach went on to call Mrs. Powers's work a probable "amalgam" of African influences rather than a style that can be traced to one ethnic community.

The second category of quilts cited by Vlach was the pieced quilt—specifically the strip pieced quilt.

Although black quilters have made all manner of pieced quilts, often using the same approaches as Euro-American quiltmakers, the strip technique is the method found most frequently in Afro-America. It has been observed in black communities in coastal South Carolina, southwestern Georgia, Alabama, Mississippi, Tennessee, southern Maryland, and in Washington D.C., and Philadelphia. This wide distribution makes the strip quilt the most commonplace domestic example of black material culture in the United States. Why a single approach to the task of quilting should be so dominant among Afro-American quiltmakers may be traced to the retention of design concepts found in African textiles.[7]

Vlach made an important statement here when he expressed the view that African American quiltmakers create all types of quilts. This sentiment appears to have been lost in more recent works by other scholars. Vlach did, however, see a direct link between the strip pattern in West African textiles and the strip construction of a particular type of quilt made by African American women.

Vlach also discussed the concept of improvisation in African American quiltmaking styles. In his view, improvisation, which is characterized by a refusal to simply repeat a pattern in its exact form, giving the artist the chance to play with form and pattern, was the basis of all African American creativity. Although Vlach was careful to qualify his statements, there is no doubt that he saw a West African influence on African American quiltmaking traditions. For this influence to exist, aspects of African culture must be retained in the cultural traditions of the African American people. "What may in the end be regarded as the most important feature of Afro-American quilting is the apparent refusal to simply surrender an alternative aesthetic sense to the confines of mainstream expectations. Euro-American forms were converted so that African ideas would not be lost."[8]

The scholar most often quoted on the subject of African American quiltmaking traditions is art historian Maude Wahlman. It appears her work was at least in part inspired by art historian Robert Farris Thompson. There was no doubt in Thompson's mind that a strong link existed between African textiles and North American quilt tops made by African American women. According to Thompson, "The cultural inheritance, it seems to me, for good reasons both stylistic and demographic, may include elements of Mande and Akan and possibly Efik influences but is in the main probably overwhelmingly Central African."[9] Thompson's belief that African American quilts are derived from Central African influences is in contrast to other scholars such as Vlach who claim the influence is from West Africa, the original home of many American slaves.

It is important to note that Thompson was looking at African American quilts within the context of art history, basing his analysis primarily on the objects themselves, although he might claim otherwise.

From Africa streamed to North America a percussive manner of handling textile color. Colors coordinate by clashing. Colors make their entrance in full sonority; they attack the eye with high-decibel reverberations. That this metaphoric linking of cloth and percussion is present in the minds of the quilt-makers themselves (as opposed to the art historian) is suggested in certain of their quilting terms. . . . When a black quilter talks, then, about "hitting" her quilt-top with color-coordinating or color-clashing passages that is her way of linking her work to the well-known dominance of a percussive mode of performance in African-American music history.[10]

In Thompson's words, "black quilters have their own lexicon. They have their own verbs of formal aesthetic analysis."[11] He based this belief on what can best be called a limited amount of fieldwork. The term of *hitting* the quilt is, by Thompson's own admission, recorded from only one quiltmaker. This is not to say that special language does not exist among quiltmakers, both black and white. However, with the data at hand it is a stretch to say that the "linking of cloth and percussion is present in the minds of the quilt-makers themselves," based on the language of one quiltmaker. Even if the term *hitting* were in widespread use,

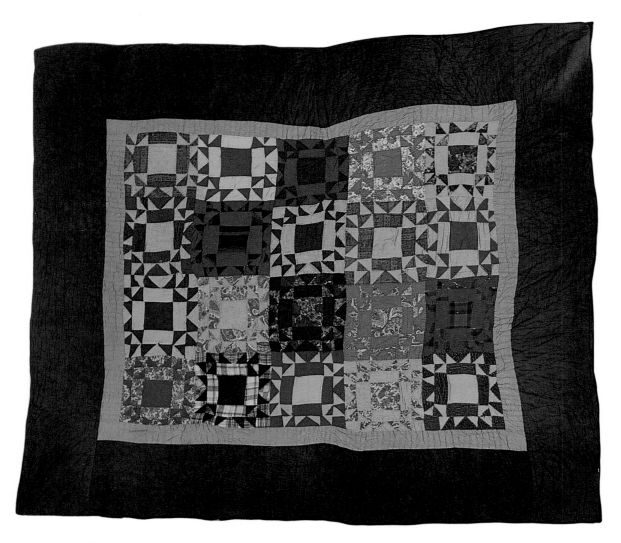

Rob Peter to Pay Paul, anonymous, Lawrence, inscribed 1965. Pieced and quilted cottons, wools, and polyester. Collection of Jon Gierlich.

The side-by-side colors with no neutrals, the use of a variety of home sewing scraps, the casual construction techniques, and the off-beat patterning might indicate to some that this quilt had African American origins. However, the maker was of Scotch-Irish and Russian Jewish ancestry, and her quilt might best be described as a product of the fabrics, taste, and standards of the 1960s.

Thompson's conclusion appears to be based on his own definition of the term. Not enough field-work has been done to interpret the communities' understanding of the link between varying forms of expressive behaviors.

However, Thompson did make a case that African American quiltmaking traditions involve the "off-beat phrasing of geometric accents." He argued that this was akin to the tap dancing phrase of "shading the count" and saw this as the factor that typified the African American quilt. "Black women thus make their measurements move for them. They shade the count. They play the fabric. They build their covers with heart and mind. The aim is innovation and discovery of new ways of seeing pattern."[12] These are concepts articulated by an outsider, not by the women themselves. It is true that quiltmakers—both black and white—use phrases that might be linked to other forms of expressive behavior, but evidence suggests that this connection is made by the researcher, not by the artists themselves. Therefore such a connection is at best speculative.

Maude Wahlman, in an article with John Scully, took Thompson's work a step further and sought to spell out the aesthetic principles that characterized an African American quilt. It is interesting to note that the authors claimed that "most contemporary Afro-American quilters are middle-aged to elderly women, living mainly in the South. . . . The tradition may be dying out with the decline of farming and the access it provided to raw cotton."[13] This statement alone reveals an extremely limited data base. The focus of Wahlman and Scully's work was the strip pieced quilt,

which they connected to West African textile production. In their view, the aesthetic principles used by African American quiltmakers could be reduced to five elements. "Afro-American aesthetic principles involve both technical knowledge and artistic choices and can be characterized by the use of five elements: (1) strips to construct and to organize quilt top design space; (2) large scale designs; (3) strong, highly contrasting colors; (4) off-beat patterns; (5) multiple rhythms."[14]

The authors referred to the "strip"—used aesthetically as well as structurally—as the most apparent characteristic of African American quilts. In their view, African Americans used large designs in their quilts and showed a preference for "strong bright colors." The concepts of off-beat patterning and multiple rhythms were taken from the work of Robert Farris Thompson. However, unlike Thompson—who implied that the quiltmakers are consciously aware of these principles and articulated them in their specialized vocabulary—Wahlman and Scully wrote, "One gets the impression that this tendency toward multiple rhythms is part of the unconscious, casual, intuitive approach."[15]

By creating a shopping list of traits found in quilts made by African Americans, Wahlman and Scully appeared to be making the assumption that a quilt could be identified as black simply by an examination of its physical appearance. This assumption is reinforced when the authors concluded, "These complex aesthetic principles, which seem most basic to Afro-American quilts, are not found in other American quilts."[16] The question must be asked, what other American

quilts are the authors speaking of? If they had a more complete knowledge of American quilts, it is doubtful that such a statement would have been made. It is not difficult to locate quilts made by white women that meet Wahlman and Scully's criteria for African American quilt production.

It may be speculated that since the authors were writing in the early 1980s they were comparing what they characterized as African American aesthetic principles to a particular genre of American quiltmaking. In the 1980s America was in the middle of a major quilt revival, during which guilds, quilt shops, and contests flourished. With this revival, which took place primarily among white middle-class women, came the articulation of a particular quiltmaking aesthetic that was defined on a national, popular level. In order to hold contests, sell publications, and promote specialty shops, some standardization is necessary. Since 1970 this standardization placed an emphasis on such things as controlled patterns, harmonious colors, calico cotton prints, and tight and accurate workmanship. The black quiltmakers studied by Wahlman and Scully appeared to be unaffected by the popular quilt revival; therefore it is inaccurate to compare their work to such a standard. A more correct comparison would be between the work of the African American quiltmakers studied and quilts made by groups of white women who lived in isolation from the quilt revival or quilts made in the 1950s and 1960s before this most recent revival began. The difficulty here is that in-depth studies of this parallel white quiltmaking tradition are not plentiful, so comparison is not easy.

The assertion that the assembling of quilt tops from strips of fabric is derived from African origins must be examined. To begin with, the techniques cited as precedents by these authors are not the same as those practiced in the New World. African strip textiles are assembled from strips of woven cloth selvage to selvage, not pieced of fabric cuttings. Once this is made clear, one does not have to look far to find that this technique is by no means unique to Africa. The manufacture of large pieces from strips of cloth is widely distributed in a geographic and temporal sense. Examples can be found from Scandinavia to Africa, from the Caucasus to the Andes. In America, woven coverlets almost always were composed of strips rather than woven whole on a wide loom. It is therefore difficult to state that the use of fabric strips is proof of African origins.

Collector Eli Leon followed Wahlman and Scully's lead in believing specific characteristics of African American quiltmaking aesthetics could be defined from the outside. Unlike Wahlman and Scully, however, Leon believed black quiltmakers created quilts that were at times indistinguishable from "standard" American quilts. It is these quilts that Leon consciously ignored in his research, choosing instead to concentrate on what he referred to as "Afro-traditional" quilts. So sure was Leon that African American quilts could be distinguished by style alone that he was willing to collect anonymous quilts and label them Afro-traditional simply by using his own criteria.

Because I expect that many of the older African-American

quilts will turn up as anonymous works, or all avenues to historical information will be . . . blocked, I feel it is imperative to devise a body of techniques to reclaim them as the products of black artisans. . . . Proof of black origins for every anonymous improvisational quilt is not, however, necessary to establish the existence of a black tradition in American quilting or to tie this tradition to its African roots. The black tradition can be established simply on the basis of the profound differences that show up in the quilts being made today. The case for continuity with African culture, a separate question, will rely heavily on the evidence gained from these older, sometimes anonymous, quilts.[17]

Leon characterized Afro-traditional quilts as improvisational within traditional boundaries regulated by attitudes and values that could be traced back to Africa. Leon admitted that many black quiltmakers were not conscious of seeking out improvisational forms but that improvisation occurred as a result of values that favored variation. Leon saw this process as distinctive from standard or white quiltmaking traditions.

It seems likely that African women in the New World, approaching the piecing of a quilt block, had skills and attitudes about "accidentals" that allowed them an alternative to measuring. Unlike some of the Europeans, whom they may have seen measuring quilt pieces, they were adept at working from a "model in their minds." If the standard-

traditional American quilt is properly executed, its final appearance is largely predetermined by the choice of pattern and fabric. The quiltmaker has only to cut and sew the pieces correctly and they will fit together to make consistent blocks and relatively predictable quilts. This emphasis on precision piecing and exact pattern replication, often yielding splendid textiles, is not conducive to improvisation. The Afro-traditional quilter, on the other hand, when she is not measuring her pieces precisely, must make adjustments as she puts the pieces together if they are to fit, since each block may be different in size and/or shape. As she deals with irregularities, drawing on a body of Afro-traditional techniques, she has opportunities to explore and excel in improvisational possibilities not open to the standard-traditional quilter.[18]

Leon went on to suggest that standard American patchwork as we know it may have been derived from African American traditions. Rather than the standard notion that blacks learned quiltmaking techniques from whites, Leon suggested that African Americans borrowed the concept of the three layered quilt from the dominant white population and used techniques known to them from Africa to develop patchwork. This tradition of patchwork was passed on to white slave owners as blacks made quilts for their masters. With this notion, Leon did not account for the strong quiltmaking traditions among northern whites.

In her book, *Stitched from the Soul*, folklorist Gladys-Marie Fry focused on slave-made quilts. Like other scholars, Fry explored the African influence on quilts made by African American women. For her that influence might be one of degrees: "Both historical and contemporary African-American quilts are shaped by a design aesthetic that differs from traditional Euro-American forms. . . . How do you categorize a large body of quilts made by African-American women that simply do not fit within any of these categories? Perhaps it could be more accurately said that African-American quilt styles are eclectic—ranging from quilts with strong African influences to those that most completely merge with Euro-American design traditions."[19] These may or may not be contradictory statements, depending on Fry's meaning when she said "shaped by a design aesthetic." Fry, like other scholars, pointed out that slaves made quilts both for themselves and for the white master. However, it was Fry's premise that slaves preferred to work under the influence of African aesthetic principles.

Instead of focusing on the issue of strip construction or improvisation as the tie to Africa, Fry focused on other, primarily symbolic, factors:

> In fact, slave quilters, who were forced by plantation rules to work within a Euro-American tradition, found inventive ways to disguise within the quilt improvisational forms and elements from African cosmology and mythology. A strong and continued belief in cosmology is evidenced by representations of the sun, the Congo cross, and the frequent use of red and white, which comes from the Shango cult of

Graham County pioneers.

Nigeria. The influence of African mythology survived in the snake motif, which is a symbol of Damballah, the West African god of fertility. Symbols of Erzulie, the Vodum goddess of love, appeared in slave-made textiles in the form of intricate flower patterns.[20]

Several times in her manuscript Fry also cited the presence of the color red in slave quilts as an indicator of African influence: "Slave preference for the color red in both their quilts and clothes has generated extensive speculation in historical literature. . . . A more accurate interpretation relates to African survivals. . . . Additionally, red and white are the colors of Shango, a religious cult that originated in Nigeria among the Yoruba and has spread throughout the New World, including the United States."[21] What Fry did not say was that the color red was prominent in many textiles made during the period 1830 to 1860, including those produced by other than African Americans. Although in many cases this may have been an aesthetic choice,

Nicodemus. The First Baptist Church is in the background.

The John Sumner residence in Morris County.

another important consideration is that red was one of the more stable dyes at that time.[22]

When searching for symbolic precedents for design motifs, we must once again be certain not to state as fact that any general similarity of form must indicate a causative connection. The circles, crosses, and lozenge shapes that are noted as African survivals are fairly basic forms. To interpret them as suns, Congo crosses, and coffins is to take certain liberties with the facts. Furthermore, there is no indication of just how widespread the use of these has been. The assertions are advanced with only two quilts offered as evidence. The connection made between the employing of flowers and Erzulie must also be viewed critically in light of the widespread use of this motif among all American quilting communities. This is not to say that speculation of such origins is to be discouraged. To state such connections as fact, however, is academically unsound.

Even though other scholars focused on uneven patterning or changes in design in African American quilts as stylistic improvisation, Fry offered yet another possibility. She explained the stylistic "imperfections" found in African American quilts as products of beliefs in the supernatural. "It was considered bad luck to make a perfect quilt or to use straight, unbroken lines. This attitude reflects the folk belief of plantation slaves that evil spirits follow straight lines, and also that an imperfect quilt would distract the devil in the night."[23] This may well be the case, but Fry offered no evidence to confirm the belief. The idea of deliberate "mistakes" in quilts has found its way into the literature of standard American quiltmaking as well. Although this idea is often cited in books, there is no evidence that quiltmakers ever put this belief into practice until they were exposed to it in print. More often "mistakes" in quilts are pointed out by researchers rather than by the quiltmakers themselves. The intentional or unintentional variations may result from many things, including the use of fabric of differing dye lots or personal aesthetic choices.

African American Quiltmakers in Kansas

All of the scholars' ideas and assumptions stated above are based on a certain body of evidence. Is there, however, evidence that runs contrary to these notions? According to the information gathered during the Kansas Quilt Project, the answer is yes. The question then becomes, should conflicting evidence be ignored to save the assumptions or should the conclusions be reworked?

Much of the evidence gathered during the KQP was the result of a series of Quilt Discovery Days in which people were asked to bring in their quilts so that information about them could be recorded. The process had certain limitations and in no way could reach all areas of the population. In response to this, an extended research phase of the project was developed. Among the populations targeted for extended research were the African American communities of the state.[24]

Research focused on the urban area of Kansas City, Kansas, and the rural western community of Nicodemus. Both communities have played a significant role in the history of Kansas (see chapter 2 for the early history of the state).[25]

After the Civil War Kansas was advertised as a good place for blacks to settle. Kansas City, Kansas, was the port of entry for many freed slaves.[26] Although Kansas City has seen a constant influx of African Americans since the conclusion of the Civil War, there have been two periods of major migration. In the 1860s and 1870s many ex-slaves entered the city, generally coming from Tennessee and Kentucky by way of Missouri. In the 1920s and 1930s a second wave of African Americans emigrated primarily from Arkansas and Missouri, where the mechanization of the cotton industry and general bad economic times had forced them to leave their homes.

Nicodemus, a small rural community in western Kansas, was settled in 1877 by a group of freedmen from Scott County, Kentucky.[27] They named their town after a legendary slave who was said to have purchased his own freedom. The African American community had a rough beginning owing to scarce resources and difficult weather conditions. A few of the original settlers returned to cities in the eastern portion of the state or to the South. However, enough people stayed so that the first school district in Graham County was organized in Nicodemus in 1879. Over the years the community has seen a decline in population. This rural community, now several generations removed from its southern slave roots, has not seen a continued influx of new settlers.

Many of the women in Nicodemus and Kansas City make quilts; however, the majority of their quilts do not meet the criteria of African American quilting described by the scholars cited above. This is true even

though the quilts studied in Kansas are generally from the same time period (from the days of slavery to the present) as those studied by other scholars, and the quiltmakers interviewed are both urban and rural. Two reasons immediately come to mind to account for the difference in quilts found in Kansas: Past researchers have ignored all but a certain type of African American quilt, and they have limited their studies to a specific and limited geographic area. The first reason is perhaps the stronger. Although both Vlach and Benberry allowed for differing styles of quilts among African Americans, Leon openly admitted he ignored all but a certain type of quilt. Thompson and Wahlman's data base was so limited that it can be assumed that they also ignored quilts that did not meet their stylistic criteria.

The second explanation for the difference in quilts found among African Americans in Kansas is somewhat more problematic. It is true that research done to date on African American quiltmaking traditions has focused on a small geographic area—primarily the deep South. The problem arises when Kansas quilts are viewed in the context of Kansas history. Many of the African Americans in Kansas migrated to the state from the South shortly after the Civil War, so it is more difficult to state that there is no connection between blacks in the southeast and in Kansas. If a cultural memory from Africa exists as an unbroken tradition among blacks in the South, would not that cultural memory have traveled to Kansas with the African Americans that migrated here? A possible explanation could be that the cultural memory has been lost through interaction with the dominant white population. This is doubtful, however, in that there were a number of social and geographic barriers in these two communities that isolated blacks from whites as effectively as they were divided in the South.

Although Kansas was an antislavery state, racial prejudice and exclusion still existed. Nicodemus was both physically and socially isolated as an all-black town in a rural Kansas county. Kansas City, Kansas, had racially restricted neighborhoods through the 1940s. This is not to imply that cross-cultural influences did not exist, but there was sufficient isolation to retain an African cultural memory. In addition, it is doubtful that isolation of any African American quiltmaking has ever been achieved or is necessary for the continuation of such a tradition. The work of Fry, Vlach, and Leon all attested to the direct intervention on African American quiltmaking by whites. Why, after all, would such a tradition survive decades of direction by white masters if isolation was essential for its continuation?

Neither can it be said that both of these Kansas communities were backwaters of African American culture. Certainly in the case of Kansas City, the African American community was not and is not culturally passive, as evidenced by Kansas City's position as one of the major centers for the development of the African American jazz tradition. If, as Thompson and Wahlman stated, African American quiltmaking traditions are akin to American jazz, then would it not follow that the same aesthetic influences of improvisation and offbeat rhythms would have been available to the African American

quiltmaker?

Another possible explanation for the variety found in Kansas quilts is that the African American quiltmaking tradition being explored in the South is not based on an unbroken African cultural influence but rather is a more recent phenomenon specific to black communities in the South. But then how does one explain California quiltmakers researched by Leon who worked within the same tradition? There are no easy answers to these questions, but perhaps a selected review of the fieldwork data collected in Kansas might shed some light on the overall issues.[28]

Residents of Nicodemus consistently recommend two women as sources on quiltmaking. Ora Switzer is the unofficial community historian.[29] Born in 1903 in a field near her present home, Switzer first learned to make quilts from her mother by cutting up overalls to make what she refers to as "comforts." The majority of Ora's quiltmaking knowledge came from the older women in the community. She recalls, "I liked to be around the older women—they taught you things. They made us lady-like. Now the young kids come around and spend time with me."

Ora Switzer joined the mission society at her church as a young woman and so enjoyed her membership that she could not wait for the weekly meetings. The routine was to work hard on quilts and then have a lesson. At the time Ora joined, the group had twelve active quilters. It was these "staunch old ladies" who refined her quilting skills. She remembers, "The older women kept you straight. If you made a crooked stitch they took it out. The women made us do such

neat work and we were really proud of our work." The quilt was put in the frame, and a clean piece of an old sheet was put on either side of the quilt so the women could work without getting the quilt dirty.

The group took in quilting to make money for the church, charging by the spool of thread. When Ora Switzer joined the group, they charged three dollars a spool. When the group finally disbanded a few years ago, the price had risen to eight dollars. When asked how many quilts she has made in her lifetime, Ora simply shakes her head and laughs. She quilted with the mission society for fifty-five years, but she also raised six children and made all the quilts and comforts for the beds.

Because of the town's small size, it is possible to interview most of the quiltmakers in Nicodemus. When asked who the best quiltmaker in town is, people always answer "Pearlena Moore."[30] Moore was born in a farm house in Nicodemus in 1929. Her mother died when she was only six months old, and she was raised among her ten aunts and uncles by her grandmother, Elizabeth Williams. Like Ora Switzer, Pearlena Moore liked to spend time with the older women in town.

At the age of eight or nine Moore's grandmother taught her to make comforts. She would come home from school and work all evening on them. The pieces came from old dresses and pants. Her grandmother would always remind her to make a double knot when she tied the comfort so that the knots would not come out—Pearlena always made three knots to be safe. Old blankets, curtains, or skirts served as linings for these comforts.

Moore's grandmother also taught her embroidery and quilting. Embroidery work is still her favorite, and it is her skills in needlework that bring her the respect of her community. In the early 1950s she joined the mission sisters at the church and was one of the youngest members. At first the ladies would not let her quilt because she would not use a thimble. She spent two years tying comforts before she convinced the ladies that without a thimble she could quilt as small a stitch as they did. As she remembers, "They were pretty particular about how their quilts were done."

Both Ora Switzer and Pearlena Moore first learned to make quilts from family members, and both women were strongly influenced by the older women in their community. Both women make a distinction between comforts and quilts. When making quilts they recall being taught to make small, straight, even stitches. This is in opposition to the often-cited assumption that African American quiltmakers are not interested in the size of the quilting stitch or other aspects of "good" workmanship. The two women are survivors of a once thriving community of quiltmakers, and their quilts and stories attest to an African American quiltmaking aesthetic that is unlike those cited in the literature to date.

There is more evidence available than the oral histories of these two women. An examination of older quilts passed down through families in Nicodemus corroborates their stories. However, one of the most telling arguments for the establishment of an alternative African American quiltmaking aesthetic is in the quilts made by Pearlena Moore.

These quilts, which are most admired in the community, involve the use of embroidery techniques and pastel colors, two characteristics not mentioned as African American aesthetic principles by Wahlman and Scully. In addition, there is evidence in the older quilts found in the community that this is not a style peculiar to this quiltmaker.

The first effort made to celebrate the quiltmaking traditions of African Americans in Kansas City, Kansas, was a show organized in 1988 by the Wyandotte County Historical Society for Black History Month.[31] The exhibit was unique in that the staff

Ora Switzer of Nicodemus.

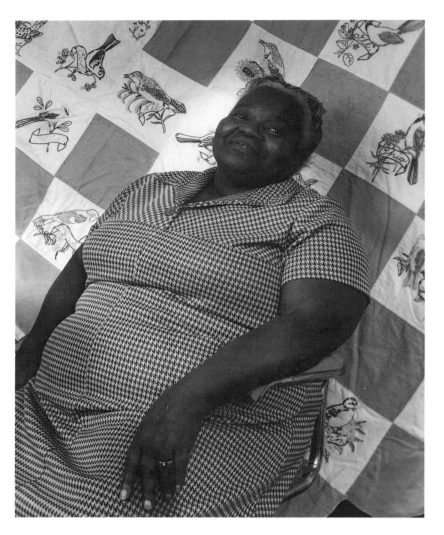

Pearlena Moore of Nicodemus.

had no preconceived notion of what an African American quilt looked like. In other words, they were simply looking for quilts made by black members of their community. As was the case in Nicodemus, the Wyandotte County show revealed that the African American quiltmaking aesthetic as described in the literature was in no way inclusive.

In Kansas City, Kansas, there is no one African American community, but rather several. By extension, not all black quiltmakers know each other or are aware of each other's work. There are, however, families and neighborhoods that share a community aesthetic. Deanna Williams, Reva Vanoy, and Yvonne Vanoy are three generations of quiltmakers from the same family.[32] The grandmother, Deanna Williams, learned to make quilts from her grandmother when she was a child growing up on the Louisiana border in Arkansas. She also learned to make batting, using the cotton out of the cotton gin. The cotton was beaten with a stick to break it down so that it would lie flat. Deanna also learned to make comforts from old wool pants. They were made quickly of simple patterns using squares of fabric. According to Williams, they were a necessity— a product of poverty. She recalls never owning a blanket until she moved to Kansas City in 1941. Here their family had a furnace, and quilts became less of a necessity and more of a decorative choice. Deanna was therefore a more prolific quilter before moving to Kansas.

While in Arkansas she often quilted with other women. Each woman had a quilting frame, and the group rotated from house to house. Deanna Williams suspended her frame from the ceiling. Although the women enjoyed the help, they also looked forward to the opportunity to socialize. Williams was raised with a very definite aesthetic in regard to workmanship. Her grandmother would pull out any stitches that were not neat or close together. According to her grandmother, poor stitches looked like "cat teeth." Although Deanna feels there are no real "ugly" quilts, she describes a "pretty" quilt as one where all the pieces fit together neatly. She likes to use "pretty," harmonious colors in her own work.

Reva Vanoy had no desire to learn quiltmaking from her mother. Instead, she took up quilting with her daughter, Yvonne, after her children were grown. Both women have been inspired by classes and their membership in the local quilt guild, which is predominantly white. The women feel that the guild not only gives them new ideas but also moral support.

Reva Vanoy, who makes bed-size quilts using repeated patterns and muted colors, gets her ideas from books and fellow guild members. Yvonne Vanoy, on the other hand, finds that she does not have the patience to make large quilts. She prefers to make wall hangings, creating her own designs. Yvonne is a professional architect who designs power plants. She feels her work does not allow her to use her creativity, so making quilts is her outlet. Both women quilt almost exclusively by hand. Sometimes Reva puts her quilt on the kitchen table and quilts without a frame. Both mother and daughter continue to make quilts because they find it to be relaxing.

Georgia Patton, her daughter, Nedra Bonds, and a neighbor, Vera Wells, make up another

Embroidered quilt by Pearlena Moore.

Nedra Bonds of Kansas City.

Opposite: Old Quindaro History. Nedra Bonds of Kansas City, Kansas, made this quilt to depict the oral history of Quindaro. Tradition in the African American community holds that Quindaro was a stop on the Underground Railroad—hence its importance in the history of Kansas City's African American community.

community of quilters.[33] Georgia Patton learned to make quilts as a little girl in rural north-central Missouri. She recalls, "Nobody had a TV or radio then. We would just sit and quilt during the evenings. We would tell stories and keep each other company. If we were sitting around the room everyone would be doing something. You know idle minds are the devil's workshop." Patton never went through a period in which she did not make quilts. However, during the 1960s she was very active in the civil rights movement, which left her with less free time. She works as a school librarian, and although her day begins at 4:30 A.M., she often takes time to piece before going to work. At school, Georgia is teaching a number of African American children how to make quilts.

Georgia Patton has inherited a number of family quilts, but they are not her only inspiration. Ideas also come from magazines and quilt shows. Although she values hand quilting, she usually has her tops machine quilted by her neighbor, Vera Wells. Patton knows of very few women who quilt by hand anymore because it is so time-consuming. However, when she was a young girl she remembers the women would count the number of stitches per inch.

Nedra Bonds first learned to make quilts as a child from her mother. Like many young girls of the 1950s and 1960s, she was too busy with other activities to devote much time to quiltmaking. While in her twenties Bonds came back to quilting through her interest in fine art. Because of this, her quilts tend to be innovative rather than traditional, and she places an emphasis on applique. As a former teacher, she is interested in making visual representations of stories of her heritage. According to Nedra, "Creativity comes in spurts—I need to get it out of my head and into the medium." When asked about her taste in quilts she replies, "No quilt is ugly because it says what that woman was feeling at the time. It's all individual."

Vera Wells, Georgia Patton's neighbor, grew up in Kansas. She learned to sew from her mother and grew up watching her grandmother make quilts. The quilts she remembers from that period were mostly wool and, in her words, "not too attractive." She has inherited one quilt made by her grandmother, however, that is considered to be especially beautiful. According to a family story it was made around 1890 and is a repeated floral pattern in red and green. The quiltmaker's inspiration was another woman's quilt that Vera's grandmother saw hanging on the clothes line.

Wells considers herself a self-taught quiltmaker; she prefers traditional to innovative quilts. She obtains most of her patterns from a box of *Kansas City Star* patterns left to her by her grandmother. Vera likes the idea that quiltmaking has no boundaries; there is, in her words, "no one to say it's bad form to do that—it's all in the maker's hands." For her own quilts Wells likes to use earth-tone colors with a little off-white to "perk it up." She says of the colors in her quilt, "I make them kind of drab."

Lillian Harrington was born in Kansas City, Kansas, in 1905.[34] As the only girl in a family with six children, she wound up doing much of the family sewing. Learning to sew in the public schools, Harrington was making dresses by the time she was nine years old. She first

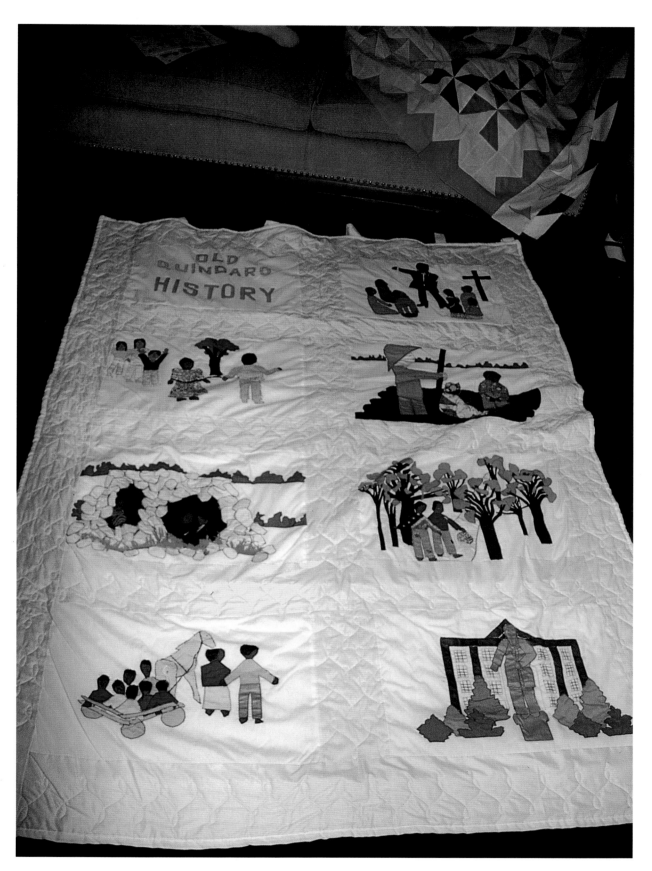

African American Quiltmaking Traditions

Georgia Patton with two of her quilts.

learned how to make quilts, however, from her grandmother, also a native of Kansas City. Lillian remembers going to her grandmother's house after school and piecing quilt blocks until it was time to go home. Her grandmother would quilt on a large frame, while Harrington kept the needles threaded for her grandmother, in lots of about a dozen.

As a child, Lillian Harrington made only one type of quilt from beginning to end. "Britches" quilts were made of discarded wool pants. The piecing for these quilts was not elaborate. An old blanket was used as batting, and the quilt was tied. Britches quilts were the only quilts that were used on a daily basis. Fancier quilts were only placed on the

beds when company was coming. Lillian remembers a constant migration of people into the Kansas City area from the South when she was a child. The southerners had beautiful quilts that they would wash regularly and hang on their clothes lines. Harrington's grandmother would become envious of the display and would dig out her best quilts to hang on her clothesline whether they had been washed or not.

Lillian has continued to make quilt tops, but she does not quilt, preferring instead to have her tops quilted by professionals. She values small, tight stitches and prefers cotton batting, which helps to produce dense quilting. Her ideas for quilt tops came from viewing the quilts of others

or from her collection of *Kansas City Star* patterns. Harrington always uses cardboard templates to cut out her fabric. She only uses cotton fabrics in her quilts. Although she likes a range of colors, Lillian is especially fond of a combination of pink and green on a white background. In fact she tends to like white as a dominant color because she feels it sets off the other colors in the quilt. Harrington has a definite aesthetic concerning her own quilts, and she expresses that she has never seen what she would call an ugly or unacceptable quilt.

Like the women in Nicodemus, the African American quiltmakers in Kansas City did not conform to the aesthetic principles spelled out in the literature.

They spoke of small, even stitches, good workmanship, and well-balanced colors, all aesthetic principles attributed to white quiltmaking traditions. They were aware of two distinct traditions: "everyday" and "Sunday" quilts, or "britches" and "special"—an idea that parallels the "comforts" and "quilts" terminology used by the women in Nicodemus, who described "comforts" as strictly functional bedcovers without an intricate pattern. "Sunday" quilts, on the other hand, were primarily decorative and, as the term would imply, were traditionally used only on Sundays when company would come by to visit. They were made according to very exacting standards and were very rarely used on the bed at night. Nowadays, however, the "Sunday" quilt is usually kept on the bed at all times.

Like the women in western Kansas, the Kansas City women interviewed are reluctant to judge the aesthetics of someone else's quilt because they believe that a pretty quilt is one that is pretty to its maker. However, both groups showed admiration for quilts that did not meet the so-called African American aesthetic standards.

Conclusion

What does the information collected in Kansas tell us about the underlying assumptions found in the literature on African American quiltmaking aesthetics? The assumption that quilts made by African Americans can be detected by a physical examination of the quilt alone is obviously false in light of the data presented. All of the characteristics attributed by some scholars to the African American quiltmaking aesthetic (bright, bold colors;

irregular patterns; the presence of movement and improvisation; and a perceived disinterest in workmanship, resulting in unmeasured pieces and large, uneven, quilting stitches) can be found in quilts made by white women and are in no way present in all quilts made by black women. In fact, the research in Kansas turned up virtually no quilts, known to be by African American artists, that possess all of those characteristics.

It cannot be concluded, however, that quilts fitting what Leon called the Afro-traditional genre do not exist in Kansas. They may indeed exist but have been unavailable to researchers for a number of possible reasons. After all, the women interviewed spoke of two distinctive types of quilts: the comfort or everyday quilt and the Sunday quilt. Perhaps quiltmakers are reluctant to show everyday quilts. African American women, like white women, have always made different types of quilts depending on their use, but it appears that scholars of African American quilts have focused on only one type of quilt. There is a great danger in this practice. When researchers fail to look at the larger scope of work done by a cultural group, they may contribute to racial stereotyping.

To use Thompson's and Wahlman's analogy between African American quiltmaking aesthetics and musical styles, it must be asked why a single African American quiltmaking aesthetic would be maintained when there is no such uniform aesthetic within African American musical forms. Would not the same individual creativity that has driven black musicians into new and varying forms of musical expression lead black women into

experimentation with multiple genres of quiltmaking? It seems unfair to assume that African American musicians work creatively within a tradition but that African American quiltmakers are reduced to being merely passive tradition bearers.

One of the major flaws within the literature to date is that the quilts made by African Americans are compared to a hypothetical European American tradition. If African American quilts are to be distinguished as a separate genre, then they must be understood within the overall context of American quiltmaking traditions. For instance, the quilts made by African American women in Kansas can be statistically compared to the more than 13,000 quilts recorded by the Kansas Quilt Project. It is possible with this data base to compare such things as the number of stitches per inch made by both white and black quilters. When this is done the same range of variation of stitch size exists for both groups. What this and other data reveal is that at least in Kansas there is no distinct African American quiltmaking tradition as described in the literature. If researchers continue to believe that an African American quilt can be judged by its appearance alone, then a great many mistakes will be made in analyzing anonymous quilts. A value judgment is being made when absolute standards of aesthetics are attributed to any one race. The irony is that if a quilt made by a white woman looks "Afro-traditional," then it is judged by some to be inferior; when a quilt made by an African American woman appears too much in line with the perceived white aesthetic, then it is assumed that the black quiltmaker is oppressed by the dominant culture. The victim of this argument is the creativity of the individual artist.

The above concerns also apply to the second assumption found within the quilt literature, the assumption of cultural homogeneity. It is dangerous to assume that race is synonymous with culture. The perception of race can be a factor in the development of a culture, particularly within a country as diverse as the United States, but it does not determine culture. Not only did the blacks in America come from a variety of tribes in Africa, each with its own distinct cultural heritage, but they have been exposed within the United States to such varying factors as class and economic distinctions, regionalism, degrees of urbanization, and popular culture.

The literature on African American quilts uses a concept of homogeneous white quiltmaking aesthetics against which black quiltmaking is distinguished. It is equally wrong to assume that all white women value a certain set of aesthetic characteristics. Quilt researcher Laurel Horton has stated, "One reason I think that whites, especially white quiltmakers, feel the need to categorize black quiltmakers as different is because whites have defined 'good' quiltmaking as showing tiny stitches and exhibiting one's control over the medium by making exact repetitions of carefully constructed blocks. Many traditional black quiltmakers consider making lots of tiny stitches to be a waste of time and doing the same block over and over as boring. There is more than one definition of what makes a 'good' quilt."[35] Horton is absolutely correct when she says that there is more than one definition of a "good" quilt. However, what is missing in her statement is the assumption that this is true of quilts by white quiltmakers as well. Although a great deal of research has been done on white quiltmaking traditions in the last few decades, it tends to focus on a particular aesthetic of white quiltmaking, one championed by the popular press. Researchers must broaden their perspective and study differing aesthetics among white quiltmakers as well.

Two other underlying assumptions about African American quiltmaking traditions found in the literature to date are interrelated. This is the assumption of African origins and the assumption that elements of culture can remain unaffected by exposure to other cultures. These assumptions are based on what anthropologist Richard H. Thompson has referred to as a primordialist view of ethnic identity.[36] This view holds that individuals will see their ethnic group as the primary determinant of their identities and will affiliate with other individuals with similar ethnic backgrounds simply because such ties are more "natural" because they appeal to a "primordial" origin. Such a view generates the notion that cultural continuity within each ethnic group is the outcome of centripetal forces found within the group itself. Social forces from outside the group as well as divisions within the group are assumed to be secondary to the overwhelming power of the primordial tie. In his critique of primordialist assumptions, Thompson thoroughly debunks this view, not only for its logical inconsistencies but for the essentially reactionary and divisive outcome that such a view forebodes for our society.

In terms of quilts, it may be interesting to point out visual similarities between some quilts made by African Americans and African textiles, even though the aesthetic link is still debatable. However, to say that African American quilts are definitely derived from African traditions is a forced view of ethnicity that refuses to acknowledge cultural flow. If a cultural memory from Africa exists among blacks in the United States and a manifestation of this memory is the "Afro-traditional" quilt, then evidence of such quilts should exist in Kansas.

A recognition of certain similarities of form will not be sufficient to prove that a connection to Africa continues as the primary determinant of the quiltmaking aesthetic among African Americans. Rather, it must be demonstrated how this connection can override other influences to which the quiltmakers are exposed. Since culture is learned, groups that come in contact influence each other. Communities may continue old art forms and techniques while borrowing heavily from other cultural groups. When this does not happen there is generally a conscious, ideologically based decision to exclude other influences—in which case the behavior is no longer traditional but has become a "created tradition." The arguments for the presence of a specific African American quiltmaking style do not include this conscious, ideologically based choice.

Ultimately, the research in Kansas suggests that black women make all types of quilts and that at times white women make quilts that meet the criteria of a posited African American aesthetic. African Americans share a common history of slavery and racial discrimination, and this shared history may influence the world view of group members. However, being black is only one aspect of an individual's identity and does not negate his or her membership in the larger American society. African American quiltmakers, like white quiltmakers, are individual artists who are influenced by their own memberships in varying communities—religious, generational, recreational, occupational, and familial. In short, each African American quiltmaker is an individual who makes aesthetic choices. These choices undoubtedly are influenced by their most immediate communities, but to claim that there is only one black community is to oversimplify, perhaps to the point of racial stereotyping.

The time has come for more quilt researchers to work toward a better understanding of culture and to broaden their aesthetic tolerance for all types of quilts made by all varieties of people. After all, there was one consistent belief shared by the African American quiltmakers who participated in this study and that was the idea that there are no ugly quilts.

Notes

The author thanks the African American quiltmakers in Kansas who shared their quilts and their stories. A special thank you is extended to Carl Magnuson and Barbara Brackman, who shared their ideas, and to Joy Harnett and Barry Worley, who completed the field photography.

1. Cuesta Benberry, "Style of Their Own—Two Black Quiltmakers," *American Quilter* 4 (Spring 1988): 21. For further discussion of this point see Cuesta Benberry, *Always There: The African-American Presence in American Quilts* (Louisville: Kentucky Quilt Project, 1992).

2. One of the earliest scholars to recognize this principle was Ruth Benedict. For an excellent discussion of the issue, see Ruth Benedict, *Patterns of Culture* (New York: Houghton Mifflin Company, 1934).

3. For a further discussion of aesthetics in quiltmaking, see Jennie A. Chinn, "'Some Ladies Make Quilts, But They Aren't Quilt Makers': Aesthetic Principles in Quilt Making," *Kansas History: A Journal of the Central Plains* 13 (Spring 1990): 32–42.

4. John Michael Vlach, *The Afro-American Tradition in Decorative Arts* (Cleveland: The Cleveland Museum of Art, 1978), 2.

5. Applique quilts by Mrs. Powers are in the collection of the Smithsonian Institution in Washington, D.C., and in the Museum of Fine Arts in Boston, Massachusetts. For more information on Harriet Powers, see Gladys-Marie Fry, "Harriet Powers: Portrait of a Black Quilter," *Missing Pieces: Georgia Folk Art 1770–1976* (Atlanta: Atlanta Historical Society, 1976), 16–23; Gladys-Marie Fry, *Stitched from the Soul: Slave Quilts from the Ante-Bellum South* (New York: E. P. Dutton, 1990), 84–91.

6. Vlach, *The Afro-American Tradition in Decorative Arts*, 45, 48.

7. Ibid., 55.

8. Ibid., 75.

9. Robert Farris Thompson, "From the First to the Final Thunder: African-American Quilts, Monuments of Cultural Assertion," Preface in Eli Leon, *Who'd A Thought It: Improvisation in African-American Quiltmaking* (San Francisco: San Francisco Craft and Folk Art Museum, 1987), 13.

10. Ibid., 18.

11. Ibid., 12.

12. Ibid., 16.

13. Maude Southwell Wahlman and John Scully, "Aesthetic Principles in Afro-American Quilts," in *Afro-American Folk Art and Crafts*, ed. William Ferris (Boston: G. K. Hall & Co., 1983), 85.

14. Ibid., 86.

15. Ibid., 91.

16. Ibid., 92.

17. Leon, *Who'd A Thought It,* 47.

18. Ibid., 28.

19. Fry, *Stitched from the Soul,* 10.

20. Ibid., 7.

21. Ibid., 44–45.

22. For further information on the nature of the effect of available dyes on quiltmaking traditions, see Barbara Brackman, *Clues in the Calico: A Guide to Identifying and Dating Antique Quilts* (McLean, Va.: EPM Publications, 1989).

23. Fry, *Stitched from the Soul,* 67.

24. Research in the African American communities of Kansas was funded by a grant from the National Endowment for the Arts. I was assisted in the research by Rebecca Barbara, Nancy Hornback, Mary Madden, Carl Magnuson, and Mary Sharp.

25. For a good history of Kansas, see Robert W. Richmond, *Kansas: A Land of Contrasts* (St. Louis: Forum Press, 1974).

26. For more information on the African American communities in Kansas City, Kansas, see Susan Greenbaum, *The Afro-American Community in Kansas City, Kansas: A History* (Kansas City: Community Development Program, 1983).

27. For more information on Nicodemus, see *Promised Land on the Solomon: Black Settlement at Nicodemus, Kansas* (Washington, D.C.: Department of the Interior, 1983).

28. The results of the Kansas Quilt Project research can be found in the Manuscripts Department at the Kansas State Historical Society—Manuscript Collection 207.

29. Ora Switzer, interview with the author, June 23, 1988, Kansas State Historical Society.

30. Pearlena Moore, interview with the author, June 23, 1988, Kansas State Historical Society.

31. The quilt show celebrating Black History Month at the Wyandotte County Historical Society has become an annual event.

32. Deanna Williams, Reva Vanoy, and Yvonne Vanoy, interview with Carl Magnuson, June 9, 1988, Kansas State Historical Society.

33. Georgia Patton, Nedra Bonds, and Vera Wells, interview with Carl Magnuson, June 9, 1988, Kansas State Historical Society.

34. Lillian Harrington, interview with Carl Magnuson, August 9, 1988, Kansas State Historical Society.

35. Quoted in Fry, *Stitched from the Soul,* 10.

36. Richard H. Thompson, *Theories of Ethnicity: A Critical Appraisal* (New York: Greenwood Press, 1989).

St. Joseph's Quilting Corner, Olpe, Kansas, 1992.

Chapter Eight

Kansas Quilting Groups: Surviving the Pressures of Change

Gayle R. Davis

FOR THE LAST TWO DECADES, QUILTS AND THE CREATIVE ENVIRONMENT ASSOCIATED WITH THEIR FOLK ORIGINS HAVE ENJOYED HIGH VISIBILITY AND STATUS IN THE UNITED STATES. FROM THE LATE 1960S THROUGH THE EARLY 1990S, QUILTS NOT ONLY MAINTAINED THEIR PROMINENCE IN TRADITIONAL ARENAS BUT ALSO reached unprecedented levels of appreciation in the worlds of popular culture and the fine arts.[1] Quilts have routinely taken center stage in settings as disparate as fashionable "country" interiors and art museums. They have also appeared as focal points of research in women's social history, art history, and material culture. In short, the United States is experiencing one of its periodic quilt revivals. However, none of the earlier revivals—in the 1860s, the 1890s, or the 1920s and 1930s—was marked by the number and variety of formal and informal organizations, commercial enterprises, and publications related to quilting that the current wave of popularity has produced.

For the social historian, quilt revivals are valuable as time-limited, discrete cultural phenomena through which to explore both the causes and effects of the mainstream culture's fluctuating attitudes toward its traditional subculture. Here I will trace the country's changing ideological needs that encouraged its most recent quilt revival and examine the influence of that cycle of surging and eventually diminishing interest on one aspect of the contemporary quilt world commonly associated with traditional culture—the quilting group. Though it is too early to determine whether or not this revival has reached its peak or when it can expect a decline, there is con-

cern about what will happen to quilting groups when that decline inevitably takes place. This study uses interviews and questionnaires completed by members of eight such groups in and around Wichita, Kansas.[2] Placing these groups within the present complicated context of quilt history, I will seek to analyze their milieu in ways that "interpret the modern context instead of reconstructing the past."[3]

The Current Quilt Revival

The nostalgic, celebratory attitudes of the larger society toward quilts in the past twenty years reflect the prevalent impulse to conserve both tangible and philosophical aspects of national traditions. Americans seem to have needed a restored heritage in defense against the perceived depersonalization of modern technological culture. The country's bicentennial celebration provided an unmatched opportunity to highlight the symbolic objects of America's past in the name of patriotism. At such moments the overall public status of the traditional culture is bound to be enhanced. After all, those who revere, conserve, or create various traditional art forms provide an element of social continuity for an ever more fragmented population.

Nonetheless, as folklorist John Vlach wrote, "in these times, not all traditions are as vital as they

once were, particularly in the area of material culture. Generally, it is those technologies with a strong domestic base—like foodways, woodcarving, or the textile arts—that continue to thrive."[4] During times of far-reaching changes in the country's political, economic, and work life, people are especially likely to seek continuity and stability where they can—in the domestic realm. Furthermore, the culture may particularly support women's domestic traditions because familiar female roles have been threatened by the growth since the late nineteenth century of women's paid employment and public responsibilities.[5]

The Depression era exemplifies one period in American history when forced role reversals in family work patterns led to a resurgence in the expression of traditional domestic values. Quiltmaking became very popular in the 1930s, as did home baking and food preservation, even though married women's time was increasingly filled by wage labor. These activities were not primarily measures of frugality, since ready-made substitutes were available and inexpensive. Instead, they signaled the centrality of the domestic role to women's and men's shaken identities. Writing of the 1930s, historian Leslie Tentler noted,

> The nonemployed wife was by the early twentieth century an

important and emotionally charged symbol of respectability for many working-class families. . . . Her work in the home allowed the family to present the appearance of stability and success to the world at large. Her domesticity was the complement to her husband's achievements as a worker and to the family loyalties of sons and daughters. Thus, a married woman's employment usually meant more to the family than a temporary expedient in hard times. It symbolized defeat, a failure of family survival strategy in an intensely competitive society.[6]

More married women went to work in the 1930s, and they struggled to maintain the family's gender role balance.

This pattern of changed roles and reaction has been repeated in the period since the late 1960s, in large part because of the social and familial adjustments required to accommodate the culture's record proportion of wage-earning women.[7] Though it is true that people have not faced the economic crisis or the family disruption of the Great Depression, women have needed to adapt to new circumstances. "The current 'emancipation' of women is also greatly the result of the sudden emergence of a whole range of previously nonexisting objects . . . [that] have considerably decreased the amount of psychic energy necessary to accomplish traditionally feminine household tasks and crafts. That is, women need not—and, in fact, no longer can—define their self exclusively with information resulting from interaction with traditional feminine objects. Thus women are free—and in essence forced—to seek new things that will help

them to define who they are."[8] Women have chosen traditional pursuits, once required in female domestic roles, as a means through which to explore some facets of their identities. A study in the 1970s concerning people's attachments to household possessions found that women prefer objects that help them perform the nurturing activities from which they derive their sense of self. "The things they cherish are signs of ties that bind the family together—shared experiences. . . . What is interesting is that many mothers in this sample also worked outside the home, yet the objects that meant the most to them were more often those signifying the traditional role of mother."[9]

In the context of traditional identity-building, quilting could hardly be surpassed as an opportunity for a woman to be "feminine": to nurture others, to provide warmth and beauty for the home, to labor selflessly to a good end, and to fill leisure time productively. Like the "ideal" woman herself, a quilt "says people, friendship, community, family, home, and love . . . [and seems] to us symbolic of some of our finer human qualities."[10] Therefore, women who quilt receive messages of social approval that translate into enhanced self-esteem, a sense of belonging in the society, and encouragement to continue. Though women are socialized to this activity, "by adopting the intentions pervading his or her culture, a person does not feel determined or coerced; usually he or she goes about building the self unquestioningly, doing 'what comes naturally.' . . . To use a thing in a culturally appropriate way means to experience the culture directly—becoming part of the

medium of signs that constitutes that culture."[11]

The women's rights movement, which saw a resurgence in the late 1960s, has also established a climate conducive to the present quilt revival. Women's rights activists, by questioning the low value society places on "women's work," have encouraged women's traditions from a political perspective that seeks to validate all work. The feminist study of previously underestimated objects of women's domestic creativity constitutes a social critique that has helped to revitalize society's ties with women's heritage.[12] Consequently, some women view quilting not only as a valued art form but also as a metaphor for their lives: "For many contemporary women, therefore, aware of the potential and power of women as a group, and of the need for group definition and consciousness, the compelling fascination of quilts and quiltmaking resides in their enactment of just such processes of bonding: the joining into wholes of separate fragments of fabric, and the joining of women cooperatively engaged in creation and constructive change."[13]

Some parts of the feminist analysis have filtered into the less-political quilt community, allowing many quilters to be more positively self-conscious in their art. Both the process and the product of quilting may thus strengthen feelings of universal ties to "everywoman's" life.[14] To ensure that the quilt artist will no longer be anonymous and that the growing historical consciousness of quilts will be maintained, many quilters now sign every quilt, and many quilting groups keep photo albums of the work they've completed. For instance, since 1975 the Dorcas Circle has kept a quilt photo album, adding a visual record to the written history of the group that has been documented since 1918 and stored in the First Presbyterian Church archives. A collection of finished quilt photographs has also been maintained by the Haysville quilters, the 76'ers, and others in this study.

Quilting Groups

In this atmosphere of patriotic, nostalgic, aesthetic, and feminist appreciation of quilting and its social history, quilting groups have proliferated.[15] Regardless of their awareness of quilt history, few of the group quilters participating in this study have ever scrutinized the cultural implications of their involvement. Most simply see their group memberships as a "natural," very enjoyable, but not especially socially significant activity. However, their perspectives and concerns, in the context of today's prevailing gender roles and social climate, confirm women's needs for traditional forms and sense of community as well as for some degree of conformity to the larger culture's conditioning processes.

Quilting groups, practical assemblies that they are, have a very long history in the traditional culture. They have been significant not only for their level of production but also as settings for transmitting quilting aesthetics, techniques, and customs and for building personal bonds among communities of women. Although more attention has been paid to the role of historic quilting groups, such associations in the contemporary world are beginning to attract scholarly notice.[16] Quilting is so popular in many Kansas cities and larger towns that each can supply quilters for numerous quilting groups. The individual collectives espouse specific priorities regarding group purpose, meeting schedules and locations, and favored quilting techniques and aesthetics. These quilting groups are the most recent variations of two historic group configurations, organized primarily according to the purposes for which the quilts are made.

One traditional grouping maintained by current quilters is that of the association whose regular quilting sessions raise money for charitable causes sponsored by a church or other benevolent organization. Historically, "every Protestant church had its Sewing Society or Female Prayer Meeting, its Women's Guild or Fancy Work Improvement Club. Ladies' Aid, Priscilla and Dorcas Societies, and African Dorcas Societies in black churches, were established in every town, city or newly settled territory almost as soon as the churches themselves."[17] The charitable quilting group still thrives in Kansas. This study included four such organizations: the Bethany Comforters at the Bethany Methodist Church and the Dorcas Circle of the First Presbyterian Church, both in Wichita; the 76'ers of the First Mennonite Church in Halstead; and the St. Peter's Church quilters in Schulte. The establishment and continuous operation of the Dorcas Circle predate the recent quilt revival. The other three groups were formed during the current period of quilt popularity. The Bethany Comforters was founded in 1973. The 76'ers, named for the nation's bicentennial and the year in which the group was founded, resumed the work begun by quilters from their church's Home Builders Sunday School Class in the 1930s, one of the earlier revival periods. The quilters of St. Peter's Church also reconvened their group based on an earlier church program. In 1984, these quilters rejuvenated the idea of a quilt bingo fund raiser that had been held in 1957. Meeting for three to six hours on a weekly, daytime schedule, all of these groups have produced utilitarian quilts as direct gifts to the needy or have created more decorative ones to auction, raffle, or award as fund-raising prizes for their causes. In both the Bethany Comforters and the Dorcas Circle, only a small portion of the members hand quilt, and the rest produce a variety of other sewn objects for charity. Three of the groups also earn money for benevolent causes on a regular basis by hiring themselves out to quilt tops for others.

Versions of the second traditional type of quilt group—customarily called the quilting bee, party, or frolic—may also be recognized in the associations of today. These quilting gatherings have been documented in novels since the late 1700s, and they were common by the early 1800s.[18] In contrast to the regular meetings of charity groups, a party was organized as a social occasion when help was needed by one of the quilters to finish her completed tops or when a rite-of-passage quilt gift was in order.[19] Sometimes the hosts invited the families of all the participating quilters to enjoy food, dancing, and other recreation after the quilting was finished. Some members of the 76'ers fondly remembered such quilting parties they had attended as children, though they admitted they were then drawn more by the food than by the quilting. These festivities are rare today, though

Bethany Comforters, Bethany Methodist Church, Wichita, 1991.

quilters in Moundridge, Kansas, with its Mennonite roots, still occasionally throw full-fledged, traditional quilting parties.

Other conventions of this second type of historical group have also been modified to suit contemporary society. Although many quilters do still gather to help each other quilt and to create quilts to celebrate a significant occasion in a friend's life or the life of the community, there is less functional urgency to the work. Instead, the party has typically been replaced by the regular meeting of a group of quilters that helps to finish quilts for members or quilts tops for others, sometimes earning money for donations to various projects the group endorses.

Four groups studied here fit this second type of collective quilting: the Quilt Patchers of Wichita, the Haysville Public Li-

brary quilters, and the two associations of quilters living near Peck and Clearwater. They were all established in the 1970s as the popularity of quilts soared in the larger culture. It was the popular—not the traditional—quilt culture that had direct influence on the establishment of these groups. For instance, the Quilt Patchers were directly inspired to form their group by a 1978 presentation by Kansan Chris Wolf Edmonds, a talented quilter well known on the national lecture circuit, an informal network developed in the 1970s to fill the needs of larger than ever audiences interested in quilts. In 1979, several Haysville women who had belonged to a quilting group called Stitch and Cackle in Wichita in the 1950s decided to organize a new group. A quilting class offered by their local public library that year attracted sufficient additional women to complete the group.

The quilters in these groups are not formally affiliated with any larger charitable organizations, although the Haysville group still meets in their library, and the Quilt Patchers meet at the University United Methodist Church. All of the original Quilt Patchers were members of the church, but the congregation did not supply enough quilters to fill the group, so the quilters opened their organization to the community. Few of the current members of the quilting group belong to the church, which has nonetheless continued to provide space. Both of these groups primarily quilt each other's quilt tops, though both have also donated fund-raising quilts to their respective meeting places, in appreciation for the use of their facilities for several hours weekly. The Peck quilters have made raffle quilts as fund raisers for their community. The Clearwater group quilts for its members, and they quilt for others, raising money to support the local quilt guild's visiting speakers and other programming.

Motivations for Joining a Quilting Group

The popularity of both types of quilting groups in fast-paced, contemporary America inevitably raises the question: In a time of increased opportunities for women, why do so many choose to become involved in an activity long associated with domesticity? Joyce Ice, studying quilters in Delaware County, New York, answered by observing that quilt-making groups remain attractive to women because the associations are flexible, "able to adapt traditional elements and incorporate non-traditional aspects at the same time . . . to meet a variety of needs."[20] In their configurations, goals, and operations as well as their personal meaning for each member, the contemporary groups both follow and revise historical quilting traditions to suit the needs of their members.

The benefits contemporary quilters derive from their groups, motivating their continued participation, have been enumerated in several studies. Susan Stewart, in her 1974 research of three traditional Pennsylvania Brethren quilting groups, located three levels on which the groups function beneficially for their constituents: "externally, the relation of the group to the outside church and community; internally, the relationship and dependency of the group members to each other; and individually, the psychological aspects of the craft and meanings it holds for each woman who practices it."[21] Stewart's conclusions effectively summarize the types of membership rewards named by the participants in this study. Of further pertinence is the fact that when the larger society's regard for quilts is high, the usual perceived rewards are enhanced by a measure of recognition even beyond that which is continuously available within the smaller traditional quilt culture. This recognition not only benefits the quilter but also promotes the maintenance of quilting group traditions.

Those functions that Stewart calls "external" include opportunities to gain information about and participate in community events. For instance, a Schulte quilter stated that the quilters at St. Peter's Church were her connections to the community news, replacing the link to local information her children used to supply when they were in the school system. When the groups provide quilting skills to raise funds for the community, the members not only enjoy the involvement, but as one Schulte quilter said, it is also sometimes easier for them to give time to the church than to give money. The quilters also gain an unusual amount of power over the monetary resources of their group. The 76'ers, for example, made the decisions to buy tables and a roaster oven for their church and to help pay for a driveway paving project. Within church-affiliated quilting groups, women thus find a way to participate in decision-making activities of the congregation even though standard leadership roles are typically filled by men.[22] This special but marginal place for women in the operation of the sponsoring churches has been recognized for years. In fact, perceiving a similar situation in her time, nineteenth-century activist Frances Willard is recorded as "ironically commenting that their charity work was the one 'department of church work where women have always been allowed an equal right with men, viz.: that of paying off church debts and raising funds for church extension.'"[23] In times of increased quilt popularity, these funds can be substantial, since well-made quilts and associated quilting services acquire a high monetary value.

The present quilt culture has expanded to include a nationwide array of guilds, research groups, shops, books and periodicals, galleries, exhibits, conferences, and classes. Therefore, quilt groups today can connect their members to a much wider "external" world than could groups that operated when interest was more narrowly confined in the culture. The wider quilt network also reaches a very di-

Haysville Public Library quilters, Haysville, 1991.

verse audience of research specialists: "The woman making quilts for her grandchildren the way her grandmother made one for her grabs the attention of the folklorist. When a woman makes quilts for art shows and clubs or learns to make quilts from a kit or class, the object attracts the student of popular culture. When the woman becomes a 'textile artist' with creations proudly protected in a refined gallery, the art historian and critic are usually nearby."[24]

When her skills are recognized, the quilter can earn a reputation for her art in the fine art or popular realm as well as in the traditional culture. Through the many systems for conveying quilt information, her renown could become national, in contrast to the local and regional limits of the contests and shows that usually define the primary public outlets for quilts in the traditional culture. Though individual members in this study do not ex-

pect public recognition to result from the cooperative structure of a quilting group, appreciation of other quilt artists in the larger society adds to the prestige some group members feel in practicing an art that is no longer widely ignored. The members of these Kansas groups do take pride in their collective successes. The Halstead 76'ers, for instance, felt gratified when one of their quilts won a blue ribbon at the State Fair for group quilting and when another quilt brought the highest bid in an annual Mennonite relief auction in Hutchinson, Kansas.

The reasons quilters have most frequently cited for belonging to quilting groups are those that fall into Stewart's second category, that of the activity's "internal" functions. Contemporary quilters, like women of the past, join groups primarily for social contacts with other women. "Sewing was thus the common denominator through which women who were strangers to each other could bridge the distances between them."[25] In current society, in which quick changes and a high degree of geographic mobility define the norm, weak ties often exist among people, even among family members. Friendships are not easily established, and they are likely to be strained by fast-paced lives. One busy and isolated Haysville quilter said her quilt group met her "need to get out among people." This is not to say that only modern women have led busy lives with too little time for social interaction. However, in the diversity of modern life, the quilting group may play an even greater role in identifying potential friends than it did in days when a quilt tradition was assumed to be part of the lives of the majority of women. The groups now "sort" people according to the shared values and world view that are conventionally associated with those interested in quilting. A Haysville quilter stated, "I feel like my quilting group meets my needs for my leisure time. I don't care for shopping, partying, etc. We really do have a lovely group." The groups routinely foster intergenerational friendships, which are unusual in today's society.[26] Several members of the Quilt Patchers remarked that having friends of all ages was important. For instance, the younger women who have small children appreciate the contact with "grandmothers" who help them realize "there's a light at the end of the tunnel" of child rearing. However, the groups rarely include members of different socioeconomic classes or racial backgrounds, reflecting the homogeneity that characterizes traditional communities in general.

Members of quilting groups have historically maintained close personal relationships with each other, as the affection and continuity provided by the group support individuals through difficult or challenging life circumstances. For instance, a quilter may join a group during the transition required after retirement or while recuperating from an illness.[27] For two newly widowed women who had recently moved to Wichita, their respective quilting groups supplied immediate, much-needed companionship. For a member of the Quilt Patchers whose mother had died, the group offered emotional support and physical help to finish a quilt top the mother had pieced, preserving one of the symbols of their familial bond. One member described this as a "love gift."

The third category Stewart identified, the "individual" function, is also apparent in several motivations specified in this study. One frequently mentioned benefit is the release of tension the women experience in the repetitive, sometimes meditative, sewing activity. At least one member from each group in this study called quilting "therapy,"[28] and many described its appeal as "addictive" to the point that they lost interest in other leisure-time, voluntary occupations. Though left unstated by participants in this study, it is logical that a person's healthy pursuit of stress-reducing activity is even more encouraged when the activity itself is widely viewed as positive.

Another individual function cited in this study was the opportunity to be creative and helpful while maintaining the traditions of quilting, a benefit named most often by long-standing members of groups that operate for church-related charities. Newer quilters in both types of quilting

groups echoed the motive of preserving the heritage of quilts, although some were not initially attracted to the art by significant personal experiences of that tradition. Instead they were drawn by the positive image of quilts throughout the culture in the 1970s and 1980s. These newcomers, upon learning the history of the art, often sought to replicate not only those techniques, designs, and materials that are reminiscent of the past but also the practice of cooperative quilting. Such sentiments were expressed by several Quilt Patchers, most of whose members describe themselves as "city girls," new to quilting as adults. One member stated, "Your conception and appreciation of quilts is completely different when you are aware of quicker methods. You appreciate the technical skills needed to put them together the old way." With knowledge of the enduring qualities of folk quilting, the new quilter can enter the traditional system whereby culture is passed on, regardless of quiltmaking's prevailing level of popularity in the larger society.

The current quilt revival and the external, internal, and individual functions of quilt groups, which meet members' needs that have been heightened by the demands of modern society, provide abundant incentives for women to participate. However, not everyone welcomes the influence of the extraordinary popularity and cultural visibility of quilts in recent years. Many see a threat to the traditional context when quilts are included in the popular culture of quilt kits, "cheater's cloth" quilt look-alikes, and classes that teach faster but sometimes technically inferior creative methods. They worry about the mercurial quality of popular tastes, reasoning that if the interest in quilting is based on fashion trends alone, the art form will disappear when quilts go out of favor. They fear that commitments to the art will be weaker if quilters participate in the traditions of the groups without having experienced the cultural heritage that informs those activities. To some, like feminist writer Patricia Mainardi, quilts also seem decontextualized and co-opted in the art world setting of high-priced commercial galleries and sterile museums. She writes, "as [quilts] are shifted from use-value to commodity-value, many troubling questions and contradictions remain. Will they continue to carry the spiritual identity of 'good objects' in their new status, or will they become merely pleasant art objects defined by a high level of craft and design?"29

One answer to these concerns is that the relatively stable value system of the traditional culture renders its quilts and group quilting more resistant to easy change than are popular fashions or movements in fine arts aesthetics. However, over prolonged periods, the influences of the popular and fine art perspectives do produce modifications in the traditional forms. This study's participants felt both positive and negative effects of the society-wide quilt revival in several areas, including the manner in which each member became interested in quilting and learned the required skills, the composition and structure of each group, and the type of quilts that were made.

Tradition and Change in Contemporary Quilting Groups

The groups' interests and skills in quilting derived from both traditional and nontraditional sources. Approximately half of the quilters in this study developed an appreciation of quilts as young children in families that carried on traditional quiltmaking. Only half of that number learned to quilt in their youth, from a female family member or a friend who passed along the expertise by example and direct lessons. The majority of the study's quilters, however, did have sewing skills or practiced other needle arts at the time that they learned to quilt as adults by enrolling in classes or workshops or by using quilt instruction books. Once they were part of a quilting group, they constantly added new skills and techniques to their quilting repertoire through interactions with the other members. For instance, one Haysville quilter had taught the others a Mennonite quilting technique called long-stitching, described as one-quarter-inch stitches using embroidery thread. She had learned the style when she lived in Goessel from a Mennonite friend (see p. 45 for an example of long-stitching).

The traditional culture can move people unquestioningly toward specific customary activities. However, when an interest in those activities is born outside of a woman's cultural heritage, she must consciously choose to learn the skills and participate in the activity. Missing is the automatic context for the acquisition of knowledge and appreciation of the tradition and for learning the skills at the encouragement and direction of a familiar person. Quilt patterns and instructions have been published regularly in the popular press since the 1870s, so the current availability of nontraditional sources of in-formation on quilting is not new. What is new is the quantity of sources and the extent to which contemporary quilters rely on them instead of on traditional modes of learning.

The way quilting skills have been acquired also affects the particular membership composition of the groups. When women who have just become interested in quilts join quilting groups, they may have a more fragile motivation for participation because there is no familial or organizational heritage to commit them to the activity. Furthermore, given the high mobility and fast pace of modern lives, contemporary quilting group members are more likely than in the past to be unrelated and unknown to other members and are less likely to share membership in other organizations or to live in close proximity. It follows that although people will be involved during revival times of high popularity, when the vogue has faded the participation of these newcomers in collective quilting will be less certain.

Instead, what characterizes the memberships of the current groups is similarities in work and family responsibilities. Those with limited time for leisure activity away from home, usually women with small children and/or full-time paid employment, find it difficult to participate in quilting groups. Without special arrangements, quilters with such time or child-care commitments simply cannot belong to the groups that meet frequently and for a long duration in weekday, daytime hours. Indeed, one Haysville quilter who had quilted since her teenage years had to give it up when she married and had five children, even though she "just ached" to return to quilting during those years. The Quilt Patchers partially solved this type of problem by collecting minimal dues from the members to offset the costs of child care when various members needed such help in order to attend the group. Other groups modified their schedules to fit the needs of women juggling full-time work and domestic responsibilities. For instance, one member of the Dorcas Circle is a teacher who attends the quilting group only during her school's summer vacation. Time availability is a very well recognized problem. It was for this reason that most subjects in Marilyn Davis's 1980 study of contemporary quilters preferred to quilt at home with their families while watching television or listening to music, rather than leaving to quilt with a group.[30]

In fact, there is special concern regarding the future of small town quilting traditions within charitable organizations. Suzanne Yabsley, writing about the collective quilters in rural Texas, could be discussing a worry of such Kansas groups: "The state's traditional church and community quilting groups still exist. In all likelihood however, these groups will not regenerate themselves when current members die or retire. With their roots firmly entrenched in rural Texas and their membership composed primarily of older, lifetime homecraft quilters, they are not likely to attract many recruits from younger urban fabric artists."[31] In the present study, the quilters of the Halstead First Mennonite Church and of St. Peter's Church in Schulte also worried that without younger women's participation there would eventually be no one to carry on the work. In recent years, the Peck quilters

were unable to replace several of their members who had begun paid employment, forcing the group to discontinue meeting for an extended period. Attributing the lack of younger quilters to the increased necessity for women to work for wages, some members despaired of a solution. In addition, in small towns or rural areas where the influences of change least affect the continuity of traditional culture, the overall population is dwindling.

Historically, church-related quilting groups have served a particular kind of quilter, the middle- or upper-class woman who has time to donate. The majority of women in this study were retired from paid work or were full-time homemakers whose children were no longer at home; many were widows. In fact, some women with time to fill during the days were particularly attached to their quilting group membership because other groups did not meet often or long enough to suit their needs. And, as a Dorcas Circle member said, sewing at home "lacks the fellowship." In densely populated urban areas, however, even the church-related traditional segment of the quilt culture is not widely nurtured. The very mobile populations of urban settings complicate the private, family-, and community-centered dissemination of traditional culture. Individuals frequently cannot make definite plans to remain in the same locale for extended periods, a fact that disrupts community involvement in any one place.

The visibility of quilts outside of the traditional culture affects not only the composition and perspective of the groups but also the types of quilts being created. All the quilt groups in this study still worked primarily on traditional quilts. However, ideas expressed in experimental avant-garde or "art" quilts have filtered into the aesthetic choices of traditional groups. As the popular quilt guilds serve as a forum for conveying information about quilt news and innovations, somewhat more receptive audiences for wider-ranging design and material innovation emerge in the quilt community. A mixture of old and new prevails. For instance, the consensus among the Quilt Patchers was that traditional hand sewing symbolized "caring" in a quilt. They explained that their preference for traditional materials, old piecing techniques, and avoidance of "fashion colors" kept the "awe" in quilts. At the same time, color innovation and exploration of all potential variations on certain traditional designs was of utmost interest to one member of that group.

The Future of Quilting Groups

In the face of the changes in quilting groups and quilt styles described here, it seems to some that the traditions of collective quilting groups are in jeopardy. This is a natural alarm, since many see traditional ways as static. Traditional systems only appear to be timeless, however, because their evolution is more gradual than that of the popular or fine art realm. The concern for quilting's future is heightened because history teaches us that the sustenance of the popular and fine art markets will eventually disappear, as new tastes gain favor in those inherently faster-changing cultural arenas.

However, it is possible to draw a more promising conclusion from these influences. It is the interplay of traditional, popu-

Women's Missionary Society, Denison.

lar, and fine art cultures that has helped to give a needed boost to quilting groups and quilting in general. Now that quilts and quilting groups have moved into all three areas of culture, they are unlikely to fade from view completely. The quilt has been made visible in a new contemporary arena by the women's art movement's investigation of "gendered" art forms since the late 1960s. Quilts have also found a small niche in the postmodern mood of the larger contemporary art scene. Through these art world efforts and the much more long-standing support of folk enthusiasts, society knows and appreciates more about this tradition. Quilters themselves, as a result, take greater pride in their work. The formal and informal records now accumulating in still-growing numbers of books,

periodicals, and exhibition catalogs and the findings of state quilt documentation projects will aid in preventing "quilt ignorance" in society in the future. The high monetary value of antique quilts, well-made quilts in traditional designs, and art quilts has increased the perceived value of the tradition and created an incentive to conserve and collect quilts and to revive support of the tradition in society. Finally, the visibility of the popular culture forms and those of the fine art world overlap but do not replace traditional quilts or co-opt the heritage, as Mainardi and others fear. Quilting activities have continued in all three cultural settings simultaneously.

A Halstead quilter in this study maintained an optimistic view of the future of quilting groups. She felt that if church

Gayle R. Davis

members perceived the imminent end of their long heritage of quilting groups, women would come forward to participate in reviving it. Her prediction has a great deal of cultural validity, both on her local level and on a national scale. History has shown that when the society moves too far from its traditional heritage and social roles, forces born of a collective ideological need for continuity urge Americans back to a full-fledged revival of interest in traditional roles for women, including domestic arts like quilting. Through it all, whether society was focused on change or tradition in any specific era, the folk quilt culture has quietly continued. I join the Halstead quilter in expecting it will be so again. Traditions like collective quilting will evolve, as they always have, to fill the changing needs of society as it experiences its irregularly rotating cycles of cultural experimentation and conservation.

According to Colleen R. Hall-Patton, "As long as the search for 'roots' continues, and folk art and country decorating remain popular, the quilting revival will continue."[32] This study also showed that as long as important traditional motivations are involved—women seeking an arena that can simultaneously include friendships, creativity, personal identity, and meaningful work—and as long as the creative sphere is important in fulfilling the needs of modern women, quilting groups will survive, with or without a general, society-wide revival.

Notes

1. For the purposes of this chapter, traditional, popular, and fine art arenas are differentiated by the various perspectives from which their representatives appreciate the quilt culture of today. The traditional view acknowledges the importance of the early designs, techniques, materials, and creative spheres of quilts as well as the role quilts play in the socialization of individuals and the maintenance of community or family rituals. The popular culture appreciates the nostalgic appeal of the quilts themselves but does not necessarily support their traditional context. Examples from the popular realm of quilting are books for self-taught quilters on time-saving construction techniques, learning to quilt in a class instead of from one's friend or relative, using mass-produced quilts, or putting the quilts away when they are no longer fashionable decorating tools. The fine art world values contemporary quilts for their aesthetics as well as for the quality of the needlework and puts a premium on innovation at least as much as on the traditional design of antique quilts. The social history related to the quilts and their makers is often of secondary, if any, importance. Since the traditional, popular, and fine art designations are not perfectly discrete terms, I intend the delineations of these areas of culture to be considered broadly.

2. My appreciation goes to the groups who agreed to participate in this study. The groups and the members who participated are (1) the Bethany Comforters at the Bethany Methodist Church, Wichita, with a membership of fifty-three women, including director Amelia Thurman and contact person for this study, Lily Webb; (2) the community quilters in Clearwater, including Rose Ellen Heitman, who named as other members Izetta Henderson, Alvere Smith, Ruth Smith, and Vada Tjaden; (3) the Dorcas Circle at the First Presbyterian Church, Wichita, including Georgia Chandler, Florence Diehl, Nina Gleason, Marieta Hatfield, Dora Kaufman, Doris Kaufman, Bessie Newman, Opal Overman, Lucille Rienuts, Ruth Roush, Marguerite Stanley, Katherine Starnes, Betsy Surtees, Mae Taylor, and Shirley Walker; (4) the Haysville Public Library quilters, Haysville, including Dollie Bradburn, Delma Carter, Betty Cattrel, Marsha Hatfield, Ruth Heyen, Ethel Margaret Klopp, Polly McPherson, Eve Ross, Clara Schlegel, Edna Shoemaker, Eloise Snow, Yvonne Sullivan, Faye Tyson, Edith Wahlen, Edna Lee Withiam, and Dorothy Woodroof; (5) the community quilters in Peck, including Rose Ellen Heitman, who named as other members Opal Rose, Winnie Delew, Liz May, Shirley McAdams, Norma Nixon, and Lucille Wan; (6) the Quilt Patchers, who meet in the University United Methodist Church, Wichita, including Karen Ackerman, Kathy Burton, Barb Chaffee, Stephanie Evans, Jane French, Ruby Hawley, Martha Houston, Doris Lusk, Trudy McLeod, Elsa Olson, and Marian Willets; (7) the St. Peter's Church quilters in Schulte, including Barbara Becker, Doris Dugan, Marlene Edgington, Almeda Faker, Vanda Hempken, Christina Hermann, Doris Komp, Veronica Lauer, Betty Schmitz, Carol Siegrist, Sherry Simon, Mildred Tannehill, Joan Wessolosky, and Catherine Winter; and (8) the 76'ers at the First Mennonite Church in Halstead, including Marylin Balzer, Ida Cooms, Eleanor Ewy, Esther Harms, Verda Johnson, Luella Mueller, Amanda Nightingale, Dorothy Ortman, Katherine Regier, Neva Regier, and Vera Regier. All references to these groups or their individual members are based on interviews conducted with the group members and on questionnaires completed by some members in 1988 through 1990. They will not be otherwise noted in the text.

3. Simon J. Bronner, "Researching Material Folk Culture in the Modern American City," *American Material Culture and Folklife, A Prologue and Dialogue,* ed. Simon J. Bronner (Ann Arbor: University of Michigan Press, 1985), 226.

4. John Michael Vlach, "The Concept of Community and Folklife Study," in *American Material Culture and Folklife, A Prologue and Dialogue,* ed. Simon J. Bronner (Ann Arbor: University of Michigan Press, 1985), 73.

5. For further discussion of the relationship between society's ideological needs and women's creative work, see Gayle R. Davis, "Gender and Creative Production: A Social History Lesson in Art Evaluation," in *The Gender of Material Culture, the Material Culture of Gender,* ed. Kenneth L. Ames and Katherine Martinez (New York: W. W. Norton, 1994).

6. Leslie Woodcock Tentler, *Wage-Earning Women, Industrial*

Work, and Family Life in the United States, 1900–1930 (New York: Oxford University Press, 1979), 141. Another time of dramatically changed gender roles was the 1940s in the United States. However, during those World War II years women were seen as a temporary, reserve labor force, with no major disruption expected in the normal peacetime roles of men and women. The married women who worked for wages in the 1940s labored along with the men for the greater good, not because their men could not find employment, as was the case in the 1930s. Depression-era unemployed men faced a psychological displacement concerning their personal worth that was far different from the wartime shifts in male gender roles.

7. Adding to the already high employment of women, the average American wife worked twenty-five hours per week more in 1990 than she did in 1980 (Research Director of the Economic Policy Institute, Washington, D.C., "Morning Edition," National Public Radio broadcast, September 3, 1990).

8. Milhaly Csikszentmihalyi and Eugene Rochberg-Halton, *The Meaning of Things: Domestic Symbols and the Self* (Cambridge: Cambridge University Press, 1981), 93.

9. Ibid., 118–119.

10. Eli Wigginton, ed., "A Quilt Is Something Human," *The Foxfire Book* (Garden City, N.Y.: Anchor Press, 1972), 144, 150.

11. Csikszentmihalyi and Rochberg-Halton, *The Meaning of Things*, 105, 50–51.

12. Patricia Mainardi, "Quilt Survivals and Revivals," *Arts Magazine* 62 (May 1988): 49–53; Charlotte Robinson, ed., *The Artist and the Quilt* (New York: Knopf, 1983).

13. Pat Ferrero, Elaine Hedges, and Julie Silber, *Hearts and Hands, the Influence of Women and Quilts on American Society* (San Francisco: Quilt Digest Press, 1987), 97.

14. Susan Stewart, "Sociological Aspects of Quilting in Three Brethren Churches in Southeastern Pennsylvania," *Pennsylvania Folklife* 23 (Spring 1974): 27.

15. Though quilt guilds are not the focus of this chapter, they have proliferated during the current quilt revival and are important links in the quilt community. They supply an opportunity for women interested in quilting to become acquainted; they introduce various well-known quilters and quilt historians to the membership in their regular program meetings; they sponsor quilt workshops, symposia, and exhibits; and they serve as a communication center for national quilting news, projects, and opportunities. Guilds are typically larger than quilting groups, and collective quilting is not their primary function.

16. See Joyce Ice, "Splendid Companionship and Practical Assistance," in *Quilted Together: Women, Quilts, and Communities,* ed. Joyce Ice and Linda Norris (Delhi, N.Y.: Delaware County Historical Association, 1989), 6–24; Colleen R. Hall-Patton, "Innovation among Southern California Quilters: An Anthropological Perspective," in *Uncoverings 1987,* ed. Laurel Horton and Sally Garoutte (San Francisco: American Quilt Study Group, 1989), 73–86; Stewart, "Sociological Aspects of Quilting," 15–29; Suzanne Yabsley, *Texas Quilts, Texas Women* (College Station: Texas A&M University Press, 1984).

17. Ferrero, Hedges, and Silber, *Hearts and Hands,* 66.

18. Carol Crabb, "Quilting Bees," *Missouri Heritage Quilts,* ed. Bettina Hawg (Paducah, Ky.: American Quilters Society, 1986), 5.

19. Special rite-of-passage quilts were given to commemorate significant moments in life, such as the wedding quilts that helped start a new marriage on the proper path. For discussions of this important aspect of the quilt culture, see "Textile Diaries: Kansas Quilt Memories," *Kansas History: A Journal of the Central Plains* 13 (Spring 1990 special issue); Linda Otto Lipsett, *Remember Me: Women and Their Friendship Quilts* (San Francisco: The Quilt Digest Press, 1985).

20. Ice, "Splendid Companionship," 24.

21. Stewart, "Sociological Aspects of Quilting," 25.

22. Ibid., 26.

23. Frances Willard, *Women and Temperance or the Work and Workers of the Women's Christian Temperance Union* (Hartford, Conn.: Park Publishing Co., 1883), 114, quoted in Ferrero, Hedges, and Silber, *Hearts and Hands,* 87.

24. Simon J. Bronner, "The Idea of the Folk Artifact," *American Ma-terial Culture and Folklife: A Prologue and Dialogue,* ed. Simon J. Bronner (Ann Arbor: University of Michigan Press,1985), 32.

25. Ferrero, Hedges, and Silber, *Hearts and Hands,* 63.

26. Ice, "Splendid Companionship," 24.

27. Ibid., 17.

28. In the 1920s and 1930s, Dr. William Dunton even prescribed quilting to women as a cure for nervousness (Thomas K. Woodard and Blanche Greenstein, *Twentieth Century Quilts, 1900–1950* [New York: E. P. Dutton, 1988], 9).

29. Mainardi, "Quilt Survivals and Revivals," 51.

30. Marilyn Davis, "The Contemporary American Quilter: A Portrait," in *Uncoverings 1981,* ed. Sally Garoutte (Mill Valley, Calif.: American Quilt Study Group, 1982), 47.

31. Yabsley, *Texas Quilts, Texas Women,* 42.

32. Hall-Patton, "Innovation among Southern California Quilters," 85.

The information in this appendix is drawn from a computerized data base of information only about the quilts recorded at Quilt Discovery Days. Quilts documented in the extended research phase of the project are not included in the database.

The Kansas Quilt Project used an IBM-compatible computer and a D-Base 3 program for the data base. Although 13,107 quilts were recorded, only 12,862 were entered in the data base as a result of such problems as incomplete release of information forms, recording errors, or incomplete information. The file for each quilt contained 55 fields.

Kansas Quilt Project Data Categories

FIELD NUMBER	FIELD NAME	INFORMATION FIELD CONTAINS (TAKEN FROM FORMS)
1	IDNUM	Identification Number
2	RESTRICT1	Restrictions
3	RESTRICT2	Restrictions
4	DEMO	Will quiltmaker demonstrate quilting?
5	QONAMEFI	Quiltowner's First Name
6	QONAMEMI	Quiltowner's Middle Name
7	QONAMELA	Quiltowner's Last Name
8	QOADDRESS	Quiltowner's Address
9	QOCITY	
10	QOSTATE	
11	QOZIP	
12	QOPHONE	Quiltowner's Phone Number
13	FIRSTNM	Maker's First Name
14	MIDDLENM	Maker's Middle Name
15	LASTNM	Maker's Last Name
16	MAIDEN	Maker's Maiden Name
17	ADDRESS	Maker's Address
18	CITY	Maker's Current City
19	STATE	Maker's Current State
20	ZIP	Maker's Zip
21	COUNTY	Maker's Current County
22	PHONE	Maker's Current Phone Number
23	BIRTH	Maker's Birthdate
24	OCCUP	Maker's Primary Occupation
25	RELIG	Maker's Religion (see code sheet)
26	ETHNIC	Maker's Ethnic Identity (see codes)
27	LEARNED	How did maker learn? (see codes)
28	FUNCT	Why was quilt made? (see codes)
29	WHERECI	What city was quilt made in?
30	WHERECO	What county was quilt made in?
31	WHEREST	What state was quilt made in?
32	DATEMEN	The owner's memory of the quilt's date
33	FOLKNAME	The name the owner gave the quilt
34	DIARY	Does the quiltmaker's diary exist?
35	PHOTOS	Do photos of quiltmaker exist?
36	SCRPBK	Does quiltmaker's scrapbook exist?
37	FOLLUP	Should followup be done?

Kansas Quilt Project Data Categories (continued)

FIELD NUMBER	FIELD NAME	INFORMATION FIELD CONTAINS (TAKEN FROM FORMS)
38	DATEEA	Documentor's estimate of earliest date
39	DATELA	Documentor's estimate of latest date
40	QUILTLATE	Was the top quilted at a later date?
41	TECHNI	Decorative techniques (see codes)
42	COLOR	Color scheme of quilt (see codes)
43	MACHN	Was it machine quilted?
44	THICK	Thickness of quilt (see code)
45	DATEINS	Is a date inscribed on it? What date?
46	INIT	Are there initials on it?
47	PLACE	Is a place inscribed on it?
48	SIGN	Is it signed?
49	STMENT	Is there a statement on the quilt?
50	STITCH	Quilting stitches per inch (averages)
51	DISCREP	Discrepancy between 2 measurements
52	BOOKNAME	Official name from pattern ID books
53	PATNUM	Official number from pattern ID books
54	VARIATN	Unofficial name for design variations
55	SLIDEMIS	Is the slide missing for any reason?

Religion of Quiltmaker

About 59 percent of the quilts were identified as being made by a quiltmaker with a known religious affiliation. The highest percentage (22.5 percent) of the total quilts recorded was made by Methodists, with the second-highest percentage (8.3 percent) attributed to Christians (either nondenominational or a nonspecific reference), followed by Roman Catholics, Baptists, Presbyterians, and Lutherans. The results are not surprising, as these five denominations rank highest among contemporary Kansans, although in different order.[1] However, Roman Catholics make up the largest percentage of Kansans who indicated an affiliation: 34.6 percent. Members of the United Methodist Church were 26.9 percent of the total.[2] The predominance of Methodist-made quilts probably reflects the strength of Methodism in the state of Kansas. In 1971, only Iowa had a higher percentage of Methodists.[3] The dearth of Catholic-made quilts when compared to the percentage of Catholics in the state and the almost complete lack of Jewish-made quilts (only six quilts made by two makers identified as Jewish in religion or ethnicity were recorded) indicate that Protestant church activities, such as Sunday School quilts and Ladies' Aid Society quilting groups, traditionally were a strong influence on quilting.

RELIGION	PERCENTAGE OF QUILTS DOCUMENTED	NUMBER	PERCENTAGE OF ADHERENTS IN THE STATE OF KANSAS [a]
Methodist	22.5	2,815	26.9
Christian	8.3	1,035	—
Roman Catholic	7.3	922	34.6
Baptist	6.7	845	15
Presbyterian	5.2	649	3.7
Lutheran	4.9	620	10.5
Mennonite	2.3	295	1.4
Episcopalian	.9	115	2.2
Quaker	.3	39	No information
Amish	<1	15	" "
Congregational	<1	9	" "
Jewish	<1	6	<1
Mormon	<1	5	1

aFigures from MRI/Capper, *Quick Facts about Kansas*, 1990 (Kansas City, Mo.: Midwest Research Institute, 1990.

Date of Quilts Recorded at Quilt Discovery Days

Total number of quilts for which we had an estimation of date was 12,462.

DATE	NUMBER	PERCENTAGE OF TOTAL
Possibly before 1840	28	<1
1840–1880	566	4.5
1880–1900	855	6.8
1900–1925	1,966	15.7
1925–1950	3,990	32
1950–1975	1,787	14.3
1975–1988	3,270	26.2

Pattern

Pattern preferences change over the years. The following patterns were found to be most popular over the whole span of almost two centuries of quilts: Grandmother's Flower Garden, 559; Double Wedding Ring, 446; Crazy Quilt, 314; Nine Patch (Nine squares), 273; Irish Chain; 199, Lone Star, 182; and Log Cabin, 125. Had we focused on specific blocks of time we undoubtedly would have seen different figures; for example, Log Cabins would have been far more popular than Grandmother's Flower Garden with nine-teenth-century quiltmakers.

Techniques in Quilts

Many quilts included a variety of techniques, so it was difficult to isolate specific types with the data system we used. We counted 3,039 quilts with some applique work but only 797 that were exclusively applique. This rather small percentage of applique quilts may be due to a problem in our instructions to the documenters, some of whom classified the seaming of applique blocks as piecing and checked that area on the forms. Others categorized such quilts as applique only. From the computerized data base we have determined the following information on techniques: quilts with applique work, 3,039; quilts exclusively applique, 797; embroidered quilts, 444; crazy quilts, 314; and whole cloth, 181. Using the data base we cannot at this time determine the number of quilts in which piecing was the sole decorative technique in the quilt top.

Quilting

We measured stitches per inch in two places on each quilt, counting the number of stitches showing on the top of the quilt and averaging the two measurements for the computer. When data on about half of the quilts were in the computer, we examined printouts and determined that the average number of stitches per inch was between seven and eight. With information on all 12,862 quilts, we found that only 445 hand-quilted quilts had better than ten stitches to an inch and only 6 had better than fifteen.

The length of the quilting stitch is determined not only by a quilter's skill but also by the thickness of the batting. We devised a gauge to measure whether a quilt was thick, thin, or in between and passed each quilt through it as we measured it. About 65 percent (7,562) of the quilts were thin; only 5.5 percent (642) were thick, a reflection of the relatively small number of warm utility quilts we saw at Quilt Discovery Days; the remaining 29.5 percent (3,045) were medium. The total number of quilts measured with the gauge was 11,609. The discrepancy between this figure and the total number of files (12,862) reflects the number of unquilted tops we recorded: 1,253.

Ethnic Origins of Quiltmakers

Interviewees at Quilt Discovery Days were asked the quiltmakers' ethnic origins. Forms had two spaces so two groups could be identified: for example, German-Irish. The total number of spaces filled was 8,084. Most quilts were identified as being made by people of British or German origins, the two groups to which most Kansans trace their heritage. Several groups were underrepresented at Quilt Discovery Days, which was one reason the KQP conducted the extended research described in chapters 6 and 7.

Ethnic Origins of Quiltmakers (continued)

ETHNIC GROUP	NUMBER OF QUILTS OF QUILTS	PERCENTAGE	ETHNICITY OF KANSANS[a] (%)
British[b]	3,385	41.8	19.2
German	3,043	37.6	19.8
Scandinavian[c]	1,066	13.1	1.9
French	389	4.8	1.4
Czech	107	1.3	<1
Native American	35	<1	<1
Italian	26	<1	<1
African	22	<1	7
Mexican	7	<1	2.8
Jewish	2	<1	<1
Slavic	1	<1	<1
Other	6	<1	—

[a]James Paul Allen and Eugene James Turner, *We the People: An Atlas of America's Ethnic Diversity* (New York: Macmillan, 1988), 225, 248–251.
[b]Includes Scottish, English, Irish, and Welsh
[c]Includes Danish, Swedish, and Norwegian
—means percentage not calculated

Immigration Patterns and Nineteenth-Century Quilts

The Kansas Quilt Project recorded 475 quilts estimated to have been made before 1901 for which the family indicated a state of origin. Of those, 51 percent (244) were thought to have been made in Kansas. The second-largest category for state of origin was Missouri, immediately to the east, through which many Kansans passed or where they stopped on their journeys west. Ohio, Illinois, Indiana, Iowa, Kentucky, and Pennsylvania were each represented by more than ten quilts, an indication of the states from which Kansas settlers emigrated. This migration pattern is reflected in the 1880 census, when Kansans listed Illinois, Ohio, Indiana, Missouri, Pennsylvania, and Iowa as the six most common states they left to move to Kansas.[4]

As noted in chapter 3 on applique quilts, family information about a quilt's state of origin could not always be corroborated by follow-up research. Often the quilt had been made earlier and farther east than the interview information indicated. However, the correlation of oral history with the census data indicates that although families may not be sure in which state a quilt originated, they are familiar with the road their ancestors traveled to Kansas.

STATES OF ORIGIN FOR NINETEENTH-CENTURY QUILTS

Kansas	244	Kentucky	17	Wisconsin	3	North Carolina	2
Missouri	44	Pennsylvania	16	West Virginia	3	Connecticut	1
Ohio	37	New York	6	California	3	Mississippi	1
Illinois	26	Oklahoma	6	Vermont	2	Rhode Island	1
Indiana	24	Arkansas	5	Colorado	2		
Iowa	19	Virginia	4	Georgia	2		

Notes

1. Figures from MRI/Capper, *Quick Facts about Kansas, 1900* (Kansas City, Mo.: Midwest Research Institute, 1990.)
2. Ibid.
3. Clark S. Judge, *The Book of American Rankings* (New York: Facts on File, 1979), 47–55.
4. William Frank Zornow, *Kansas: A History of the Jayhawk State* (Norman: University of Oklahoma Press, 1957).

Acknowledgments

The Kansas Quilt Project would not have been possible without the quiltmakers of Kansas. We are grateful to them and to the quilt owners who so generously shared their quilts.

All photographs, unless otherwise credited, are from the collection of the Kansas State Historical Society. A special thank you to the following institutions for their help in obtaining photographs: the Kansas Collection at the Spencer Research Library at the University of Kansas, the Riley County Historical Society, the Johnson County Historical Society, the Denver Library, the Denver Art Museum, the Spencer Museum of Art at the University of Kansas, and the Smithsonian Institution.

We had help from so many people; below is a list. If we have inadvertently left anyone out we want to apologize.

The Kansas Quilt Project: Documenting Quilts and Quiltmakers

BOARD OF DIRECTORS

Barbara Brackman, *Lawrence*
Barbara Bruce, *Overland Park*
Jennie Chinn, *Topeka*
Nancy Hornback, *Wichita*
Mary Madden, *Topeka*
Eleanor Malone, *Wichita*
Mary Margaret Rowen, *Lawrence*
Helen Storbeck, *Winfield*

CONSULTANTS

Dorothy Cozart, *Waukomis, OK*
Gayle Davis, *Wichita*

REGIONAL COORDINATORS

Delores and Stan Dorsch,
   Bird City
Betty Lou and Neal Anderson,
   Plainville
Mary and Tom Sharp, *Fort Riley*
   (now of Georgetown, TX)
Shirlene Wedd, *Holton*
Jacqueline Holcomb, *Liberal*
Muriel Wolfersperger, *Peabody*
Eleanor Burenheide, *Emporia*
Ann Harrison, *Liberal*
Shellee Morrison, *Wichita*
Elly McCoy, *Chanute*

MAJOR CONTRIBUTORS
(over $500)

National Endowment for the
   Arts
Kansas Arts Commission
Prairie Quilt Guild
American/International Quilt
   Association
Quilters Guild of Greater
   Kansas City
Dema Zupan
Ross Foundation

DOCUMENTORS

Barbara Brackman
Barbara Bruce
Dorothy Cozart
Nancy Hornback
Eleanor Malone
Ruth Montgomery
Ann Reimer
Wilene Smith
Terry Thompson

PHOTOGRAPHERS

Jon Blumb
Jane Braverman
Ron Bruce
Bob Cross
Gail Hand
Paul Hornback
Virginia Lamb
Mary Linn
Nancy Maes-Simonetti
Margot Mead
Deloit Peterson

Shawna Peterson
Helen Storbeck
Barry Worley

Kansas State Historical Society Staff

Art Debacker
Pat Debacker
Joy Harnett
Earl Kitner
Bobbie Pray
Dolores Rose
Rick Schmidt
Nancy Sherbert
Becky Siple
Christie Stanley
Dot Taylor
Sarah Wood-Clark
Barry Worley

Editorial Assistance

Marilyn Holt
Laurel Horton
Larry Jochims
Craig Miner
Bob Richmond
Dale Watts

University Press of Kansas

Dorothea Anderson
Elizabeth Barstow
Susan McRory
Christine Mercer
Cynthia Miller
Jan Butin Sloan

Donors

Alma Abbot
Ethel Abrahams
Anna Mae Ackerman
Alveda Adams
Agenda Club
Aglaian Club
Rita Alberdine
Georgia Aldridge
Betty Alexander
Elaine Alexander
Alma Allen
Dorothy Allen
Patty Allen
Arlene Anderson
Erma Anderson
Mary Anderson
Nancy Anderson
Velma Anderson
Anthony Quilt Guild
Mrs. Victor Arick
Doris Armstrong
Judy Arnold
Attic Window
Merilyn Austin
Mariana Aylward
Barber County Savings and Loan
Maurine Barber
Rebecca Barber
Norma Barclay
Mona Barker
Margaret Bartley
Jan Basley
Joan Beck
Belle-Hayne Unit
Tyla Bennett
Lavina Belle Berner
Besel Roofing & Heating, Inc.
Lois Beyer
Bonnie Biles
Robert Billings
Teresa Binder
Binney & Smith
Joyce Black
Cheryl Blacklidge
Pamela Blankenship
Jon Blumb
Blue Valley Quilters Guild
Margaret Bonanomi
Judy Bond
Camilla Bookwalter
Bourbon County Quilters Guild

Helen Bowers
Pat Bozeman
Mary Ellen Brace
Eunice Bradley
Dorothy Brands
Kathleen Brassfield
Jane Braverman
Marguerite Brenner
Frances Brinegar
Dorothy Brinkman
Deola Brinley
Becky Brown
Helen Brown
Pauline Brown
Suzanne and Roger Brown
Carol Brubaker
Della Bruce
Ron Bruce
Jane Buckley
Alice Burch
Debbie Burgess
Dee Burns
Marsha Burris
Norma Wasinger Butler
Florence Cade
Leonard C. Cake, Jr.
Marlene Calhoun
Pamela Calhoun
Calico Country Quilt Shop
Calico Kiddies
Doris Callaway
Anita Cambera
Caroline Camp
Christine Campbell
Jeanne Cardenas
Aline Cargill
Brenda Carlson
Alice Carpenter
Dr. and Mrs. Paul Carpenter
Dava Carrell
Cathy Carroll
Pam Carvalho
Deborah Catlin
Central Kansas Thread Benders
Chanute Bank of Commerce
Peggy Chapman
Chase County Historical
    Society, Inc.
Chatty Cathy Quilting Guild
Norma Chestnut
Kimy Christie
Katy Christopherson
Citizens Mutual Savings & Loan

Association of Leavenworth
Georganna Clark
Debbie Clarke
Jean Clarkson-Frisbie
Norma Claus
Mildred Clemens
Virginia Clevenger
Naomi Clifton
Emmaretta Cockrill
Coldwell Bankers Shoenrock
    Realtors
Darlene Cole
Mrs. John Collins
Wilma Combrink
Barbara Conant
Josephine Conley
Patricia Connet
Bertilla Conroy
Hazel Cook
Irene Cook
Marilyn Cook
Sharon Cook
Dona Cooper
Mary Corn
Country Stitchers Quilters Guild
Elaine Craft
Susan Craig
Francis Cramer
Kim Crane
Belinda Crawford
Crazy Quilters Guild of
    El Dorado
Orvil Criqui
Michelle Crisler
Ramona Crosley
Bob Cross
Mary Curry
Cut-Up-Quilters Club
Ellen Czarnowsky
Delores Darland
Betty Davidson
Dorothy Davidson
Barbara Davis
Josephine Davis
Olive Davis
Ruby Davis
Art DeBacker
Pat DeBacker
Louise DeForest
Luann Delgado
Miriam Dennett
Denny's Collectables
Karla Devan

Elaine Dill
Lois Donaldson
Donna's Designs
Mary Douglass
Mrs. Charles Driscoll
Margaret Duckworth
Lorraine Dungan
Betty Dunlap
Geneva Dunster
Mary Dusenbury
Cathy Dwigans
Elizabeth Dysinger
Michelen Eakins
Sharon Eastep
Amy Edgerton
Charlene Edmonds
Mertie Edmondson
Kay Ehlen
Martha Elledge
Billie Elliott
Vivian Elliott
Emma Ellis
Carolyn Elmore
Dorine Elsea
Linda Emery
Emma Creek Quilters
Emporia Regional Quilters Guild
Marie Emrich
Judy Ermey
ESA Sorority #1723
Fern Eubank
Berneice Ewertz
Sara Farley
Louise Feldt
Ella Ferree
Winnie Fields
First Community Federal S&L
    of Winfield, Derby and
    Arkansas City
First National Bank & Trust of
    Leavenworth
First National Bank of Medicine
    Lodge
First National Bank of Winfield
First State Bank of Lansing
Erma Fisher
Mrs. Gerald Fisher
Annette Fitzgerald
Carolee Flask
Rosella Flowers
Bonita Folck
Carol Ford
Sarah Foreman

Fort Riley Historical Society
Fort Riley National Bank
Lucinda Foster
Vera Fox
Steve and Emily Frazier
Phyllis Fredrickson
Mary Ann French
Jane French
June Friend
Georgina B. Fries
Anita Fry
Rachel Fuller
Edna Funk
Barbara Gaeddert
Gladys Gall
Margaret Garrett
Jacqueline Garton
Mary Gaunt
Joan Gerber
Dorothy Gilbert
John V. Glades Agency
Jerry and Lola Glenn
Marilyn Glenn
Glenwood EHU
Mary Beth Goering
Grace Goff
Shirley Goodnight
Margaret Gragg
Grantville Country Quilters
Inez Graves
Jean Gray
Ruth Green
Pauline Greenhaw
Colleen Grieder
Jane Griffith
Rosie Grinstead
Dorothy Groene
Jeanie Guilfoyle
Lee Gunter
Mrs. William Guy
Gyp Hills Quilters Guild
Anne Haehl
Betty Jo Haines
Ora Haines
Amy Hake
Willa Ruth Hall
Marie Hammerbacher
Gail Hand
Martha Hansen
Cathy Hanken
Dennis Harbaugh
Sue Harmon
Gladys Harms

Elsie Haynes
Heart of Kansas Quilters
Mrs. Heart's Attic
Mary Louise Heaton
Ruth Hehrlee
Colleen Heitman
Roberta Helling
Marilyn Helstab
Thelma Hendricks
Ruth Herman
Martha Hershberger
Sandy Heyman
Linda Highbarger
Bernita Hill
Clyde Hill
Sara Hill
Roslyn Hoch
Peggy Jean Hogan
Joyce Hogoboom
Shirley Holmes
Home Savings Association
    of Chanute
Cathy Honken
Emily Hooper
Paul Hornback
Dorothy Houseman
Martha Houston
Margaret Hubbard
Hubbard's Drug
Eva Hudson
Polly Huff
Pat Hughes
Mary Hutcherson
Sandy Hysom
Bonnie Ipson
Laraine Isaac
Anna Jackson
Arvid and Susan Jacobson
Donna Jacobson
Carol Jenkner
Judy Jennings
Alva and Bessie Jester
Karla John
Judee Johnsen
Chris Johnson
Debbie Johnson
Doris Johnson
Georganna Johnson
Gladys Johnson
Mrs. James Johnson
Maxine Johnson
Theresa Johnson
Norma Johnston

Florence Jones
Marilyn Jones
Tresa Jones
Carol Jordan
Maurine Jost
Vera Kaiser
Kansas Capitol Quilters Guild
Kaw Valley Quilters
Robert Kearley
Carolyn Kelsey
Mrs. Jay Kelso
Kerr's
Dorothy Kimbell
Kiowa County Extension
    Homemakers Council
Marilyn Kirby
Vivian Kirkpatrick
Anna Klema
Norma Kline
Helen Kanpp
Regina Kobuszewski
Frances Kohrs
Marjorie Konopaska
Konza Prairie Quilters Guild
Eva Lou Koons
Virginia Kreider
Terri Kretzmeier
Miriam Kruse
Joan Kuck
Nancy Kuenhle
Inez Kuestersteffen
Carol Kuse
Virginia Lamb
Mrs. Robert Lamborn
Janet Langsdorf
Diane Lane
Thelma Lanier
Carlene Larson
Pam Larson
Winnie Laughlin
Whitt Laughridge
T. R. Laven
Hazel Leady
Pearl Lear
Leavenworth County Extension
    Council #884
Dorman Lehman
Mildred Leighty
Mildred Lemert
Marcia Lemmons
Bessie Letourneau
Florence Lewis
Margaret Lightner

Edna Lindquist
Mary Linn
Linn Branch Historical Society
Vona Clark Little
Marilyn Livingood
Sammy Locke
Kay Loftus
Martha Lohman
Karen Lone
Verna Long
Inez Loyd
Marjorie Loyd
Vivian Luthi
Lenora Lyman
Nancy Maes-Simonetti
Kathie Maestas
Carl Magnuson
Jilann Mahoney
Vicki Malone
Mary Manlove
Ella Manske
Manufacturers State Bank of
    Leavenworth
Nancy Marin
Ona Mae Marmon
Ann Martin
Dean Martin
Eleanor Martin
Anita Martz
Carolyn Maruggi
Dorothy Mast
Marilyn Mathews
Augusta Matlack
Ann Mawhirter
Vera Mayhew
Mildred McAllaster
Dorothy McBee
Margaret McClellan
Velma McClung
Mary Ellen McCorgary
George McCune
Alice McElwain
Rosemary McEwen
Wilma McGown
Betty McGuffey
Phyllis McKay
Barbara McKee
Susan McKelvey
Olive McKenzie
Connie McKim
Keith McKinney
Trudy McLeod
Beth McMillen

Sarah McMillen
McPherson Quilt Guild
Margot Mead
Joan Meili
Laverns Merklin
Lois Melia
Patti Mersmann
Ruth Meserve
Ruth Meyer
Rebecca Meyerkorth
Miami County Quilters Guild
Roxine Michael
Lenora Mick
Anita Middleton
Midwest Grain Products
Karen Milberger
Tracey Miles
Berta Miller
Margery Miller
Pauline Miller
Bernie Misznow
Ann Mitchell
Bill and Jean Mitchell
Jean Mohler
Nadine Mong
Ruth Montgomery
Dorothy Moore
Jean Morris
Kay Morse
Henrietta Moser
Verna Mosiman
Mud Creek Quilters
Teresa Mulhern
Mary Ann Mull
Marian Muslow
Tony Muñoz
Mutual Savings Association of
    Leavenworth
Eleanor Nelson
Jean Nestor
Loretta Nettleton
Jeanne-Marie Neuroth
Karen Nicols
Karen Niles
Janelle Nolte
Londa Nonken
North Carolina Quilt Project
Northeast Kansas Quilters Guild
LaRue Nuest
Helen Nyhart
Sylvia O'Donnell
DeLila Offutt
Nancy Ohlde

Dianna Oishinsky
Rosalie Osburn
Ottawa Quilters Guild
Mary Ellen Page
Mary Pacey
Jane Palmer
Palmer Trucking
Parker's IGA Foodliner
Katharine Parker
Pearl Parker
Ruby Patton
Helen Pawling
Sharon Payne
Judy Peddicord
Ruth Perry
Caroline Peterson
Deloit Peterson
Shawna Peterson
Sarah Pfeifer
Nola Pickett
Kate Poorey
Roseann Porter
Zelph Powell
Sheila Prichard
Karen Priess
Jayne Prockish
A Quilt Shoppe, Etc.—
    Mary Lou and Joe Rodell
Quilts 'N' Things
Quilters Guild of Parsons
Marge Ragle
Josephine Rago
Ruth Rago
Coralee Ramsay
Ruth Randgaard
Elizabeth Raymond
Lorraine Reed
Price R. and Flora A. Reid
    Foundation
Ann Reimer
Lois Rhodes
Janet Rhodes
Ruth Richards
Harriet Richardson
Janice Riley
Marie Riley
Vivian Ritter
Glenda Rodgers
Sheila Roesler
Frances Rogers
Bonnie Rosen
LaVerne Rosenberger
Ruth Roudebush

Irene Rowe
Jonell Rowland
Betty Rutherford
Alice Sabatini
Linda Sader
Saltbox Sampler—Gloria Case
    and Karen Overstedt
Erna Saltzman
Lora Belle Sander
Margaret Sangster
Frances Schaffter
Vivian Schauf
Barbara Scherer
Lucille Schoonover
Irene Schwilling
April Scott
Ailene Seeman
Bettie Seibel
Glenda Selterstrom
Sequel Club
Mary Severns
Judy Severson
Bev Seyfert
Kim Shannon
Peggy Shapland
Barbara Shaver
Pattye Shaver
LaVerna Shaw
Connie Shea
Whitney Short
Sue Sielert
Karen Sim
Vivian Singer
Mary Skipworth
Sarah Sleeper
Tom and Teri Slover
Anita Smith
Margaret Smith
Phyllis Smith
Wilene Smith
Leslie Snodgrass
Dr. Phyllis J. Howard Soine
Betty Solberg
Janice Sowder
Elaine Sparlin
Esther Splattstasser
Teddy Spencer
Judith Splechter
Carolyn Spillman
Nancy Staley
Sybil Standley
James and Nedra Starkey
State Bank of Winfield

Norman Steers
Marge Steiner
Stitch On Needlework Shop—
    Steve and Leslie Ahlert
Betty Stoll
Cinthia Stolte
Betty Strand
Little Strangers EHU
Okley Strawn
Donna Stroh
Marsha Struby
Jean Studebaker
Ruth Sturges
Dorothy Sullivan
Sunflower Piecemakers
Sunflower Quilters Guild
Vera Surface
Anne Sutlief
Nancy Swanwick
Jean Swartz
Camilla Swenson
Rose Wasson Swift
Deb Talamantez
Carol Taranto
Betty Taul
Joan Taylor
Mardell Taylor
Marian Teall
Linda Tegethoff
Regina Tenbrink
Margaret Tharp
Bettie Thoeming
Dorothy Thomas
Flora Thompson
Judy Thompson
Terry Thompson
Jean Tomson
Tonganoxie Sunflower
    Quilters Guild
Topeka Needlework Guild
Nancy Tosh
Louise Townsend
Hazel Tracy
Darleen Trimble
Pauline Trubshaw
Blanch Turner
United Telephone Co. of Kansas
Elizabeth Unruh
Mrs. Lloyd Unzicker
Janet Verity
Nola Vice
Chelcie Vincent
Grace Voight

Janice Wade
Sandy Wagerle
Sadie Waller
Evelyn Walden
Leona Walker
Walnut Valley Quilters Guild
Frances Walter
Fran Walters
Winnifred Wamhoff
Mary Washburn
Pamela Washburn
Cynthia Washburne
Betty Webb
Lillie Webb
Marilyn Webb
Shirley Wedd
Ida Weltha
Sue Wettstaed
Jean Weniger
Paula Whisenhant
Barbara White
Lori Whitehair
Judy Whitehill
Marjorie Whitfield
Whiting State Bank
Elizabeth Whitman
Mary Wiley
Genevieve Haskin Williams
Willing Workers EHU
Marian Willits
Sally and John Willome
Maxine Wilson
Winfield Daily *Courier*
Patty Wise
Peggy Wixson
Edna Wood
Woodson County Women
Cletes Wranosky
Malvina Wright
Yates Center Branch Bank
Cindy Yeoman
Esther Yohon
Walter Yost
Margaret Youngberg
Alice Youngman
Donna Zellers
F.W. Zschietzschmann

IN HONOR OF:

Doris Armstrong
Alice Parsall Brady (Mrs. H. B.)
Pearl Coker (Mrs. A. B.)

Katharine Baeddert
Wilamina Kramer Barber
Bhlandena Hull Barnes
Jane Buckley
Alice Carpenter
Dicy Carter
Chelsea Lea Catlin
Zoe Hoofe Clark
Josephine Craig
Ella M. Bechtle Croyle
    (Mrs. George M.)
Esther Curry
Patricia Howard Drewry
Sally Dunn
Zella Emrich
Helen Ericson
Nella Mae Weir Fankhauser
Irma M. Folck
Grace Goff
Rosie Grinstead
Betty Hagerman
Mrs. Theresa Hall
Pearl Harman
Myrtle Hefflefinger
Ema Heitschmiet
Dorothy Hjorth
Faye Hogoboom
Margaret James
Lucyle Jewett
Rosa Lee Jounkin
Ula Noffsinger Kelsey
Mrs. Bertha Stewart Lemert
Faye Lewis
Edna Lillich
Ida Looney
Estelle McConnell Loyd
Gladys Burton Manka
Georgia McAllaster
Hulda B. McCall
Ruth Meyer
Jean Mitchell
Muriel O'Connor
Ruth Fern Larson O'Neal
Belle Paquette
Anna Laurie Dunkle Pautz
Lavisa Jeanette Peddicord
Mrs. Marion Peterson
Veril S. Pettit
Alice Jane Phillips
Della Phillips
Rachel Rago
Elizabeth Schesser Randall
Bertha Stucky Reimer

Mrs. Letha Rice
Eva Rowe
Mary Schuvie Sauer
Laura Schneider
Velma Schnuerle
Judy Severson
Mary Pawling Sharp
Elaine Sparlin
Dora Staker
Lizabeth Stauf
Pharby Taylor
Mary Emma Tryon
Dorothy Vetter
Mrs. Goldie L. Webster
Lora Housholder Wedd
Margaret Friesen Wiens
Josephine Willis
Della McCoy Wolf
Dema Zupan

DATE DUE

GAYLORD			PRINTED IN U.S.A.